To Marion and Gerry —
This story of a
great man. Thank you
for your wonderful friendship

Dorothy

9/30/06

BERNARD FALL

Memories of a Soldier-Scholar

DOROTHY FALL

FOREWORD BY DAVID HALBERSTAM

Potomac Books, Inc.
Washington, D.C.

Library of Congress Cataloging-in-Publication Data

Fall, Dorothy, 1930-
Bernard Fall : memories of a soldier-scholar / Dorothy Fall.— 1st ed.
p. cm.
Includes bibliographical references and index.
ISBN 1-57488-957-5 (alk. paper)
1. Fall, Bernard B., 1926-1967. 2. Historians—Vietnam—Biography. 3. Historians—United States—Biography. 4. Fall, Dorothy, 1930- I. Title.
DS556.489.F35B47 2006
959.70072'02—dc22

2006006640

ISBN-10: 1-57488-957-5
ISBN-13: 978-1-57488-957-4
(alk. paper)

Printed in the United States of America on acid-free paper that meets the American National Standards Institute Z39-48 Standard.

Potomac Books, Inc.
22841 Quicksilver Drive
Dulles, Virginia 20166

First Edition

10 9 8 7 6 5 4 3 2 1

For my daughters
Nicole, Elisabeth, and Patricia
In memory of their father

CONTENTS

LIST OF ILLUSTRATIONS   ix

FOREWORD   xiii

PREFACE   xvii

ACKNOWLEDGMENTS   xix

1 THE LAST DEPARTURE   1

2 ON WHAT RESTS OUR DESTINY?   9

3 GERMANY   37

4 FIRST ENCOUNTER   45

5 THE FIRST TRIP   55

6 THE YELLOW BAMBOO AND THE PRUNE TREE   83

7 WASHINGTON   99

8 THE PURPLE ORCHID   111

9 SPEAKING TRUTH TO POWER 125

10 HOWARD UNIVERSITY 139

11 STREET WITHOUT JOY 149

12 CAMBODIA 161

13 THE OMEN 179

14 SURVEILLANCE 189

15 TO TEST ONESELF 205

16 OPPOSING THE WAR 221

17 RETURN TO THE STREET WITHOUT JOY 237

EPILOGUE 257

NOTES 267

BIBLIOGRAPHY 273

INDEX 277

ABOUT THE AUTHOR 285

ILLUSTRATIONS

ART
BY THE AUTHOR
CREATED BETWEEN 1955 AND 1997

Hong Kong Harbor   1

Sailing Boats in the Tuileries Royal Gardens, Paris   9

Nuremberg   37

Bernard from my student sketchbook   45

Planting rice   55

Place du Théâtre, Paris   83

Night view from our apartment, Washington, DC [1]   99

Palm Trees, Indochina   111

Baby Nicole   125

Howard University   139

Notre Dame Cathedral, Paris   149

Wat Phnom, Phnom Penh, Cambodia   161

Papeete Harbor, Tahiti   179

Oracle   189

Indochina village   205

You Won't Forget[2]   221

Village on the River   237

[1] Private collection

[2] Collection of Myra MacPherson

PHOTOGRAPHS

The Fall Family   11

Forces Françaises de l'Intérieur identity card   19

Bernard in the Compagnons de France   20

Lisette with Soeur Emmanuelle   24

Bernard and his army buddy, Rémy Malot   31

The armored truck "Babette"   33

Bernard instructing his squad   34

Bernard at the Nuremberg Tribunal   38

Bernard with the map he created for the Nuremberg
    Crimes Tribunal   39

Bernard listening to testimony   42

Bernard and Dorothy   49

Bernard at Syracuse   51

Dorothy and Bernard at the Military Ball, 1952   53

Boarding a plane to Laos   65

On a supply drop mission   66

Bernard in the Delta   71

Bernard writing his dissertation   90

The infamous jeepster   104

French veterans at the Jeanne d'Arc monument   108

Dorothy, painting and pregnant   113

Ngo Dinh Diem   116

Dorothy, Nicole, and Bernard in Nice   131

In Ubol   133

Bernard with Gen. Amkha Soukhavong   135

Bernard's students with Nicole and Elisabeth at the
    annual garden party   146

Nicole is introduced to her new sister, Elisabeth   150

Marshall Andrews   152

A book party for *Street Without Joy*   154

At Pich Nil, Prince Sihanouk's hideaway in the
    Cambodian mountains   166

Prince Sihanouk visiting Dorothy's exhibit 175
Bernard interviewing North Vietnamese Prime Minister
Pham Van Dong 178
Bernard presents a copy of *The Two Viet-Nams* to
Madame Nhu 183
Lisette, Uncle Auguste, Bernard, and Aunt Marcelle in
France 186
Copies of documents from Bernard's FBI file 196
Copies of documents from Bernard's FBI file 197
Preparing to go up in a bomber 211
Combat Reconnaissance toward Konbrai 213
Bernard in a Vietnamese village 217
Taking pictures on a bombing run 220
Bernard with Walter Cronkite 223
Bernard and I.F. Stone 228
Howard University President and Mrs. James Nabrit 230
A special farewell luncheon at the French Embassy 234
The last family photo 236
Bernard with journalist Jim Pringle 240
Bernard at Camp J. J. Carroll 241
Bernard interviews a prisoner 245
Patricia, Dorothy, and Elisabeth in Lai Ha 258
Meeting Gen. Vo Nguyen Giap 264

FOREWORD

In the spring of 1999, my wife and I went to Dien Bien Phu where fifty-five years earlier the Vietminh had defeated the French after a fifty-six-day siege in one of the most famous and most important battles of the twentieth century, a battle that in a dramatic way signaled the end of the colonial era. I had long wanted to visit Dien Bien Phu. Back in 1954 when the battle had taken place, I had been a junior in college and the managing editor of the college daily, and there had been much talk of America reinforcing the French and sending troops there. That had meant greatly increased draft calls, including quite possibly sending someone like me. So I paid close attention to the battle. Though the Americans eventually decided not to engage the Vietminh there, Dien Bien Phu had made a deep impression on me. I found it remarkably easy to identify with the men on both sides, who were about my age—the French garrison caught in the constant squeeze of the noose of the siege and the young Vietnamese who were fighting this difficult war for independence, almost always with less in the way of weaponry than their Western opponents.

Now all these years later, the American war with the Vietnamese over for nearly a quarter century, travel to Hanoi and the North finally possible, I was there on assignment for a magazine, walking the battlefield with my wife. Yet despite all my work and study, the battle seemed to elude me on the first day. I simply could not get the feel of it and could not imagine the final hours as the French garrison came to the end of its struggle. The Vietnamese do warfare, especially guerrilla warfare, very well, but they did not do tourism well, not yet anyway. They are not very good at battlefield monuments and not very good at highlighting a story that is so profound and moving on both sides. They are better at living history than knowing how to honor it.

So that night we returned to our very simple motel where on occasion the air conditioner worked, and where my wife and I stayed three nights (ordering the same meal every night and getting something very different each time). That first night I stayed up and reread for the umpteenth time *Hell in a Very Small Place*, my old friend Bernard Fall's classic book on the battle. It is a great, great book, one of the most important nonfiction books of the last fifty years, a stirring bit of history and a cautionary tale for American presidents. (What, one wonders, would have happened had the men who were the architects of the second Iraq intervention read it?) It has a prominent place on even the smallest shelf for anyone wanting to understand the Vietnam wars, French and American, and in addition for anyone trying to understand the twentieth century. It is nothing less than a magisterial work.

And I stayed up past 4:00 a.m. rereading the section on the final hours of the battle. The next day when I walked the same battlefield, I had it down, and the pieces tumbled together. I could see Dien Bien Phu as the young men on both sides had in those desperate minutes. It was not surprising that it came together, for the book, like the man who wrote it, was brilliant, and intensely human and passionate in the best kind of way.

Bernard Fall was a great figure of the Vietnam wars, both the first and second: historian, journalist, and most of all, a great teacher. Someday someone may write the great definitive history of both wars and perhaps eclipse his work, but I am not so sure of it. The most important thing about Bernard was that he was the man who taught us about that small fierce country's past when we most desperately needed it. He allowed us to under-stand how the past had shaped the present back when it really mattered and when the shelf of books on both wars was still very small—tiny really—and when the leaders of the most pow-erful nation in the world did not yet know that they would be the architects of the least attractive part of their country's twenti-eth century destiny in that country. Thus what Bernard did and wrote was singularly important. He was what you might call an action historian.

He was in all ways a wonderful man. He was bright and full of energy and zest for life, talented and fearless, and above all generous, as this remarkable, tender, and insightful memoir by his widow shows. He was not in love with the war, but he was excited by the fact that his own life was so rich, that he, an émigré from Hitler's Europe, had created so important an incarnation in a nation that had reached out to him so generously and where people in general cared so little about his antecedents. He truly loved America. He had come here from France as a Fulbright scholar and stayed on to teach, loved the openness of the coun-try, and decided to become an American citizen near the end of his life. Because the sum of what he wrote about Vietnam was so pessimistic, the architects of that war, who became in time the architects of a Great American Lying Machine as the war went on, needed to try to diminish his credibility. One of the worst of their canards—they attacked all of us in those days (we were too young or too left, or too innocent, or in my case, too idealis-tic)—was that he wanted America to lose because he was French and the French had lost there. Nothing—and I mean nothing—could have been further from the truth. Even before he received his citizenship papers, I thought of him as the most American and least European of men. He exalted in the freedom and op-portunity that this country had given him.

When I first met Bernard, I belonged to a small group of correspondents who were constantly under attack because of their pessimism. It was the early sixties, and we were young. I was twenty-eight, which was about average, and my pal Neil Sheehan was even younger, twenty-five. We were good at what we did, and we sensed instinctively that it did not work, but we depended on Bernard for the reason *why* it did not work. At the time we were considered by two administrations to be "enemies of the people." Five of us, all of us in that unofficial way taught by Bernard, went on to win the Pulitzer Prize. Not many professors can claim that five of their students did so well in such a short time. But then Bernard was teaching not just at Howard University—he was teaching the largest graduate class in the nation. The whole country was learning from him, if a bit too slowly.

He was a not a war lover, but he honored the men who fought it on both sides. The men who fought it reciprocated. Charley Mohr, one of the great *New York Times* reporters who covered the war, liked to tell of the time that he had come back from an operation late at night only to find that the mess hall was closing down and they would not feed him. Just then Bernard walked in, and dinner was immediately served to both of them. "But why did you feed him and not me?" Charley asked the mess sergeant. "Because he is Bernard Fall and you are not," he responded.

Bernard was brave to the end. He did not merely live with his prophecies, no matter how accurate they were. He had to see them, had to be there, to feel the battle and talk to the men who were fighting there. And it cost him his life. Those who knew Bernard Fall honor him to this day, and forty years later I still mourn him—the intellect, and the courage, and the laughter.

David Halberstam

PREFACE

Soon after my husband, Bernard Fall, died in Vietnam in 1967, I knew I must write his story. Bernard's life was one of truth, courage, honor, and destiny. In 1971, I was given a six month leave of absence from my job with the U.S. Information Agency to begin this book. In my husband's basement office I found a myriad of documents and writings to research for my project. I went to France and interviewed Bernard's friends from the French Resistance during World War II. His best friend in the army and his school teacher, who knew him as a young immigrant in France, sent me letters full of stories about Bernard. I contacted other Resistance friends who now lived in the United States. Others contacted me. A former girlfriend gave me letters he had written to her in their teenage years during the war. I traveled to the Bronx to talk to a man who had lived in the same villa in Nice with the Fall family before police came and tore their family apart. I tried without success to obtain Bernard's FBI file, from the days when J. Edgar Hoover suspected him of being a French spy, or at least disliked what he was writing about the war in Vietnam. Above all, Bernard's sister Lisette spent hours telling me about their early years.

I began to write. But my daughters were young. They needed my attention and my six months were soon up. I packed all the materials into cartons and put them away for another day.

Twenty-four years later, with the publication of Robert McNamara's *In Retrospect*, I knew that the day had arrived. In his book, McNamara wrote that when it came to Vietnam, he and the government found itself setting policy for a region they knew nothing about. He claimed that they "lacked experts to consult to compensate for their ignorance."[1] In truth, there were plenty of experts, inside and outside of government. My husband Bernard Fall, right here in Washington, was one of the country's outstanding experts. But McNamara was not interested in learning the truth.

About the same time, I saw in the newspaper that President Bill Clinton had issued a directive to the FBI to be more forthcoming in releasing people's files. In 1995 I applied, for a second time, for Bernard's FBI file. After five years, the file arrived, and enough of it was not blacked out to show how extensive the Bureau's snooping had been.

I resumed my interviews and with few exceptions I taped them all. I traveled to Vietnam and interviewed Gen. Vo Nguyen Giap, whose forces had defeated both the French and Americans in wars that lasted some thirty years. In the early part of the book, I have quoted Bernard verbatim and have honored his insistence on writing Vietnam as two words separated by a hyphen, Viet-Nam.

Bernard was an eminent writer, military analyst, and scholar. His legacy is one of dedication to finding the truth and exposing it, regardless of the consequences. Although he has been dead nearly forty years, his dedication to the truth and to realism in our nation's foreign policy should still be an inspiration and an important lesson to us today.

ACKNOWLEDGMENTS

Dᴜʀɪɴɢ the long gestation period of this book I have been sustained by the encouragement of many people.

I am grateful to Patrick Anderson for transforming my rambling text into a comprehensive and readable book, a challenging task.

I thank David Halberstam who, because of his friendship and regard for Bernard, generously offered to write the foreword to my book.

From the very beginning Myra MacPherson has been with me with her support and advice. My agent Ronald Goldfarb has believed in this story since he saw my first chapter twenty-five years ago and finally succeeded in having me finish the entire book. I thank publisher Don McKeon for his encouragement and patience.

Gen. Vo Nguyen Giap was kind in writing his thoughts about Bernard for me. Mr. Huu Mai has been extremely helpful in many ways in this venture.

Seth Resnik read much of my original draft and pointed out the essentials to improve it. A number of writer friends read early parts: Ann Crittenden believed in this book, offering her help and critiquing my proposal; Joy Billington Doty, Jack Casserly, John Jacobs, Kevin Buckley, and Marilyn Heilprin read early chapters and spurred me on. My thanks to Marc Pachter and members of the Washington Biography Group, including Pat McNees and Florence Rubenfeld, who offered helpful comments on my early work.

A special thanks to Megan Desnoyers of the John F. Kennedy Library, curator of the Bernard B. Fall collection, and to Michelle De Martino, who catalogued Bernard's voluminous correspondence for my use.

David J. Steinberg gave warm support. He and Ralph Greenhouse supplied much background on WAHRAF (Washington branch of the Human Relations Area Files).

I am indebted to Gail Hansberry, who located a number of my husband's former students, including Ella Meisel Kelly and Rey Madoo, who supplied background on Howard University students of that era.

There are many who helped in different ways. Lady Borton shared her research findings. Horst Faas, Richard Pyle, Tran Van Dinh, and Henry Gallagher helped prepare me for Vietnam. Peter Hickman, David Chandler, Max Kraus, and Sika and Charles Meyer supplied their memories of Cambodia. Lucien Stervinou helped with French translation. Marion Goldin found me a long-lost source. Polly Berteling typed early tape transcriptions. Judith and Milton Viorst helped at the beginning. Father Robert Drinan phoned me periodically to make sure that I was on track with my writing. John Black wrote a song entitled "Dorothy," whose lyrics urged me to finish my memoir.

Numerous individuals, although not mentioned in the text, shared their memories of Bernard and helped in other ways, including Joe and Elsie Paull, Pierre D'Ornano, Joel Halpern, Arthur Dommen, Barry Zorthian, Christopher Goscha, Inpeng Suryadhay, Dorothy Reese Bloomfield, Michèle Merowka, Tom Ware, Bill Weidenbacher, Randy Fertel, Bill Dunlap, Gilly Burlingham, Morse Byer, Claudia Gertie Hall, Phillip Heymann, Frank Sieverts, Robert McLellan, Patricia Berger, and Ralph and Glika Rappaport.

My grandson Blake Bernard Fall-Conroy produced a Bernard

Fall web site and set up a filing system for his grandfather's published articles for easy retrieval. Robert Quinn produced a special Bernard Fall web site.

I am indebted to Bernard's sister Lisette Fall Biret for her contribution, without which I could not have written this story in its entirety. Gertrud Barnert, daughter of Bernard's beloved Viennese aunt and uncle, supplied background on their lives. Renée Kurz Wiener gave me letters that Bernard had written to her as a teenager. Charlotte Sorkine Noshpitz and Catherine Palinker shared their French Resistance stories.

I am especially grateful to Harvey Resnik for his constant urging that I write, for his belief in this book and the importance of my story.

To my wonderful daughters, Nicole Françoise Fall, Elisabeth Anne Fall, and Patricia Madeleine Fall Salamy, and their children, I give this loving tribute to their father and grandfather.

1

THE LAST DEPARTURE

I WATCHED as he packed his suitcase, the largest one, the one that would do for a long stay. I said nothing, although I wanted to beg him to stay. He kept packing, engrossed in the details of the trip. The shirts and trousers, the razor and comb. I brought him his date book and he cast me a wary glance. My husband, Bernard Fall, was once again leaving me to visit his mistress.

That September of 1966, he had begun a sabbatical year from Howard University in Washington, D.C., a break after ten years as a professor of government and international relations. He would leave not only me but the admiring students from whom he demanded perfection in his friendly but firm manner. He was a popular figure on campus both because of his teaching style and his international reputation as a leading expert on Vietnam. The war there was raging, many of his students had friends there or might be drafted themselves, and most of them believed he understood the realities of the conflict far better than President Johnson and the other leaders who wanted them to fight and possibly die in that distant land. His involvement with Vietnam had begun with his first trip there in 1953. It had become a passion that occupied virtually all of his time and thoughts. That was why I called Vietnam his mistress. Twelve thousand miles away, it beckoned him, like a siren's song, to come unravel its mysteries and expose its truths. I had grown to accept his obsession and, as Bernard increasingly was a voice of reason in a bitter national debate, I supported him, even though part of me feared that his passion would one day destroy him.

That autumn had begun well. It was one of those rare periods in life when everything was right. Our third daughter, Patricia Madeleine Marcelle, had been born on September 20. Bernard's lingering kidney infection seemed to be under control, thanks to the huge pills he took for it. I was planning both for a January exhibit of my paintings and for what I hoped would be a glorious seven months in Hong Kong, where our daughters and I would await Bernard's visits from Vietnam.

Bernard was a powerful man both in physique and intellect. He was a muscular six footer who worked eighteen hours a day on his research and writing, stopping only for classes, lecture commitments, and romps with our children. But in 1963, Bernard had suffered a life-threatening illness, during which he lost one kidney and was left with the other so impaired that he had doubts about his physical well-being.

2

Along with a vast enthusiasm for life, he was blessed with extraordinary intellectual gifts. His total recall, combined with the ability to interpret mountains of data, resulted in the penetrating analysis that distinguished his books, articles, lectures, and conversations. His conclusions were often controversial, unacceptable to those with established, safe opinions. When Bernard was attacked for his views, he fought back relentlessly. He would not compromise with those whose ideas he believed were false or based on ideology rather than fact. He was further blessed with a gift for languages. Nothing pleased him more than to surprise a stranger with his fluent French, English, or German.

He had, while still a teenager, become a warrior, fighting with the French Resistance against the Germans, and he carried a warrior's mentality into his intellectual life. He could be abrasive and he intended to win every argument, devastating his opponent with the depth of his information and the power of his mind. Despite all this, he had an underlying gentleness. When this man with the crew cut and big grin entered a room, children and animals ran to him. He had a ready smile and a quick wit, even when discussing the most serious subjects.

During this sabbatical year Bernard intended to write a book on the Vietcong, the South Vietnamese Communist force then battling the might of the U.S. military. He had received a Guggenheim grant to support this, his sixth trip to Vietnam since 1953. He had to go, because he believed passionately in firsthand research. Unlike the armchair scholars he disdained, he would accompany troops on operation into Vietcong-held territory. He would interview prisoners and travel through the countryside talking to the soldiers, peasants, and local officials.

As a dedicated scholar, who was also a first-class journalist, he had to do this and I accepted it, but with trepidation.

This time, at least, the girls and I would be near at hand. At that time, Nicole was nine, Elisabeth was six, and Patricia was just an infant. On previous trips, Bernard had taken us as far as France. After visiting his family there or doing research in the

French army archives, he would take off for Vietnam, leaving us in Europe to travel a bit before we returned home. It was our family joke that he bribed us with those trips to Europe.

This year the plan was that Bernard would precede us to Asia by several months. Our newborn daughter needed time to build up her immunity before we took her to the other side of the world. Also, the exhibit of my paintings was set for January. So we decided that, while Bernard would leave for Vietnam after Patricia's birth, I would wait until early February before leaving for Hong Kong with the girls.

What plans we had! We might return home via Communist China, which was forbidden to Americans at that time, but open to us thanks to Bernard's French passport. Perhaps we would even journey to Moscow via the Trans-Siberian Railroad. Also, Bernard was urging me to come to Vietnam. "Just leave the kids with the nanny," he said. "You could sketch the soldiers in battle. And don't forget to pack those hiking boots of yours. They'll be great for trekking through the jungles of Vietnam."

I had no answer to that. As the mother of three young children, how could I expose myself to such danger? The notion seemed absurd.

After Patricia arrived on September 20 I waited nervously for Bernard to announce his departure date, but he did not. Before his other trips to Vietnam he had been filled with enthusiasm, but this time we both felt foreboding. The war had become so massive, so violent. We watched the ever-growing "body counts" reported on the evening news. The war haunted us as it did millions of others.

In those uncertain days, I watched as he played with the baby, then held her quietly, gazing at her, perhaps wondering if he would see her grow up. I would sometimes catch him looking at me in this way, when he thought I was asleep or not looking. I had never seen him do that before. Yet I said nothing, nor did he. He would go. He had to.

We both had much work to do that fall. Bernard had his book *The Two Viet-Nams* to update, articles to write, and lectures to deliver. I had my exhibition to prepare for. Bernard wrote while I painted. Our baby grew. I secretly hoped that he would give up the commitment he had made. I was delighted as he continued to accept commissions for articles and lectures into October and then November. I naively imagined that this could go on forever.

Friends gave dinner parties in anticipation of his departure. The longer he stayed the more he was feted, until I began to have an uneasy feeling that there were too many farewells and they were all too final. After all, we would be gone for less than a year. French Ambassador Charles Lucet gave a luncheon in Bernard's honor that brought together our closest friends. Two of the guests were men Bernard particularly admired, the columnist Walter Lippmann and Senator William Fulbright.

On November 19 we celebrated Bernard's fortieth birthday. The next day he announced his departure date, December 8. The articles were finished and the lectures given, and now the dreaded day approached. I felt like Cassandra before her fate at Troy.

Two couples, close friends of ours, came to call the evening before his departure. Marcus Raskin, who came with his wife Barbara, was a former disarmament advisor for President Kennedy and had cofounded the Institute for Policy Studies. Marc had approached Bernard two years earlier with an idea for a book. Deeply concerned about the U.S. involvement in Vietnam, he wanted to put out a compilation of official documents and interpretive comment on the country and the war. Joining forces, the two men produced *The Viet-Nam Reader,* which became a basic text for the anti-war movement. The book not only explained the background of the war but proposed a diplomatic solution for ending it. Marc was later indicted, along with Dr. Benjamin Spock (author of *Baby and Child Care*) and others, on a charge of "conspiracy to counsel, aid and abet violations of the Selective Service Act." Marc was acquitted after a trial in Boston. The other four men were convicted but acquitted a year later upon appeal.

Our other guests that night were Tony Cistaro and his wife, Jean. Bernard and Tony had a different kind of bond. They had met in the summer of 1965 when my husband was on his fifth trip in Vietnam. Bernard had gone into Chau Doc province planning to go out daily with the Special Forces patrolling the Delta. He had arrived on a convoy and would have to leave by his own means, although Gen. William Westmoreland had put two helicopters at his disposal.

Tony represented the U.S. Agency for International Development in Chau Doc. He had read Bernard's books and was delighted to meet this man whose work he so respected. As they talked, they discovered that they would be returning to Saigon the same day. Tony always drove up for supplies because plane flights were so irregular. What happened next became a favorite joke between them. Tony thought that a ride to Saigon in one of the Army's helicopters sounded like a fine idea. But under Bernard's questioning, he admitted he usually drove.

"You do that often?" Bernard pressed. "Is it secure?"

"Well, we have been shot at on occasion," Tony admitted. "But it's secure enough that *I'll* drive it."

"Great," said Bernard, always eager for a new adventure, "then I'll go up with *you!*"

The trip took several hours. Bernard relished riding shotgun— almost literally, with a submachine gun in his lap—on the lookout for VC. A close friendship began on that trip. Several months later, on a similar trip with two other men, Tony's truck was blown up by a land mine. Sgt. Carl Torello and Maj. John Arnn, whom Bernard had met, were killed. Tony was a mass of broken bones when he was found by friendly Vietnamese.

We learned of this disaster months later when Tony was brought to nearby Bethesda Naval Hospital. His wife Jean called us and we went to see him. He was in a plaster cast from the neck down. We talked about the damage done, the internal injuries, the bones to be mended. Tony did not know that he had been admitted as a terminal patient.

After that, Bernard visited Tony weekly, no matter how busy he was. Slowly, Tony shed his cast and the pulleys which held his legs and left arm taut. He finally left his hospital bed and one day appeared at our house in a wheelchair.

He was still walking with the aid of crutches on that December evening when he and Jean arrived. The six of us talked quietly, mostly about Vietnam. "When are you coming to Vietnam?" Bernard asked Marc, taunting him affectionately. "Come with me and really learn about the country." He often chastised his intellectual friends who wrote about the war from afar. Sometimes he succeeded in goading them into a trip there. Eventually Tony, who tired easily, rose to leave.

"Don't do anything foolish," he said.

"Don't worry," Bernard joked, "I won't do anything as foolish as *you* did."

At the door, the two men embraced. Suddenly, Tony had tears streaming down his face. No one spoke. He feared, as we all did, that he would not see his friend again.

That last morning, I watched as Bernard packed the khaki shorts and shirts, the safari jackets, the mess kit, that enormous jar of pills—three a day for nine months—the film, the cameras, and the galleys for his new book on the battle of Dien Bien Phu, *Hell In A Very Small Place*. I finally summoned my courage and appealed, "Bernard, don't go." His only reply was, "You know I have to." He had stayed too long already.

We focused on last-minute matters. He gave me instructions on forwarding mail, and lectured the children about being good. "I want you both to work hard and to be good students and to mind Mommy," he told the two older girls. We discussed the details of my trip to Hong Kong. Finally, the suitcase was closed, the Leica camera and portable tape recorder were ready to be hoisted onto his shoulder, and his reading material for the flight was assembled.

He said I should not drive him to the airport. His taxi arrived all too soon. The driver came for his suitcase. At the doorway

Bernard bent to kiss the girls, then me. At the bottom of our steps, as he neared the taxi, he turned and gazed at us. It was a grave, definitive look. He climbed in, closed the door, and waved to us as the cab sped off.

I never saw him again.

2

ON WHAT RESTS OUR DESTINY?

I<small>N</small> 1925, in Vienna, Anna Seligmann married Leo Fall. He was 32 and she was 29. Anna had come to Vienna from the town of Mosty Wielkie in Galicia, which was formerly Austrian but after World War I was made part of Poland. Her parents had died in the cholera epidemic of 1914, leaving Anna, at eighteen, in charge of her four younger sisters, Marcelle, Paula, Hilde, and Lotti.

Well-educated and trilingual, Anna found work as a secretary. The two youngest sisters, Hilde and Lotti, were temporarily put in an orphanage. Marcelle eventually made her way to Paris, where she married a chauffeur, Auguste Biret, who was a Catholic from Brittany. Soon Marcelle sent for Lotti, the youngest sister, who eventually married Daniel Dedina, a tall and handsome blond Catholic.

Leo Fall, also from Galicia, had come to Vienna at the age of fifteen to look for work. He was a soft-spoken, gentle man who loved music and was distantly related to the composer with whom he shared his name. Together, Leo and Anna opened a women's clothing store on Franz Joseph Quai in Vienna. Bernard was born in 1926 and Lisette, his sister, two and a half years later. Bernard, as the first son in a Jewish family, was doted on, and his strong-minded mother also pushed him to make good grades in school, which he did, so much so that his parents affectionately called him "Herr Professor." Lisette often felt neglected as she watched her older brother win his plaudits, including a prize for skiing at the tender age of five. His ability to ski would later serve him well as a teenager fighting with the maquis in the French Alps.

By age five, Bernard was a voracious reader and was permitted to start school early. His favorite books were about war, soldiers, battles, and far-off exotic lands. Lisette gave up playing with dolls to play soldiers with him. They recreated the French and Indian War, the Napoleonic Wars, the exploits of Genghis Khan. The piano became their fort as they scrambled along the top of it or hid underneath.

Anna's sister Hilde had married Franz Freistedter, an Austrian civil servant, and their book-filled apartment became a treasure trove for Bernard. One Saturday afternoon he discovered there a book that he soon loved. It was a large, colorfully illustrated volume entitled *Der Weltkrieg in Bildern* (World War I in Pictures). There were pictures of weapons, soldiers, trenches, army commanders, and members of the Imperial family. During each visit he poured over the book, barely able to part with it when it was time to leave. Years later, after the war, Franz gave Bernard the book as a gift.

Franz could not have given it to him earlier because Leo would not have allowed the book in his home. He had fought in the Austrian army during the war depicted in the book and he despised the glorification of war. He became a pacifist and early on announced that Bernard must study medicine "because when there is a war, the doctors are never on the front lines." But, Lisette later told me, Bernard would reply, "When I grow up I want to be a general, sitting high on a horse, with a long sword, in a beautiful uniform with many medals on it."

On Sundays, when Leo's store was closed, he would set out to amuse and enlighten his children. He might take them to a Laurel and Hardy movie or to the Prater, Vienna's giant amuse-

The Fall family. Left to right: Lisette, age nine, Anna, Leo, and Bernard, age eleven.

ment park, or to a circus. A circus clown once gave Bernard a tiny harmonica. In later life, he always carried a harmonica with him even though he did not play it well. I thought it reminded him of his happy, all-too-short childhood. The family had season tickets to the opera, but Bernard and Lisette remembered that Wagner would put Leo to sleep. For Bernard's part, as an adult he would not attend anything more serious than *Carmen* at the Paris Opera. All this added up to a happy, bourgeois existence for Bernard and Lisette, a tranquil childhood blessed with material comforts and intellectual riches.

Then, so swiftly, Hitler rose to power. With the *Anschluss* of March 1938, Germany annexed Austria and took control of the most important Austrian banks and industries. In September, Bernard's school was closed to Jewish students. Twice, he was beaten by boys in an anti-Semitic, supposedly patriotic youth organization. Humiliated, he withdrew deeper into his books, dreaming that he was part of a military group and could fight back.

Soon his parents' store was confiscated by the Germans. Leo wanted to flee with the family to Spain and from there to the United States, but Anna insisted that they go to France. Her sister Lotti came from Paris for the children. She had brought the passports of her two sons, who were four years younger than Bernard and Lisette. The railroad station was teeming with the Gestapo as the parents kissed the children good-by. Leo, a religious Jew, wept at the sight of the little cross that Uncle Franz had pinned on Lisette's lapel to protect her on the journey to Paris.

The train was crowded as Lotti and the two children looked fearfully at the others in their compartment. Lisette was dressed in boy's clothes and her long hair was stuffed into a cap. Bernard crouched down so that his long legs would not betray that he was twelve, not eight. An unsuspecting Austrian guard let them pass and at the border they pretended to be asleep and the Swiss official checking passports did not disturb them.

Paris in November of 1938 was in political disarray following the Munich Conference. Upon their arrival there, the children were separated. Bernard went to live with Aunt Marcelle and Uncle Auguste, who were childless. He quickly learned French. Aunt Lotti and Uncle Daniel took Lisette, who had more trouble with the language and missed her brother terribly. Bernard entered school at which he continued to excel.

As the months passed, the situation in Austria further deteriorated. The Viennese Nazis were even more zealous in their anti-Semitism than the Germans. Tens of thousands of Austrian Jews were jailed and their possessions stolen. Anna and Leo decided to join their children in France, but Leo stayed behind to make provisions for his mother and sisters. Because Poland was still neutral, Anna reinstated her Polish citizenship. In June 1939, she crossed northern Italy by train and then traveled in a fishing boat to France. Lacking a visa, she entered the country clandestinely and made her way to Paris.

By August, Leo had found a lawyer he entrusted with the care of his aged mother and two sisters. Despite his efforts, they were subsequently deported to a concentration camp, where they perished. Leo also reclaimed his Polish nationality but nonetheless encountered great difficulty as he tried to reach his family. He was arrested as he tried to enter Switzerland and was returned to Austria. His second attempt was through Germany where he was arrested and spent three weeks in jail before he was freed and reached Belgium. He hid there for eight months, unable to enter France without a visa and desperately writing to his family.

In Paris, Anna found her children separated but well cared for. Determined to reunite her family, she took Bernard and Lisette to Nice, in the so-called Free Zone of France, confident that Leo would manage to join them. She sold her jewelry but her money soon ran low. After relocating several times, she moved into the Villa Beauregard, in the hills overlooking Nice on the rue Pessicart. It consisted of forty rooms, each occupied by a family.

The children walked seven kilometers to a school run by Monsieur and Madame Culas and attended by twenty young refugees from the villa on rue Pessicart. Bernard, already speaking excellent French, struck Monsieur Culas as an animated and brilliant child. Bernard was becoming very French, more ardent and patriotic than the French themselves. He became attached to the schoolmaster who treated him with such respect and affection. Monsieur Culas had been a professor of science at the Collège Sisowath in Phnom Penh, Cambodia, from 1929 to 1932, and he spoke with enthusiasm about Indochina. I always thought that was the start of Bernard's love of that distant region of the world. He would see Monsieur Culas again during the war and throughout his life he maintained a correspondence with his beloved schoolmaster.

War came to Europe on a sunny afternoon as Bernard stood high on the hill of the rue Pessicart, overlooking the blue Riviera. The city below remained unchanged. "I always imagined that it would be raining or night when war breaks out," he later wrote. "Here I was. It was a perfectly sunny Riviera day and I was standing on a hill waiting for the thunder and the rains to come down and nothing happened. In a way I was quite disappointed that war would start on this perfectly banal, beautiful day."[1]

That was Bernard's recollection, many years later, of September 9, 1939, the day the European war officially began, when he was twelve. Actually, the war was still far from Nice at that time. But the German blitzkrieg soon moved westward and in the early days of June 1940, amid the chaos as Hitler's armies swept into France, Leo managed to cross the border from Belgium, only to be deported to the French internment camp of Saint-Cyprien. He huddled there with hundreds of other refugees in vile conditions, but finally was set free and in August 1940, a year after leaving Vienna, he joined his family in Nice.

The four of them lived together at the Villa Beauregard. It was a kind of kibbutz, administered by the Nice Refugee Committee, a group of French Jews with local funding. It had been set up through a foundation supported by the writer Sholem Asch and was intended to prepare families for a life of agriculture in Israel. Additional support came from ORT (Organization for the Distribution of Artisanal and Agricultural Skills) and JOINT (now the American Jewish Joint Distribution Committee), two American-based organizations that sought to help Jewish refugees. The villa had five acres of land where the families grew the food they needed to survive. Men from many countries and all walks of life learned to spread manure, empty septic tanks, and raise chickens. Leo told Lisette that he no longer recognized himself as the man who had owned a women's apparel store in Vienna.

Nice was part of the so-called Free Zone. While the Germans occupied Paris and half the country, the collaborationist Vichy government ran the unoccupied or Free Zone. In occupied France in August 1940, there were 300,000 Jews age six or above who were forced to wear the yellow star of David. Their businesses were closed and they were removed from all governmental, commercial, and industrial activities. Jews were forbidden to have telephones or to attend theatres, restaurants, and libraries. Thousands of French Jews fled to Vichy France, which already had an influx of refugees from other countries.

The Vichy regime, on its own initiative, had already begun anti-Jewish programs but the Nazis wanted more. In the summer of 1942 they demanded that the Vichy government turn over all foreign Jews. The Villa Beauregard fell victim to that edict.

At one o'clock in the morning on August 26, the men came up the driveway, then up the stairs. Lisette and Anna watched from the window. It was a clear night and the moonlight reflected on the steel helmets of the French police. There were six or eight of them, including one doctor. The terrified families thought the soldiers had come for the men, because they wanted workers to be transported to Germany, but would not take the women and children. The men hid as best they could, in the villa or outside.

"Leo, it's the police!" Anna called down to her husband, who had been sleeping on the ground floor, in case of such a raid as this. He jumped out of the window to the garden where other men had been sleeping. They had seen these raids before in Germany and Austria.

The police spread out, pounding on the doors. Those not quickly opened were kicked down. They entered the room where the Fall family lived. Bernard was in bed with a fever. "He has a sun stroke and can't be moved," said Anna. She was desperate that they not take Bernard. "We'll see about that," a soldier replied. "Meanwhile, get ready. And the little girl, too." The doctor came over. Seeing that Bernard was feverish and sweating, he agreed that the boy was very sick. They would need an ambulance to transport him. "All right," the policeman said, "we'll leave him here. But we'll be back for him tomorrow."

It took three hours to round up what remained of the forty families in the villa. By four o'clock everyone was ready. Lisette had dressed, bewildered by what was happening. As Anna prepared to leave, she went to Bernard. Tears streamed down her cheeks. "Good-bye, my child. Be a good boy." "Good-bye, Maman. I'll be seeing you soon."[2]

Women, children, babies, and those men who had not escaped—Bloman, Greenbaum, Hirshel, Grabowski, Igel— all were taken. Only two of those men would return. They were taken in buses to the military barracks known as Caserne d'Auvare.

On August 26, the morning after the raid, before the police could return to claim Bernard, a man named Henry Frankiel came to the Villa Beauregard. He was a Jew and a French army veteran. He and his family lived at the bottom of the hill on rue Pessicart. He knew people in the villa and had warned them there might be a raid. Henry found Bernard in bed, still feverish. Wrapping a blanket around him, he took Bernard with him on his large military bicycle to the Frankiels' house where the boy remained until the raids and deportations subsided.

Meanwhile, Anna and Lisette were among hundreds of terrified prisoners at the d'Auvare barracks. The children and babies settled on straw strewn about on the cement floor, while adults waited in a long line for water. French policemen pointed submachine guns at the women and children. Thirteen-year-old Lisette, too terrified to move or eat, clung to her mother. As hundreds more were brought in, they all mingled in the filth and heat for a week.

Finally, just before the prisoners were to be shipped out, they learned it was possible for children to be spared deportation. The Vichy government, while agreeing to German demands, had insisted that children, the aged, and the infirm be permitted to stay behind. The parents of children under eighteen had only to sign a paper. It was an agonizing decision for any mother. Anna and the other parents did not know what lay ahead. Would the little ones be better off going to an uncertain fate with their parents or released with nowhere to go? How would the children survive alone?

Anna did not hesitate. She told Lisette, "You must find Bernard," and signed the release. It took three policemen to tear the child away from her mother, but Anna kept telling her, "You must find your brother." In so doing, she saved her daughter's life. Lisette and eleven other children came out of the barracks on the night of August 31 and thus were spared death at Auschwitz with their parents.

The French Red Cross gave the children rides back to Nice, where they spent the night sleeping on the grass outside the Red Cross building. In the morning Lisette set out on foot for the Villa Beauregard, only to find it empty. There was no sign of Bernard. Not knowing what else to do, Lisette stayed there, eating whatever she could find in the garden. She hid there alone, sleeping in her parents' bed, for several weeks.

One day, as Lisette was gathering potatoes from the garden, a peasant spied her and said, "My poor child. You mustn't stay in this big house all alone." The woman took her to her home in the country.

Leo, having escaped from the raid, was in hiding, sleeping on a mattress with four other men in the apartment of a family named Zeiger. The Zeigers, like the Frankiels who had taken in

Bernard, were naturalized French citizens who were safe from the roundups, which were thus far restricted to refugees from other countries.

In time, through a message she left with the Jewish Committee, Lisette found her brother and father. Bernard and Lisette took a room on the Avenue Georges Clemenceau. It was in the Villa des Fleurs, which belonged to a woman of Polish origin called Madame Richard. She needed money, so she rented out every room in her apartment. A Madame Lanselle and her young son occupied the room next to Bernard and Lisette, and they looked to her when they desperately needed help. Lisette cooked whatever they could find to eat. Food became increasingly scarce. At one point, she and Bernard cooked and ate a cat.

Leo, as an adult Jew and a foreigner, remained in hiding. When he felt it safe, he would visit his children. This gentle man, who had seen his life destroyed and his wife carried away, was increasingly distraught. He began to look for guidance from his young son, who in contrast was increasingly resolute. From learning to survive under perilous circumstances, Bernard had become self-reliant at the age of sixteen.

Soon Bernard was living a double life, passing himself off as French and non-Jewish even as he became involved in Zionist and anti-Nazi resistance movements. One of his first moves, which probably saved his life, was to join the Compagnons de France, a paramilitary youth group. Bernard would in later years refer to them as "the Boy Scouts" but they were more than that. France had suffered a humiliating defeat by the Germans in 1940. In an effort to rebuild the morale of French youth and to teach them to obey and trust their leaders, the Vichy leader Marshal Pétain created the Compagnons. They eventually had 100,000 members. The boys wore uniforms, saluted the French flag, sang patriotic songs, and attended camps that provided work for unemployed and homeless youth between ages fifteen and twenty. The Compagnons provided an organized existence with a patriotic overlay but, unknown to the authorities, also served as a cover under which Jewish boys like Bernard could seem "respectable" even as they engaged in Resistance activities.

At sixteen, Bernard joined the Compagnons and wore its uniform—black beret, dark blue shorts, colored tie, and the khaki shirt with its emblem of the Compagnons, a white weathercock on a red background. All his life he liked uniforms. He attended meetings, helped the aged, and, for several weeks in the summer, participated in chopping down trees in the forest near St. Etienne. But that was not all he was doing.

Bernard's work in the Resistance seems to have evolved over a period of time, but in later years he tied it to a specific event. As he told an interviewer in 1966: "I joined the underground on a sunny afternoon of November 8, 1942." That, he explained, was the day—eleven days before his sixteenth birthday—that U.S. and British troops invaded North Africa. That day, as he recounted it, an older man, a former lieutenant colonel in the French Air Force, organized "fifty of us—young ones, reserve officers, boy

Forces Françaises de l'Intérieur (F.F.I.) identity card.

19

scouts"—to hijack a tanker and sail it across the Mediterranean Sea to Algeria, where they could join with the Allied forces.[3] Unfortunately, about thirty miles out, an Italian torpedo boat stopped them and forced them to return to Nice. As Bernard told it, he was released because of his age "but it was a pretty close thing and from there on in I was wedded to the underground—that was it."

Because of his membership in the Compagnons, its uniform, and his forged identity papers, Bernard was able to move about freely. He was soon working with at least three Resistance groups that operated in the vicinity of Nice and Cannes. One was the clandestine group MJS (Mouvement de la Jeunesse Sioniste or

Bernard in the Compagnons de France, a Vichy paramilitary youth organization, March 1944.

Zionist Youth Movement), who worked in mostly nonviolent ways to resist the Germans. The MJS hid Jews, provided them with forged identity papers, and helped them escape from France. Bernard was an ardent Zionist in those days, but by the end of the war his attitude would change and he rejected his Jewish identity. One major reason for this was the willingness of the Jewish Committee, the organization of Jewish elders who worked with the Vichy police, to give up the names of the refugee families in the Villa Beauregard to the police. In one traumatic night, he had seen his family shattered, his mother taken away, never to be seen again. Whatever justifications the Jewish elders might offer, he could never forgive such betrayal.

Bernard also worked with the Armée Juive, a more militant Jewish Resistance group whose members took an oath to fight to the death against the Nazis. One of his companions in AJ was Pierre Lanselle, who had joined the Compagnons with Bernard. Lanselle later told me that Bernard was well aware of the danger of his double life. "He was marked by the war, always idealistic, tall in his uniform with its silver braid and chevrons. He was a solitary voyager needing to see the thing *sur place* [on the spot]. For us, it was the exhilaration and determination in the struggle against the Germans."

Bernard always wanted to operate in the open, insisting that one had to fight back against oppressors with physical force. Later in life, he would refer to his own strength as his "machine." It was his machine that throughout his life made possible his constant work, and gave him the strength and resilience to perform, to fight, to think, and to write.

Through his membership in the Compagnons, Bernard was able to attend a technical school in Cannes. There, Bernard and Lanselle distributed false identity papers. They traveled to Grasse where they stole an official stamp for the papers from an office in the town hall. In the village of St. Vallier de Thiey, a comrade manufactured huge numbers of identity cards. They were helped by Catholics who provided false ration cards and identity cards.

A Monseigneur Clément was a key ally. It was thus that Bernard's name was changed from the Germanic "Berthold" to the French "Bernard"; he became Bernard Roger Fall, born in Montpellier on November 19, 1926, his actual date of birth. After the war, he retained Berthold as a middle initial as Bernard B. Fall.

Pierre Lanselle told me that while working with the Armée Juive they formed a camp for Jewish children who were in danger of being deported. They fed them hundreds of cans of food they stole from the Compagnons. They smuggled arms, sabotaged bridges, and blew up trains. They eliminated informers and collaborators, and they didn't hesitate to kill Germans. Once several of them found a German soldier in the toilet on a train that stopped in Grenoble. They killed him, took his supplies, and fled.

Years later, in a lecture, Bernard explained (in a scholarly third-person narrative) how he and his colleagues used terror as a weapon and why they changed their tactics:

> At first, they tried to kill German sentries, German soldiers. It seemed terribly heroic in the beginning. But the Germans would take fifty hostages and execute them for each killed German soldier, which was unproductive in terms of kill ratios. The French population was tired of bearing the brunt of their guerrilla activities. That worked against the guerrilla. So finally, in 1943, by trial and error, they switched to killing French collaborationists. There was a triple advantage to that: (a) the French collaborationist would not be armed, which helped, (b) the French Vichy rarely would take hostages in reprisal for the killing of a collaborationist, (c) for every collaborationist killed, there would be another five thousand Frenchmen who wouldn't give the time of day to the German Army henceforth. Now, *there* was the kind of deterrent effect we were actually looking for, the kind that would isolate the German troops from the population, in fact insulate them. There would be complete loss of contact

with the population without creating any kind of adverse reaction toward us. This is precisely the secret of the guerilla operator in this particular field. Terrorism in this particular sense becomes a strategic weapon and not a tactical weapon.[4]

After the Allied landing in North Africa in November 1942, the Germans invaded the Free Zone of France and the Gestapo tried to force the French to hand over their French Jews. At the same time, the Italians moved into eight zones east of the Rhone. The Italians, who at that point were more anti-German than anti-Semitic, claimed many Jews as their prisoners and installed them in hotels or let them escape to the Resistance. Bernard always kept a warm place in his heart for the Italians.

With the arrival of the Germans, Nice became a city of terror. The raids increased and people went underground, changing their identities. Lisette could not remain in the room on rue Georges Clemenceau. Her life was saved thanks to the efforts of Moussa Abadi, a Syrian Jewish student of medieval literature who had decided to stay in France when the war came. He worked to save Jewish children through a network he operated with the support of Monseigneur Paul Rémond, Bishop of Nice. The bishop provided an office where Abadi manufactured identity papers. Abadi found hiding places for five hundred children primarily in local Catholic institutions.[5]

Thanks to Abadi's efforts, Lisette was one day told to go to the bus stop at the Galleries Lafayette and to follow a nun in a white habit. Lisette followed the nun, Sæur Emanuelle, up to the Convent de Clarisse, at the top of Cimiez, the hill which had been the heart of ancient Nice. She remained at the convent for three years, taking care of the younger children. Moussa Abadi would come periodically to train Lisette and bring additional children and new identity papers. Many were taken to Switzerland or sent to another convent or to live with a Christian family. Part of Lisette's job was to teach the young children their new names. "Don't make a mistake," she would warn them. "Other-

Lisette with Sœur Emmanuelle at the end of World War II, April 1945.

wise, you will die." During a bombing in 1944, she hid the children safely under a mattress, but she herself was injured by a
falling brick.

Leo Fall was captured in 1942 and, as his wife had been, sent
to the military barracks, the Caserne d'Auvare. He developed a
hernia and was sent to the Hôpital Pasteur, from which he escaped under the lax eyes of the Italian guards. In November 1943
Leo developed peritonitis. Bernard rushed him to a private clinic
thought to be safe. The operation went well. Bernard visited him
and they discussed where he would hide once he recovered. But
that night the Gestapo raided the hospital and found Leo. He
died during the night, after being tortured and beaten. Bernard
later told an interviewer that his father had been part of the un-

derground, but I've never seen evidence of that and it would not have been in character.

Bernard arranged for his father's funeral. With their pistols in hand, Bernard and ten of his young companions in the Resistance formed a procession, four of them carrying the plain wooden casket containing the body of Leo Fall, who was freed at last from the torment he had endured for four years. Up the hill from the Boulevard Henri de Cessole they marched, prepared for combat with the Gestapo, to bury this decent man with proper respect. At the top of Cimiez, because other cemeteries were denied him, he was laid to rest in an unmarked mass grave, with the last rites of the Hebrew people.[6]

The young men who helped Bernard bury his father were his companions in another Zionist underground group, the EIF, or Éclaireurs Israélites de France. Henri Pohoryles was their leader and coordinator in Nice. Bernard sometimes spoke and wrote of two other members of the group, Ernest and Serge. He said Serge spent his days and nights manufacturing false papers. His food was brought in and he never left. Only one person knew the address. His laboratory specialized in making photocopies of decrees of naturalization and identity cards for the members of the Armée Juive. A courier transported the papers, the blank forms, names, and photos to Serge. After he had done his work, the courier took the precious documents to the appointed place.

Bernard said that Ernest, whose real name was Oury Appenzeller, was handsome, blond, tall, and Aryan looking. He and two others formed a resistance group that executed informers who betrayed Jews to the Gestapo. Bernard recalled Ernest as a man of exceptional audacity, who kept on his desk a card with the names and addresses of traitors to be killed. After the war he settled in Israel, where he was an architect, but he died of cancer while still young.

Bernard's friends in the EIF in Nice were in need of weapons. Under the cover of the Compagnons, Bernard was free to move about, transporting the weapons. He even traveled to Paris. One member of the group, Charlotte Sorkine Noshpitz, later told me that Bernard would send them packages of breakfast cereal with the components of a pistol hidden inside. Another of the friends he made during his work with the resistance was Renée Kurz, an attractive young woman two years older than he. Years later she told me how Bernard lost the goodwill of her mother. He arrived one evening at her mother's apartment in Nice with a suitcase and asked her to hold it for him. Not until Bernard returned several days later did the woman learn that the suitcase was full of weapons.

Renée continued, "He came to Nice to see his friends from the underground. Those kids were family at that time. It was the only genuine warmth or affection he had anywhere because the Compagnons de France and that military stuff offered no warmth. I think that's why he came to Nice. That's where he spent his free time and also, Lisette was there." Bernard would visit Lisette at the convent, arriving in his Compagnons uniform, a rifle slung over his shoulder. Despite the danger, he said he would not go into hiding, that he preferred to die with a weapon in his hand.

In a May 21, 1944, letter to Renée, Bernard immodestly listed his activities at the Jules Ferry School in Cannes: "Here I am, always first in French as well as in geography, history and mechanics. I play the genius. At the moment I am reading Maeterlinck: I must say that it is arduous." On one trip to the convent, he chatted about Freud with Sœur Emmanuelle. He was reading whatever he could get his hands on. He read a great deal of Clausewitz's military writings and could quote him at length.

He was seventeen years old and alone. Renée, two years older, thought him in part a little boy, very much in need of compliments. "He did deserve them, snatched them up readily," she told me.

"He tried to do a tremendous job at a very young age by himself. He needed those kudos very badly. He was an extremely bright boy who at twenty wrote letters like other people do at forty. They read well, with humor, so polished, so precocious.

All alone at sixteen, you grew up fast. He picked a route for himself and went straight after it. He educated himself. Did all this without any support, under his own steam."

She told me that Bernard manifested a matter-of-fact attitude about the tragedies in his life and that at seventeen he wanted to be married. "He didn't have a family. He didn't have a country. Marriage would give him a vestige of stability." She thought of him as a younger brother and Bernard called her his best friend.

In late May 1944, after the Allies bombed Toulon, an important shipping port, Bernard and his companions went to help the survivors. They worked two days and nights, often as bombs fell. "You heard the screaming of the dying and you dug in the rubble," he wrote to Renée. "From time to time your pick-ax touched something soft. Then, making use of your hands, you disinter parts of a cadaver, a trunk, a head from which the skull had been torn off. Sometimes a mother pressed against her child. And you tell yourself, one has to help these unfortunate ones. You no longer think of the rest, nor of the sun that is setting over the road nor of the golden hills of the Esterel. You are under the gas fumes, fumes that torture, that cover the rescue teams, the delayed action bombs that killed four buddy volunteers."

After the Allied invasion of Normandy on June 6, the Germans were increasingly drafting Frenchmen for work projects. To protect himself, on June 22, Bernard requested and received authorization from the secretary general of the Compagnons of Vichy for assignment to a city in the French Alps. He left Nice and struck out on his own. He made his way north, past Grenoble, to the territory around the city of Annecy, south of Geneva. He was seeking elements of the maquis, the guerrilla groups fighting in the Alps. But first, he joined Renée on a mission to transport Jewish children across the border into Switzerland. Each week they would find a new passageway across the border. Sometimes they were forced to turn back. When they were successful, the children were given to Jewish groups and put into camps.

One of their friends, Marianne, was caught by the Germans and killed. Her mutilated body was found in a mass grave.

Finally, assigned to the 2e Bureau FFI, the Forces Françaises de l'Intérieur, Bernard left Annecy in July for Haute-Savoie, or Upper Savoy, in the French Alps. He went first to visit his old school teacher, Gaston Culas, now a Resistance leader, and living in Conjux on the edge of Lac le Bourget. Monsieur Culas had left Nice for Haute-Savoie in the fall of 1942, after the refugee children were forced from the Pessicart villa. Bernard arrived at the door of his old mentor, after having earlier been stopped by Resistance fighters on the other side of the lake. They found Bernard suspect, particularly since he was dressed in military clothing and was armed. But when he told them he was looking for Monsieur Culas, Bernard was taken directly to his former teacher's home.

He remained more than a month with this Resistance group, during which he participated in the sabotage of a railroad and engaged in combat in Chindrieux. The town, elevated at the north end of the lake, was a surveillance point for the Rhône. A nearby bridge was of great importance for the defense of Haute-Savoie. Both the Germans and the maquis were in the mountains with the bridge between them, partly blown apart. Skirmishes were fought and men on both sides were killed. The Resistance fighters attacked and the Germans counterattacked. The French were in a bad position. The Germans issued an ultimatum for them to surrender. The situation was resolved when two battalions of regular French army units came to the rescue. By then, following the Normandy invasion, French forces were fighting the Germans and the Resistance fighters increasingly worked with and joined them.

On November 21, 1966, Bernard was interviewed by Dick Hubert on a radio show called *Celebrity's Choice*, where guests discussed their lives and their favorite music. He gave this summary of his Resistance work:

So, I was then in Upper Savoy—from there on I was on the Wanted list, I was in a real *maquis*. Now, *maquis* was really a combat outfit. There was no such thing as living at home like a solid citizen and then go out and shoot up a few Germans and then go back home and stay camouflaged. Oh, no, you actually fought all the way through. So, for us there was nothing except the endless tunnel. Either the Americans, British, and the Free French landed and we would be saved or you'd just die—that's all there was to it. There was no giving up or being a prisoner—you landed in a concentration camp for extermination. . . . We were in the Alps, we were fighting our own war. The Americans weren't anywhere near us and we had some pretty grim German troops on the other side.[7]

Bernard engaged in advance reconnaissance for the FFI and served as an interrogator of German prisoners. He also saw combat under the leader, who called himself Chef Blanc, for the liberation of Aiguebelle, a village at the base of the mountains. Arriving there, they found the village in ruins. An Austrian Alpine battalion had burned down chalets, destroyed tunnels, and killed the Resistance fighters along their route. The houses of Aiguebelle were in ashes, autos were burned in ditches, and bridges were blown up. Bernard was increasingly inflamed by the tactics of this vicious enemy.

Throughout his years in the Resistance, Bernard kept a record of his activities. It was dangerous for him to carry such material with him. If he was captured, the Germans would know he was a fighter and he would be shot or tortured for information. But it was basic to Bernard's character to want documentation, facts, a record, whatever the risks.

In August 1944 Bernard left for Maurienne, where a major battle was raging. He was behind the German lines at Col de la Madeleine, the mountain pass, where units of the Resistance combined with the regular army. The French were immobilized by the force of the fire of the Wehrmacht and several of them were killed.[8] During this campaign, Bernard served as the guide for a Commandant Hunter of the Royal Canadian Artillery, who was probably part of a Jedburgh team that had parachuted in. These teams usually arrived in groups of three—a British or American officer, a French officer, and a radio officer. They were to provide radio communication between the Resistance forces and Allied Headquarters. By then, Bernard had picked up some English, and he practiced it with Hunter. During an operation to destroy a small fort, Bernard was wounded by a grenade and sustained injuries to his right forearm and left leg. He continued fighting, entering combat in the valley of Tarentaise.

During lulls in the fighting, Bernard would sometimes pay unannounced visits to Renée in Nice. She found him still very young but excited about his military feats. She told me, "He tried very hard to build up his own manhood, the business of being a man, the military man aspect and how tough he was, thinking if he said something flattering or affectionate, it might be a sign of weakness. Very proud of his maleness. Having to prove himself. It was very logical. It was this that kept him alive. He always felt that he wanted to make his mark on the world." Renée added that sometimes she became angry when he criticized her while emphasizing his own masculinity.

As the Allies liberated more of France, the men of the FFI were integrated into the regular French army. On September 14, 1944, Bernard was attached to the First Alpine Division of the Sixty-ninth African Artillery Regiment, Fourth Moroccan Mountain Division. He learned how to lash mortar shells to mules for transport through the mountains. He told me that at one point he was in charge of a field bordello, made up of women who traveled with the Moroccans. He guarded German prisoners and saw combat in Leysse. At Briançon his datebook has comments about German artillery shooting from above. *"Pas drôle.* But we have good morale. Next to us a shell falls. One dead, 5 injured."

By November the cold of the mountains was intense. To

Bernard with his army buddy Rémy Malot, circa 1945.

Renée, Bernard extolled the magnificence of the panorama: "The white mountains that appear to crush us in a dark blue sky. With that, a radiant sun that makes us forgive a constant cold temperature of minus 15 degrees. The pure air renders you joyous just to breathe it. Your skis are permanently attached to your feet. These buddies of the African army are very nice. We are learning to swear in Arabic."

In the early days of January 1945 their company was quartered in old fortifications of Grenoble called the Bastion IX. His close army buddy Rémy Malot later told me that he and Bernard were lodged in a dark old stable. Ten men slept on straw mattresses on the concrete floor at night and during the day it became a classroom. "We are happy and don't ask for more," Bernard wrote to a friend. "You would laugh at us, each morning ten soldiers march off, notebooks in hand." They were there to learn wireless telegraphy and codes. Rémy was one of the instructors. Ten boys, and a dozen girls of the AFAT (Auxiliaries Féminines de l'Armée de Terre), attended, all about eighteen years old. Rémy said that Bernard was not gifted at Morse code but he worked hard and learned it.

Rémy found Bernard reticent about his past. "He was calm and reserved though loquacious. He wasn't able to feel or show affection as he would have if he had had a normal existence in

31

the bosom of his family. Because of the tragic events of his child-hood, he was marked by the events, traumatized. He didn't open up his heart on the subject of what had happened to his family."

On January 18, Rémy was promoted to corporal with a team consisting of Bernard and another corporal, Chauvin, whom he described as a bit of a loafer. A radio transmitter was installed in a Renault convertible. However, none of them knew how to drive. A driver took them to Jausiers, a small town near Barcelonnette, where they were installed in two rooms in a small house, one for them and a smaller one for the transmitter. Their bedroom was under the roof. There was a double bed in their room but no sheets. Rémy and Bernard shared the bed. They put their six single blankets together. Chauvin slept on a rubber mattress on the floor. The war was winding down and they had little to do. They ate, wrote, and went to Barcelonnette. They wrote to girls they had known in Grenoble and together they read the girls' replies. Rémy recalled this as fine camaraderie. Little by little they spoke of personal matters, of their past life, of their fami-lies. They came to think of themselves as family, as brothers. It was "*our* aunt" or "*our* sister." Later, when they were married they spoke of "our" wife.

Paris had been liberated and Lisette, living there with the Birets, would send Bernard packages containing American canned goods. Regularly at 10:00 a.m. and 4:00 p.m., out would come Bernard's large hunting knife and he would attack his pâté or his corned beef. At the beginning he didn't share his bounty. He would take a tiny piece of bread, rub it on the pâté and say to Rémy, "Taste how good it is, my pâté." One day, vexed, Rémy said to Bernard, "Pass me your knife." "I cut off a slice of bread and spread it with the famous pâté. Bernard said nothing and afterwards we shared *our* pâté."

Rémy recalled Bernard as someone who cared about his appearance: "We were noted by the brilliance of our shoes and the pleating of our trousers. It became a mania, above all for Bernard. He had patches on the knees of his American fatigues,

Bernard with the armored truck he named "Babette."

but these pants would be creased. He was already attired in everything made in the USA. When he could unearth an American shirt, leggings, a cap, parts of a U.S. uniform, he was happy."

In his 1966 interview with Dick Hubert, Bernard discussed how he still associated that period of the war with the music of Glenn Miller that the GIs played: "We finally linked up with the Americans, of course, then I was transferred to the French regular army. . . . To me, the whole Western campaign—the whole end of World War II—is always going to be Glenn Miller. I can't hear, can't even today listen to Glenn Miller without quite breaking up over it."[9]

Bernard signed up for classes that would qualify him to become a staff sergeant in an artillery squad. For three weeks he learned about the functioning of machine guns, mountain Howitzers, and assault guns. Bernard was thrilled one day when he could fire a shell into the German sector. Perhaps it was to avenge the death of his parents.

But mostly his sector was calm. The war was elsewhere, in Alsace and Belgium. One day in April there was an offensive with big guns firing all day. But when all their munitions were exhausted, the Germans surrendered. It was the end.

Bernard and Rémy were no longer needed. Early in May, the two comrades walked to the Italian border, watchful for the mines that were always present. They took photos and enjoyed the beautiful weather and did not think of war. On May 8, the day of the armistice, they descended from the mountain in the telegraph car with the top down. It was a joyous time.

The artillery left. The rest of their company went to Italy. Their superiors had other concerns. Finally, Bernard and Rémy were reassigned to an infantry regiment stationed in Barcelonnette. They reported to Briançon where they were installed in the Hotel Pasteur. Later they were ejected from the hotel and assigned to the Berwick barracks. Their commander found a way to requisition their convertible. Even without it, Rémy and Bernard found girlfriends. Then Rémy went to Italy with another unit, while Bernard stayed on in Briançon.

The two friends saw each other again around 1950. Rémy, a career officer, had by then served in Vietnam. For Rémy, Bernard

Bernard instructing his squad how to use a weapon, 1945. "When they don't understand," he noted, "I get annoyed and start making large gestures."

was his best friend. He thought that he was Bernard's as well. "He was a good guy, too intelligent for the average soldiers of the era who, because of that fact, were a bit skeptical of him. He was an intellectual lost in the midst of peasants."

With the war over, Bernard's Aunt Lotti returned from America, where she had been living on Long Island with her two sons. She hoped to open branches of her travel agency in Paris, New York, and Buenos Aires, and wanted Bernard to head the Paris branch. She would supervise from New York. Bernard found her offer tempting. It would include his own apartment, a car, and a percentage of the profits. To Renée, he wrote, "Very acceptable, don't you think?" But then he listed his doubts:

> What about all my luminous ideas, my cherished freedom? It's a difficult problem because I sense that this is a turning point in my life. One senses the fresh air of an abyss. Here would be assured calm, a stable life and on the other side there is the filth, the squalor, the lice, the hunger and thirst, frustration, the injuries and, in the end, little money. But you feel life, as you and I understand the term. To live, to breathe each mouthful of air twice, as we did at la Foux.[10] That is what I would have to sacrifice and that seems hard to do at nineteen.

He said that if his request for transfer to Austria was accepted, he would remain in the army for another year. If not, he would accept his aunt's offer.

He reminisced to Renée about their time together in Grenoble. "I am happy that the word Resistance evokes in me, at the same time, the radiant sunrise on Lake Annecy, the patrols in full sun in Maurienne, the glowing nights of the burning villages, or the howling of the Germans that we had tied to a post. On what rests our destiny?"

Bernard was demobilized on March 19, 1946. He was nineteen and a half years old. His years as a guerrilla fighter would shape his life, and would lead him halfway around the world to Vietnam. Upon his demobilization he requested naturalization and his French citizenship was granted on the basis of his military service. He was awarded *la Médaille de la France Libérée,* the medal of liberation of France.

3

GERMANY

AFTER his demobilization, Bernard went to Paris where once
again fate took a hand in shaping his future. His aunt Lotti had a
friend named Jean Brandes who was working as a translator at
the war crimes trials in Nuremberg. Bernard, who clearly was
not sold on a future as a travel agent, immediately made contact
with Brandes. Soon Bernard, still not yet twenty, but with his
sterling war record and his fluency in French and German, was
also working in Nuremberg as a translator. In his own way, he

was continuing his war against the people who had killed his parents and devastated the world of his childhood.

Jean and Bernard roomed together for a few months before Jean moved on to another job with the U.S. military government in Berlin. Jean later told me: "My relationship to him was very similar to my relationship to my son, with a certain fondness. We had a strange mixture of friends—an English WREN, former intelligence officers who went back to the U.S. to teach French, Sara, an attractive woman captain in the U.S. Army. In the evening we would get together in the officers club and drink. Bernard fit in perfectly, although young, as though we had known him for a long time."

In less than a year, Bernard was promoted from translator to research analyst and investigator. He worked from February 1947 to November 1948 for the office of the U.S. Chief of Counsel, mostly on the trial of Alfred (or Alfried) Krupp and eleven other

Bernard in uniform of the office of the chief counsel at the Nuremberg Tribunal.

officials of the Krupp industrial empire, who were charged with numerous war crimes, including the enslavement of concentration camp inmates and prisoners of war to work in their factories. Gustav Krupp was originally to be tried, but he had begun showing signs of senility in 1943 and his son Alfred took over management of the firm and became the key defendant in the trial.

Bernard kept records of his work. They show that he located, investigated, and interrogated German war criminals as well as their victims and other potential witnesses against them. He researched Krupp's files dealing with arms output and produced reports and charts showing the firm's growth and profitability. One of the defendants was Friedrich von Buelow, the Krupp director who handled counter intelligence and liaison with the Gestapo. Bernard drew an elaborate chart of von Buelow's duties, the people he supervised, his contacts with the Gestapo, and his role in obtaining slave labor from prisoner of war and concentration camps.

Bernard located a woman in Seattle, a survivor of both a concentration camp and one of the Krupp plants. He wrote asking if she would provide a sworn statement of her experiences at the Krupp works, and she added information about the movement

Bernard (right) with the map he created for the Krupp trials at the Nuremberg War Crimes Tribunal 1948.

39

of five hundred Jews to Auschwitz from the Krupp plants. Bernard even used captured German newsreels to produce a documentary on the role of Krupp under the Hitler regime. Perhaps the achievement that pleased him most was taking an affidavit from Alfred Krupp on his Nazi party activities.

On September 16, 1947, Bernard wrote a report on his exchange with Krupp, in which he noted dryly:

> Subject states that while he did not believe in a German victory in 1943, he expressed in an appeal to Krupp workers the hope in a coming retaliation for the Allied air raids on the Ruhr. . . . Subject states that he could not do otherwise than to follow the German leaders. States that several common points existed between Nazi ideology and Krupp's tradition.

The case against the Krupp officials was overwhelming. On July 31, 1948, when the trial ended after eight months, Bernard wrote in his diary: "Victory for us. Krupp condemned." The tribunal convicted eleven of the twelve defendants of flagrant violations of the laws of war. All were sentenced to prison, including twelve years for Alfred Krupp.

However, in 1951, U.S. High Commissioner John J. McCloy commuted or reduced the sentences of numerous Nazis found guilty by the tribunal. He commuted Krupp's sentence and allowed him to return to the ownership of his munitions empire, despite outraged protests from Gen. Telford Taylor, chief prosecutor in the Krupp trial, and countless others around the world.

In 1951, Bernard published an article called "The Case Against Alfred Krupp" that reflected his contempt for Krupp and his empire:

> As Alfred Krupp's father once pointed out . . . the Krupp plants continued to produce and carried on research on prohibited weapons during the whole post-Versailles period,

without the help and orders of the Weimar Republic. In Gustav Krupp's own words, Krupp continued to train his staff for war production under the very noses of the allied "snooping commissions."

Krupp was neither "compelled" nor "threatened" by the Weimar Republic to make illegal use of his factories. He did so of his own accord, freely and willingly. . . . It is public knowledge that the Krupp firm had embarked upon such a criminal course of conduct: foreign plants were pilfered and plundered, slave laborers were beaten, starved, and killed. . . .

Without batting an eyelash, the Krupp works used the poor wretches from the concentration camps for the heaviest jobs that were to be found. The whole town of Essen—Krupp's hometown—saw every day the rag-clad column of five hundred Czech concentration camp inmates, all girls from fifteen to twenty, march to their assigned place of work at Krupp's: twelve hours without food and without protective clothing in the armor plate rolling mill.

And what, Herr Krupp, happened to those girls? Is it true that, with U.S. paratroopers hammering at Essen's gates, they were hurried away to the extermination camp of Bergen Belsen and murdered there, so that no tales of this, your "private" concentration camp, would leak out?

However, two girls survived, some of the female SS guards were found, and the most subtle arguments of the defense failed to shake this terrible accusation.

As to Krupp's famous "social welfare program," it included also the abortion station in Voerde, where foreign female workers were aborted so that they would not divert any of their time from Krupp's armament projects to the care of their newborn babies.[1]

Soon after the Krupp trial ended, Bernard left his job and returned to Paris. He had gone directly from the army to Nuremberg and many people, including Jean Brandes, Sœur

Listening to testimony at the Knupp trials.
Bernard is in the rear left with his hand on his chin.

Emmanuelle, and Monsieur Culas, were urging him to pursue his education. College was not expensive in Paris and his aunt Marcelle offered to help. Before the war she had married Auguste Biret, then a chauffeur, and they had opened a bookstore, the Librairie Biret on the Champs-Elysèes, near the Arc de Triomphe.

Bernard attended the Sorbonne for a year, and then left to work as a Child Search Officer for the International Refugee Organization in Munich. Thousands of Jewish children had become separated from their parents during the war and his job was to work with German and Allied authorities to try to put families back together. He interviewed displaced persons and civilians in an effort to locate children who had been put in hiding with non-Jewish families and elsewhere during and after the war.

It was a mission dear to his heart but after a reduction in staff he found a new job, also in Munich, as manager of distribution for the U.S. Army newspaper *Stars and Stripes*. In Munich, in the postwar era, he managed to have both an active social life and to continue his education. On the social side, many people were making up for lost time, and he danced into the night, skied at Garmisch, and had numerous relationships with young women. For a time he was engaged to an attractive Hungarian woman named Eva. He was 22 and she was 24. Eventually they quarreled and she went to the United States. Bernard wanted her to return and marry him but she was unsure. After his death, I read letters she had sent him and it was clear that they were in love but also that she resented the fact that he was sometimes highly critical of her. It would not have helped, if she knew it, that he was also seeing another woman. For whatever reasons, she chose not to resume their romance.

In Munich, Bernard studied for one semester at the Ludwig Maximilian University. He also enrolled in a program the University of Maryland had set up at six centers in Germany. It was primarily for American soldiers but he managed to qualify. He had worked with Americans in Nuremberg, and his English was improving, but he perfected it in Munich, studying alongside Americans in classes that were conducted in English. He proudly reported to his family that he was first in his class in both International Law and American Foreign Relations.

Despite his love of France, Bernard was increasingly drawn to America. He had worked with Americans, studied their history and politics, and mastered their language. He had learned that he could excel in the classroom and that he might have a future as a scholar. He began to explore the possibilities available to him for graduate study in the United States. His diary for December 18, 1950, recorded another turning point in his life: "HURRAH, my application for fellowship has been accepted!!!" He had won a Fulbright fellowship, started by a great American senator to encourage international education. He was to do graduate work at Syracuse University in New York. When he arrived in the United States in October 1951, he did not feel like a foreigner at all.

4

FIRST ENCOUNTER

I GREW UP during the Depression in Rochester, New York, the youngest of four children. My parents, Isadore and Esther Winer, were part of the generation of Eastern European Jews who fled the pogroms of Russia in the early years of the twentieth century. They met in Chicago as teenagers and married in 1913. Their first child, my sister Mary, was born the next year. Although Mary was sixteen years older than I, she was my role model when I was growing up. Rochester was a cultural center and she exposed me to ballet, to the theater, and above all, to art. She taught me to draw and, after giving me a beautiful wooden box of oil paints, showed me how to use them. My older brother Richard went off to the University of Illinois to study chemical engineering when I was four. Once Mary and Richard left home, my companion was Morris, our redhead in a family of brunettes. Six years my senior, he had taught himself to play the piano and he would drill me on the titles and composers of the pieces as he played.

Although uneducated themselves, my parents knew that education was the key to advancement for their sons. For the girls, a good marriage would suffice. Mary, who married when I was ten, was keenly intelligent and well read. She became a painter and a part time "commercial artist," the term used then for today's graphic designer and illustrator. At an early age, I decided that hers was an ideal vocation for a woman. I assumed I would marry in my early twenties, as women did then, but a career in art would allow flexibility while I raised children and ran a household.

I was eleven when the United States entered World War II. Morris was drafted into the Army and participated in the invasion of Italy. He quickly learned Italian and developed a lasting love of Europe. Mary's husband Arty served on battleships in the Pacific. Richard, a brilliant engineer, spent the war years working on the invention of the bazooka. My mother proudly hung the banner with two stars in our window, signifying that the household had two men in service.

I spent the war years safe at home with my parents. They would read in the Yiddish newspaper, the *Forward*, of the devastation in Europe and the persecution of the Jews. My father, a tailor, was a pocketmaker for the men's clothing manufacturer Hickey-Freeman, which during the war made uniforms for the armed services. My parents were Socialists, and my father was active in the Amalgamated Clothing Workers Union. My lifelong belief in fighting for what is right and defending the oppressed stemmed from the lessons my parents taught me.

They did not attend a synagogue but culturally they were very Jewish. To marry out of the faith was a sin. I knew enough not to date non-Jewish boys or at least not to bring them home. I prepared for a career as an artist. I did not even consider another field even though in high school I excelled in math and had excellent grades. But when it came time to plan for my future, my parents said they could not afford to send me to my school of choice, Syracuse University. The less expensive Rochester Institute of Technology would prepare me for my art career. They thought an education would be wasted on me, since I would soon marry and have children.

I told this to Miss Coulton, the college counselor at Benjamin Franklin High School, who firmly declared, "You should be going to a university. Have your mother come in to see me." My mother did go see her and, that evening, after talking to my father, she informed me that I could attend Syracuse after all.

"What did Miss Coulton tell you?" I asked.

"She said that if you go to a university, your chances of meeting and marrying a professional man would be much better."

I was forever indebted to my advisor for her understanding of my parents' priorities.

At Syracuse I majored in graphic design, which then was called advertising design. I also took excellent courses in English, philosophy, and psychology. I minored in painting, thus following in my sister's footsteps, although she did not have a university degree. To help with college costs I worked in the summer as a sales clerk in a variety of places. During the school year, I worked in the university library. To cut costs, I lived in a cooperative, a house where we women students did our own cooking and cleaning. In my senior year, I became active in extracurricular activities. I joined the Tri-Orange party, which was considered more democratic than the other, more preppy, fraternity-oriented party. We plotted the coming election for senior class officers. We needed an independent on the ticket and because I had not joined a sorority I became the vice presidential candidate. Somehow, I won, although my presidential running mate lost.

Besides being class vice president, I was cochair of the Human

Relations Committee, which sought to introduce students to social problems through speakers and discussion groups. That year, we had lectures on human relations, anti-Semitism, and race relations, and we wrote to Negro high schools in major U.S. cities to give them information about Syracuse and possible scholarships.

We wanted to expose students to other cultures, and therefore decided to have a series of lectures by foreign students. After sociology professor Byron Fox addressed our group on world poverty, my cochair Joan Altstedter and I asked him to recommend foreign students who could speak to us. He suggested a French student who was a Fulbright scholar studying at Syracuse's Maxwell School of Citizenship. Joan phoned to invite him to talk at our next session. She reported to me, "He doesn't sound French, and he doesn't even have a French name: Bernard Fall. He wants us to meet with him at the Cosmo for coffee on Tuesday evening at eight."

To publicize this talk by a Frenchman, I produced three-dimensional posters and put them up around the campus. They featured an entirely stereotyped Frenchman. He sported a twirling mustache, wore a black beret, and I had a real cigarette hanging out of his mouth through a hole in the board. At the end of the cigarette, to simulate smoke, I glued a flowing ribbon of nylon, which I cut from an old stocking. I let my creative urges run wild. "Are We It? A Frenchman's View of the U.S., March 5, 1952," the posters proclaimed. I also produced fliers which included a small drawing of the Arc de Triomphe and the handwritten phrase "Ah! Paree!" I had of course never been to Paris.

On Tuesday, Joan and I met our Frenchman, who proved to be an attractive, six foot tall, clean-cut young man with a crew cut, who was wearing an American Army bomber jacket, blue jeans, and loafers.

"Who is that idiot who did those stupid posters?" he asked.

I admitted to being the idiot, but Bernard only laughed.

He didn't even sound French. He spoke colloquial English

with a midwestern twang and a barely perceptible accent. He told us that was because he'd taken a course in remedial English given to American GIs in Germany.

I was soon in awe. Bernard was not like anyone I had ever met. The students I dated were still boys. Bernard spoke candidly of his life in France, his roles with the Resistance and with the French army, the fate of his family, and his work at the Nuremberg trials. I was both shocked and fascinated by this self-confident young man who had already experienced so much of life.

In his talk the next afternoon Bernard introduced himself, noted that he was a "straight-A student," and talked about his experiences during the war. He discussed the differences in the democracies of France and the United States. He admitted that in the United States a person can start out poor and rise through hard work more easily than in France. However, he said that in France, racial discrimination is forbidden by the French consti-tution. He discussed the two conflicting trends that were then

Bernard and Dorothy, class marshals at Syracuse University commencement, 1952.

timely and of great importance to him: one was French distrust of Germany, and the other was a move to unite the two countries militarily through NATO, the North Atlantic Treaty Organization.

I still have a copy of the student newspaper that quoted part of what he said: "France is war weary, having lost two million men and having had four million casualties because of invasions by Germany. The U.S. has not had that many casualties and deaths in her entire history. France is now hanging on in French Indo-China, sending over her lieutenants as soon as they graduate from officer training school because of the increasing rate of fatalities every day. She wants a unified international army with Germans and Frenchmen in the same divisions, but she is afraid of a separate German army even supposing the army would follow allied military policies."

Despite his wartime experiences, he expressed no bitterness against the Germans. He was a pragmatist who believed both countries must move ahead and build better relations. He had German friends and later took me on a tour of the places he had lived in Germany. I was the one who would sometimes refuse to buy German products, not Bernard.

After he finished his talk, I thanked him and thought I would never see him again. So I was surprised the next day when he called and asked me to go with him to see the movie *The African Queen*. It was the beginning of a fascinating journey. I would spend the rest of that spring of my senior year falling in love, incapable of concentrating on my studies. He was falling in love too but it did not keep him from studying.

We talked, took walks, met for coffee, and visited with his friends. We didn't go to bars because Bernard didn't drink. He was a French chauvinist, critical of Americans and what he considered to be our lack of culture, but he delighted in America too. He loved our movies, comic strips, and popular music. He joked that he was a happy low-brow. He dressed in blue jeans or khakis, sported a crew cut, used American slang, and seemed entirely comfortable in this American environment. His car, a white Willys Jeepster, was often parked in front of the library and I would leave cryptic notes to him under the windshield wiper. He was taking flying lessons and one day I went and watched him go up with the pilot, who later took me up for a spin. Bernard taught military affairs to the ROTC at Syracuse. It was a way to use his hard-won military knowledge to earn extra money.

Roma Stibravy, a fellow student, recalled of Bernard: "He already had a well established reputation as accessible, affable, and kind. At the Maxwell School he was much revered, held in awe by students because of his experiences during the war. And being such a brilliant student, everyone looked up to him and admired him. He was everyone's good friend. That was his personality."

At Syracuse, Bernard taught ROTC classes, 1951–52.

Maté Mestrovic, son of the Croatian sculptor Ivan Mestrovic, was at Syracuse because his father was teaching there. I often saw him at Bernard's apartment on Ostrom Avenue. They spoke French together as they discussed European affairs, which Maté thought would be Bernard's future area of specialization: "He seemed to have a purpose in life. He seemed to be an individual with a calling, a man seeking a mission. But it wasn't clear what that mission was. He wanted to accomplish something of significance. He had tremendous energy. He was Jewish but he had no bitterness. He was objective."

In May, we drove to Rochester to visit my parents and to see the lilacs in bloom at Highland Park. I took my two roommates, Iris Roth and Betty Pierson, and another girlfriend along because I didn't want my parents to think Bernard was my boyfriend. The idea of a French boyfriend who might lure me off to Europe would only have upset them. It didn't help that he was Jewish because Bernard presented himself as French, not Jewish. He spoke German to my parents, who answered in Yiddish.

After commencement, Bernard went down to Washington for a summer course at SAIS, the Johns Hopkins School of Advanced International Studies. He had finished his course work and his master's thesis, "Illegal Rearmament of the Weimar Republic," which drew upon his knowledge of the Krupp trial, but he would return in the fall to begin his doctoral studies. I returned home to Rochester to start my career in graphic design. Despite the separation, we both intended for our romance to continue.

Dorothy and Bernard at the Military Ball, 1952.

5

THE FIRST TRIP

"M<small>AYBE</small> we'll get married when I come back from Indochina,"
Bernard said, as I lay in his arms. He had been discussing his
plans for the coming year, plans for travel, adventure, and re-

search, plans which did not include me. I said nothing but reflected on the sincerity of his comment. It seemed a tentative marriage proposal at best.

We were spending weekends together, that fall of 1952. I would come from Rochester to Syracuse, a ninety-three-mile trip by Greyhound bus. Here in his Ostrom Avenue apartment we had a private life, at least for now.

Bernard was fulfilling the course requirements for his PhD, and I was back in Rochester. After my graduation, I had quickly found an interesting and challenging job with a one-man design firm that handled a variety of accounts. I had a week off in late August and used it to visit Bernard in Washington, D.C., where he was attending the summer session at SAIS. Important events had happened that summer. He was taking a course called Nationalism and Colonialism in Southeast Asia, taught by Amry Vandenbosch, a visiting professor of Dutch origin from the University of Kentucky. Vandenbosch's area of specialization was Indonesia. He had served as an interpreter in France during World War I and this may have contributed to his warm feelings for this young French graduate student. For Bernard, the friendship would change his life.

Of course, Indochina had touched him before. His beloved teacher in Nice, Monsieur Culas, had sparked his interest with stories of Cambodia. More recently, Bernard had been receiving letters from his army friend Rémy, who was serving in Vietnam. The letters painted a realistic picture of the war against the Vietminh rebels. After one battle he wrote: "We are fighting against the Vietnamese regulars, perfectly equipped and armed à l'américaine' [that is, with American arms captured in Korea], supported by the Chinese Communists. We didn't come out of it unscathed and in the final analysis . . . I believe that Indochina will only be pacified after a third world war . . . or she will be completely lost for us."

Bernard found it fascinating to study a country that France had occupied for almost one hundred years and where its forces

were fighting once again. Bernard's paper for the class was entitled "Political Development in Indo-China." He had embarked
with his usual enthusiasm on his research, only to be frustrated
by a dearth of solid material. Few books existed on the area, and
those often offered little depth. He did find books, reports, and
periodicals in the Information Division of the French Embassy.
He managed to produce a hundred-page paper complete with
maps, analysis of the economic, political, and military situations,
and photographs of the Vietnamese and French armies.

Professor Vandenbosch gave his paper an A+. More impor-
tantly, he told Bernard that, with his French background, he ought
to specialize in Vietnam. The political and military situation there,
he said, would be an ideal subject for his doctoral dissertation.

Bernard found the notion tantalizing. Here was an opportunity to make a contribution to the understanding of a country
that had become so pivotal in France's colonial empire. To write
such a dissertation, he would have to *go* to Indochina for first-
hand research—that was to him the only way to obtain the facts,
perhaps even the truth.

Of course, for Bernard the lure of Vietnam was more than
intellectual. He would be returning to the excitement of war, to
risk-taking and the camaraderie of soldiers, all of which intoxicated him. He knew he would need six or seven months to do
adequate research in Indochina, then several weeks in Paris for
research and interviews. He decided to do it.

Or, as he put it in an interview in 1966, "By pure accident,
one sunny day in Washington, D.C., of all places, in 1952, I got
interested in Viet-Nam and it's been sort of a bad love affair ever
since."[1]

For me, the prospect of him 12,000 miles away, and in physical danger, was profoundly disturbing. I didn't want him to risk
his life and I didn't want us to be separated that long. I had to
wonder if such a trip was compatible with his avowed love for
me and our plans of marriage. Bernard soothed my anxieties with
assurances. The work was so important, he said. He would be

cautious and would hurry back to me. Given my love for him, I had little choice but to agree.

Bernard finished his course work at Syracuse ahead of schedule and spent the next months completing the requirements for his PhD. Having some extra time, he took a class called "Marriage and the Family, Home Economics 103." With his usual caustic wit, he said that he wanted to prepare for the fate in store for him. But it was a welcome gesture.

With Bernard going away for more than six months, I decided to leave Rochester. I was there only for proximity to him. I, too, wanted to travel and to have new experiences. At my brother Morris's urging, I decided to join him in San Francisco. Morris was a man of intelligence and taste who became a teacher and actor, and he loved San Francisco for being so cosmopolitan, like cities he had known in Europe after the war. I felt sure I could find a job there in graphic design. For transportation, Bernard put me in contact with Mary-Margaret, a thirty-seven-year-old former WAVE (women who served in the U.S. Navy) commander in Syracuse. She had finished her studies and was planning to drive across the country to Sacramento. I had driven very little but assured her I would help.

On May 6, 1953, Bernard left for Indochina. He would pay for the trip with his savings, and would be on a tight budget, but he was proud to be acting with no outside financial aid. He was his own man. One military-style duffle bag was sufficient to hold his necessities for a seven-month journey that would take him literally around the world. His new short-wave radio and precious Leica camera were slung over his shoulder as we said goodbye.

Although he had little money, he took with him other assets. He had a letter of recommendation to the political advisor of the Vietnam National Government from the French Embassy in Washington, D.C. He had his resourcefulness, his intelligence, his unabashed friendliness, and his imposing presence. Moreover, as a former officer in the French army, he would be able to travel throughout Vietnam with the French military much more freely than most civilians. He had been promised access to documents that had high security classification and permission to quote from them. In all these ways, the French and Vietnamese authorities showed extraordinary cooperation to a young PhD candidate. Of course, Bernard also sought and obtained information from the other side—the unofficial representatives of the Democratic Republic of Vietnam in Paris and Burma.

During his absence Bernard almost daily wrote me long, reassuring, fact-filled, wonderful accounts of his experiences. His descriptions filled the pages of letters typed single-spaced on both sides of tissue-thin paper. To economize further on postage, he would lighten the letters by ripping the lining out of the envelope, so that the whole missive was a transparent bulk, difficult to read, but full of fascinating stories, drawings, maps and diagrams. These were not just love letters. They amounted to a diary that later provided the basis for his book, *Street Without Joy.* As he put it in the preface of the book, first issued in 1961: "The upshot of my personal experiences and interviews which I could not use for my research went into a diary in the form of letters to the American girl who is now my wife. In those I tried to render the feeling of the atmosphere in which we were living and in which this war was being fought."[2]

In one early letter he defended his long and dangerous trip and suggested that the separation would test our love. He said, "Oh sure, I admit that it would be safer to be a soap salesman, or to be an insurance company manager. Or, my family still wants me to take over the bookstore in Paris. On the other hand, you know that my heart wouldn't be in it. It's like the Indochina trip: I'm as scared as the next guy of getting hurt, but I couldn't look myself in the mirror if I'd backed out of it just because I feel yellow inside. . . . In any case you'll have (and so will I) six–seven months to feel how it is."

On his flight west, he stopped in Hawaii to visit friends and ask about a teaching position at the university. I found that I could imagine a languorous existence there. Of course, as a student of warfare, he also visited Pearl Harbor and contemplated the historic attack there a dozen years before. In Manila he encountered both terrible heat and a painful challenge. Pan American had lost his vaccination certificate and he faced the choice of either being completely revaccinated in one sitting or enduring fourteen days of quarantine. He chose the former and suffered the resulting fever and a sore arm. He wrote to me about all this. Often, humorous illustrations decorated his letters. He sent a sketch of his radio plugged into an outlet, fizzling because he had not known that the Philippines used 220 voltage current instead of the America's 110. His letters were often laced with his bawdy humor, which did not always amuse me.

Still, I treasured those letters, and still do. In those days, with long-distance telephone calls too expensive for anything but emergencies, letters were our only communication for eight months. His letters almost always closed with declarations of his love. Once he said, "Very often I have the feeling that you're along with me on the trip and that I'll find you just around the corner. Also, many a thing that I enjoy, I actually enjoy it because I'm sure you'd enjoy it if you were here. My guess is that I'm just plain crazy about you." My own letters were mundane in comparison. I told him I loved him and missed him. Yet I began to grow a layer of protective emotional armor to help me cope with his risk-taking, to help me feel less vulnerable.

On Saturday, May 16, Bernard arrived in Hanoi. His flight from Hong Kong's Kai Tak airport had been harrowing. "Near the point of no return, and a bare three miles from Communist Hainan Island, the port #2 engine *conked out*," he wrote to me. "Let us be charitable . . . everybody felt pretty doggone crummy, particularly when we jettisoned the reserve gasoline to lighten the ship—which made us sitting ducks for sticky weather over the airport."

Then Indochina appeared. From the air the Red River Delta was beautiful, with vibrant green rice, the water of the paddies reflecting the sky. "It looks just like one big garden, with all [the] little villages very neatly surrounded by trees and shrubbery, and French military roads showing their regular tracings against the erratic boundaries of the fields. As we lowered through the overcast for the landing, you began to see the scars and the marks of the watchtowers, gun emplacements."

He found Hanoi a vibrant place, run by a joint French/Vietnamese administration. Its French colonial buildings gave it an aura of former times, despite the war. Under their great leader Ho Chi Minh, the Vietminh were leading a war of liberation. Living in the mountains of the north near the Chinese border, Ho and his generals began their struggle for independence after the defeat of Japan. At first, the British had replaced the Japanese in the south and Chinese forces had come to occupy the north. Then the French returned. Ho sought support from the United States, which sent a military team parachuting into the jungles of northern Vietnam to help Ho's forces with arms and training. Ho wrote to President Truman asking for further aid, but both the Truman and Eisenhower administrations felt they owed their allegiance to their French allies. Ho then sought and received support from both Communist China and the Soviet Union. By 1953, the French had been fighting the Communists for seven years. Just how the war was going was a matter of dispute, one Bernard would investigate closely.

Bernard took a room at the raffish Metropole Hotel while waiting for something better to turn up. He found that he could eat well for as little as eighty cents at inexpensive restaurants. He soon made friends. He translated for an NBC television reporter in a Vietnamese post office, which earned him a lunch invitation and an introduction to foreign correspondents who could be helpful to him. One morning Bernard requested permission to travel with the French army: "Showed them my resignation as an officer and was reclassified a sgt. Apparently with my qualifications, I cannot be lowered below that without committing a misdemeanor, and I don't feel yet like robbing someone."

Another letter alarmed me with reports of fighting near Hanoi: "Since early this morning the heavy artillery booms along the perimeter. Quite a lot of it, too. . . . You see, the 'rice war' begins. Twice a year, when the rice crops are collected, the Viet-Minh tries to get the rice, which constitutes its wherewithal not only for food purposes, but also as money (a Viet-Minh soldier gets about 20 pounds of it a month as pay) and as a means of foreign exchange. And, believe me, in the Asian southeast, 'a grain of rice is worth a drop of blood.'" It was a phrase he would use again, when writing about the gap between the countries of Southeast Asia that grow more rice than they consumed and those that had to import rice.

He urged me to come to Vietnam. He offered various options. We could be married when I arrived. Or I could come as a student and study art in Saigon. Or we could marry later in Paris or San Francisco. In retrospect, any of those options would have been exciting, but I was still a sheltered girl from Rochester, not yet ready to risk such adventures. This would change in time.

Bernard's mail, by the way, was heavily censored. He was not supposed to write about the military situation but he often did, until the censor warned, "Just stick to love letters to your fiancée, none of this military information."

A week after his arrival Bernard met with Michel Cans, a high-ranking French political officer. Cans handed him a batch of files from the archives and said Bernard could use his office if he wanted to peruse this classified material. Soon after that, he invited Bernard to a dinner at his home. It was a stag affair with both French and Vietnamese officials on hand, including the chief of the Information Division, the vice mayor of Hanoi, and the director of the Cabinet of the Governor for North Vietnam. It was clear that Cans liked Bernard and wanted to help him. For his part, Bernard was favorably impressed by the officials he met. At the conclusion of the evening he was invited to accompany the governor on one of his trips to contested areas where the government had set up frontline civil administration groups.

Thanks to his new friends, Bernard was offered a free room and bath in one of the houses reserved for the office of the commissioner of the republic. "Very nice room and furniture (it's got—thank heaven—a fan), and a six foot four submachine-gun toting Senegalese in front of the house. Boy, am I going to get my taxpayer's money's worth out of the French Republic!"

On May 27, Mary-Margaret picked me up in Rochester and we set out across America in her beige Chevrolet convertible. We were pulling a small trailer that made the car sway rather violently at highway speeds and I had a devil of a time keeping it under control. Still, we averaged five hundred miles a day as we sailed through the Midwest. We stopped in Chicago, where I visited relatives I had heard about since childhood but never met. In a Kansas restaurant on June 2, we watched on television the coronation of Queen Elizabeth II. In Boulder, Colorado, we stayed with friends of Mary-Margaret's and I had my first and last horseback ride. Finally, on June 6, Mary-Margaret dropped me at the station in Sacramento and I caught a bus to San Francisco, where Morris immediately took me on an evening tour. I was enraptured by the shimmering lights of this beautiful city, a world away from the grayness of Rochester and also from Bernard in Indochina.

On Saturday, May 30, while I was driving through the Midwest, Bernard joined the Vietnamese governor of North Vietnam and his staff on an inspection tour of the northern provinces. Their heavily armed convoy navigated what Bernard said were the worst roads he had ever seen. He said he was more worried about getting thrown out of the vehicle than about the Vietminh who might be lying in ambush. He wrote, "The countryside has a charm of its own: the rice which is nearly ripe, the little fields full of water with their little dikes around them, the buffaloes wallowing in the mud to get the flies off their back, the farmers (call them Viet-Minh after working hours) with their cone-shaped hats—and then, a new element that looks as strange here as an armored knight riding down Fifth Avenue, the French forts. Built along strictly functional lines, high square towers of concrete pillboxes, they have an air of early-gothic castles and give the whole place an eerie out-of-this-worldliness."

At the seaport of Haiphong they crossed the Red River in ferries. They reached the isolated French outpost of Quang-Yen and visited a nearby, newly built village housing refugees from the war. Bernard expressed his sympathy for their living conditions, but noted "yet, they're the lucky ones—houses and land if the Viet-Minh doesn't burn everything down once it's ready."

At Quang-Yen they inspected a training camp for Vietnamese non-commissioned officers. These men would soon lead new commando battalions intended to defeat the Vietminh at their own game, by ambushing their convoys, burning their villages, and similar acts of violence. Bernard said these men "looked really good and tough, believe me." At lunch, he joined some junior officers who declared that "their students are good and they'll WIN this war."

Climbing a road that was more like a goat path, they arrived at a Christian village high in the mountains. Although led by Catholic priests, the residents greeted the soldiers and dignitaries with Buddhist cymbals and gongs. The village had its own armed units and, from its mountain perch, defended itself against the rebels. Then the visitors started their ninety-mile return trip to Hanoi. It was a one-day trip, because the government officials would not have been safe in that territory overnight.

Soon after that Major Saylor, chief of the U.S. military assistance group, invited Bernard to fly to a place called Ban-Ban, in Laos, in a mission to parachute ammunition in. Bernard wrote to me: "I didn't want to stay behind because it was a frontline job and it was Sunday anyway and I needed some fresh air—well, I got a nice fat parachute strapped onto me, shook hands with the pilot, a civilian named Al Kusak, from *Rochester, N.Y* . . .

and the loading began." The plane, a C-119 "Flying Boxcar," normally had huge doors in the back from which ammunition and jeeps could roll out. But Bernard explained that this plane had no doors, the rear was wide open and when they were over the drop zone the plane raised its nose and "whoosh, the whole load of shells disappeared out of the gate. . . . The sky now is not horizontal but appears at the left hand corner of the cockpit as the pilot put the plane on one wing to 'peel' it out of the way of the falling load." As they flew away, the Vietminh were firing at them with heavy machine guns. Fortunately, there were two French fighter planes in the area to fire back.

Bernard was thrilled by the adventure but I was alarmed. No one else on the plane even wore a parachute. Even if he parachuted, he would not have survived in Vietminh territory.

He wrote to me in a humorous vein that a problem in finding the enemy was that the Vietminh sometimes disguised themselves as women. It was easy to do since Vietnamese peasants of both sexes wear trousers and large conical hats. "Then when (if) they get licked, they just plain mix with farm women working in

Bernard boards a plane to Laos, 1953.

65

On a supply drop mission, 1953.

the next best field. Go and fight a war like that. Now, how are you going to find out real quick whether you've got a real or a 'phony' woman in front of you? Touching the breasts in a country that's as flat chested as the rice paddies is senseless and they're easy to fake, but an inquisitive hand at a certain place (even over the clothes) puts you—so to say—'in the clear' on the spot." This anecdote was illustrated by a figure with bare buttocks and a conical hat captioned, 'checking the enemy.' He concluded, "This is a real case of CHERCHEZ LA FEMME."

He began having medical misadventures. A front tooth broke off on a stone hidden in some fried fish he was eating. He also was battling dysentery, and debated whether he'd be better off drinking whiskey than the water—but it was a moot point, because Bernard never touched alcohol.

He wrote to me about his evenings with a French colonel he liked and respected: "In any other country, this guy's words would have been called at least 'pinko,' but I know him well enough to know that he isn't even a liberal. He has, however, an excellent grasp on the situation here. He said: 'This is not a military war; it isn't even a political war. It's strictly a social war. As long as we don't destroy the mandarin class and abolish excessive tenancy rents and give every farmer his plot of land, this country is going to [go] Communist as soon as we turn our back.'"

Bernard recounted tales of the war for page after page. He was delving into the Hanoi library, which he found had excellent resources. He filled his calendar with appointments to meet with French and Vietnamese administrators, journalists, the military. His love affair with Vietnam was growing daily.

One of the most important questions he addressed was the reality of the military situation in the Red River Delta. A French briefing officer assured him that with 900 forts and 2200 bunkers in the region, "We are going to deny the Communists access to the eight million people in this Delta and the three million tons of rice, and we will eventually starve them out and deny them access to the population." Bernard asked if the Communists held anything inside the Delta. Pointing to his map, the officer said, "Yes, they hold those little blue blotches, 1, 2, 3, 4, and a little one over here." Bernard asked how he knew that. "It is simple, when we go there we get shot at; that's how we know."[3]

At Hanoi University, where Bernard was doing research, his new Vietnamese friends laughed at the officer's claim of French control. They told Bernard the Delta was controlled by the rebels. Those who had been back to their villages assured him the village chiefs were Communists, no matter what they said to the French when they passed through. One student after another said the same.

Bernard suspected the students were right. But how could one man document the political reality of such a huge area? Then it occurred to him that any real government would surely do two things: collect taxes and educate children. He therefore went to the Vietnamese tax collection office in Hanoi and studied the village tax rolls. It was obvious that most of the Delta hadn't paid taxes for years. If the people in the Delta were paying taxes, it was to someone other than their French-supported national government.

He went next to the Office of Public Education and examined the school teacher lists. Teachers in Vietnam were assigned by the central government. He discovered that the same places that did not pay taxes also were not being assigned teachers from Hanoi.

Drawing on his school and tax data, Bernard drew up maps that showed the difference between what the French military claimed and what his data revealed. He concluded that the Communists controlled 70 percent of the Delta inside the French battle lines. The French held Hanoi, Haiphong, and other large garrison areas, but the countryside was largely under Communist control.

Bernard's examination of the tax rolls and teacher placements was a classic example of how he approached his work. He had great sympathy for the French officials in Vietnam. He had sympathy, too, for the Vietminh war of liberation, particularly since he had fought in a guerrilla war. In one letter, he said, "In all fairness, 'chapeau' ["Hats off!"] to the Viet-Minh. They don't even have any decent hospitals or medical supplies." But his personal feelings were not the issue. He was a scholar, a seeker of truth, and he believed it was invariably available to those who put aside ideology and looked for it.

In San Francisco I was living in a former mansion, now divided into room and board accommodations for young, single working adults. The house was perfectly situated, perched on a ridge in Pacific Heights on the corner of Broadway and Laguna. The picture windows, spreading across two walls of the dining room, offered a breathtaking view of San Francisco Bay.

I had quickly found a job with an advertising agency. The trip to work was a daily adventure. I caught the electric bus on Union Street, then changed to a crowded cable car, precariously hanging on to the outside rail for the rest of the bumpy trip to our Stockton Street office. After designing rather dull retail ads during the day, I satisfied my creative needs by attending an evening ceramics class at the California School of Fine Arts. I threw pots on the wheel and learned about glazes. On weekends, I would walk down the hill to the Marina, watercolor pad and paint box in hand. What a delight to sit and paint, inspired by the colorful boats, the warmth of the cream-colored houses and the incredibly blue sky and water. I was excited by the abstract possibilities, the vast geometric patterns formed by the city's buildings on the San Francisco hills, visible as far as one could see.

Late in June, returning from a series of field trips, Bernard was delighted to find a letter confirming that his article "Indochina: The Seven Year Dilemma," had been accepted by the *Military Review*, the prestigious publication of the U.S. Army's Command and General Staff College at Fort Leavenworth, Kansas. The four-thousand-word article opened with a history of the area, then described the Vietminh, the war situation, the French tactics, and the outlook for the future. Bernard was thrilled to have the piece approved, because it would be read by senior U.S. military leaders and foreign military officers around the world. It was the first of many articles he would publish in the *Military Review*.

In late June, he wrote to me about his work and some of the people he had met in Vietnam: "Re your recommendation that I stay out of trouble—well, I guess I should but it is intellectually dishonest to write about a thing (in non-fiction) that one does not experience directly. If I came to Indochina it was to collect first-hand knowledge and actually SEEING it makes you understand the how and why of a few things. Right now, I'm attached to an outfit that is in charge of liaison work that is attached to the Vietnamese to beat the Viet-Minh at their own game. That's all I can say. It is terrifically interesting and the guys that are in this type of work are the highest-class type we have out here."

Bernard had the utmost respect for the French officials who had brought their wives and children to Vietnam. He mentioned one wife who was doing pacification work fifty miles out in the countryside. Another with a small baby was living with her husband, a French officer, in a dangerous village. I read this in San Francisco and was ashamed of my reluctance to go join him.

He added this alarming account of his visits to the countryside:

> There are the peaceful villages with luxuriant hedges close to the road, hedges behind which the Viet-Minh love to lie in wait for a vehicle . . . so you just gun the engine and hope that you'll see them before they see you. We passed an artillery convoy and again hit one of the ominously calm villages all by ourselves, the same duck pond, mud huts, luxuriant orchards, and out again on the highway. A few miles further, all of a sudden [we] heard the harsh staccato of automatic weapons, then some more of the same, and a few minutes later, the heavy booms of gunfire. The artillery convoy had been ambushed in the village through which we had passed. They just let us through because they were waiting for the bigger game behind us. The whole thing was a matter of sheer, unforeseeable luck, because for a while we had toyed with the idea of staying with the convoy for more protection. Well, the convoy was lucky. They lost only one dead and a few wounded, and they let the Viets have it. In the south today, a train blew up on a bridge and fell into a ravine. . . . Situation not so hot right now.

He returned to Hanoi on July 1. He had completed his study of the minorities of Vietnam and now he was working concurrently on the National Guard, the local militia, and the Communist government. As July 4 approached, Bernard told me he would not be invited to the ceremonies at the U.S. Consulate. He had antagonized the vice consul over lunch by telling how he and many Frenchmen felt about the execution of Julius and Ethyl Rosenberg, the alleged atomic spies, two weeks earlier. "Better apply for my re-entrance visa to the U.S. from another consulate now, I guess."

Bernard labeled this photo, taken "somewhere in the Delta, June '53:
Something's happened. An armored task force, loaded with infantrymen,
rushes in. This is an everyday occurrence."

I continued to find Bernard's absence difficult. In response
to my complaints, he wrote, "I could have chosen any damn subject on earth, including the milk distribution in Monroe County
and its effects on commercial relations with Canada (doesn't that
sound great?), or in any case, and in view of my M.A. research, a
subject on Germany. It would have been the easy way out—and
I've never taken the easy way out in my life and I'm not going to
start at 26. The Indochina thing was a challenge and I just had to
meet it. Just like Mallory, the British mountain climber, who was
once asked why he tried to climb Everest: 'Because it's THERE,'
was his answer.

"P.S. I forgot to tell you that James Mallory died on Everest,
trying to climb it, but that's pushing the comparison too far for
my taste."

On July 11, he wrote that he planned to go to Son La and Lai
Chau, the fortress two hundred miles behind Communist lines,
to study the "administrative set-up" there. He urged me not to

worry if I didn't get a letter for a few days. Six days later he wrote to me:

> Lai Chau . . . I just can't describe it. Shangri-la at the edge of nowhere. It's the most wonderfully interesting place I've yet been to! The flight over Ho Chi Minh territory was uneventful, although you'll read (by the time you'll get this) that we've just launched the biggest parachute operation yet made behind Ho's lines. I pray for the guys that jumped into that jungle. . . . Lai Chau is in a valley bottom where 3 rivers meet, with an airfield that is nothing but a cow pasture. I shudder to think how they get a plane into the place. . . . People are cut off from the rest of the world and the calm here, save for the chirping of grasshoppers and an occasional shell of ours, is really eerie. The young Frenchman who, by himself, is the gov't here, is very friendly and so is the commanding officer, a colonel, and I'm getting the info I need. We have sparse electric light for 2 hours in the eve—but thank God, it's so nice and cool up here! Everything's so very friendly, yet when you think that we're 200 mi. behind Communist lines with Red China a few minutes away—and those fellows here with not the ghost of a chance to get out of here IF . . . but nobody thinks of it and that's good.

As Bernard said, the French outpost at Lai Chau was highly vulnerable. A few months later, in November, the French military withdrew from it and moved about sixty miles south to the presumed greater safety of Dien Bien Phu. He continued:

> Our offensive seems a full success—thank God. The kids caught 'them' with their pants down and captured big stores of brand-new Soviet weapons there, we went up to a hill position—the real jungle (there are tigers here!) and WHAT roads! We've heard of units here that walked four days to make 15 miles. Last night, two enemy agents crawled in to

within 2 mi. from our hq. otherwise the country is so wonderfully quiet and peaceful. . . . They've got their own type of
elementary democracy with a little parliament called the "Tai
Council" AND THEIR GIRLS ARE REALLY ALL THEY'RE
CRACKED UP TO BE! They bathe stark naked in the river
and are really a sight—no bras needed around here! The
regional commissioner here, a kid a year older'n I, is known
all over the place, so that traveling is fun. I am sorry that
you're not with me to enjoy all this—your sense of shape
and color would actually get so much more out of this than
I with my Poli Sci.

He waded through two rivers to get to an outpost that consisted of a few French and German legionnaires, two machine
guns, and a radio. "And that's a *point d'appui (P.A.)*—a strong-
hold—I wonder how they just don't go nuts and start seeing
things. . . . No, here we are, maybe 1200 strong, and nobody but
ourselves to look for help."

While in Lai Chau, Bernard received a letter which arrived in
a mail pouch dropped via parachute by the French Air Force. The
letter had been forwarded from his Syracuse address. It was a
summons to appear in traffic court because he had not paid a
parking ticket. When he eventually returned to Syracuse, he explained the situation to traffic court judge Truman Preston, who
kindly dropped all charges.

Late in July, Bernard went to a lot of trouble to buy me a
lovely gift. Knowing that the customs duty on anything in gold
or silver would be prohibitive, he decided to send me another
type of gift. It would be personal, decorative, and genuinely Vietnamese: two love scrolls, each six feet tall. With a Vietnamese
friend along as interpreter, he visited a man versed in the arts of
poetry and calligraphy, a wispy-bearded elderly chap wearing the
black turban of a "notable." They engaged in a lengthy traditional ritual which began by their bowing low to one another,
then drinking the offered tea in a noisy manner, to show appre-

ciation. Finally Bernard explained that he planned to be married, to a girl in America, and wanted to express his love to her in a fitting way. As Bernard recounted it:

> Thus we got to the heart of the matter (1 1/2 hours after the introduction; the morning was shot). But we had to agree upon the text. Do I really love her? Very much, indeed. (Important question, because in a country where you might marry several women and have a concubine or two, to boot, there are about two dozen different words to express "love for one woman only," "love for a concubine," etc.). She's going to be my only woman. And are you going to be separated for a long time? A few months anyway. And afterwards you intend to stay together forever? Oh, yes! And he starts scribbling on a small piece of paper. We just sit in respectful silence and wait. He then reads aloud what sounded like very nice chatter and my friend seemed quite pleased. Anyway, we two were to stay united for life like iron and copper. Sounds like a lot o' kettle, doesn't it? So, I duly appreciated but asked whether the metallic components could be modified? Well, of course, he understood. Our feelings were more delicate . . . and he started scribbling again and the following met with general approval: "For all our life we will be attached to each other and stay together in eternal conjugal love, just like the yellow bamboo and the prune tree."

Bernard wrote me without details that he had been offered a job in Indochina and declined. He explained: "Do I want to make a career of Indochina? Nope. Do I want to get my block knocked off sooner or later? Nope. Do I want my girl to catch a lot of tropical diseases? Nope! So, why the hell stay out here?" I replied that I was delighted he had decided not to make Indochina his permanent career. Of course, in a way, he had.

Bernard wrote that while winding up his work in Hanoi he had hit "pay dirt." Wanting to find out what goes on in the mind of the Vietminh diehard, and why certain people come over to the French side, he had read two hundred case histories that the government had compiled. They showed that women, children, farmers, political commissars, and soldiers had all risked their lives to leave Vietminh territory and come to areas controlled by the government. A good deal of information was included on each person and Bernard studied it closely.

In one case a Vietminh company commander had walked into the French lines because he was scolded by his superiors and thus "lost face." Of all those interviewed, only a sixteen-year-old girl said that she hated the Vietminh and thought that they were bad for the country. People showed a respect and admiration for the "Can-Bo," the name for the Vietminh political, military, or financial commissars.

Bernard drew unexpected conclusions from this data: "Funny when you think that every Vietnamese around you, that grimy beggar, the flower girl, the vagabond salesman of odds and ends, they may all be part of the fanatical group that does more to keep the Viet-Minh alive as a political force than any of the Chinese-delivered Soviet (and U.S.)-made guns ever could." As Bernard saw it, the defectors did not come to the government for ideological reasons or because they hated Communism and sought democracy. "They came because we have better food, medicine, and no French bombers to worry them. The Viet-Minh merely sheds its weak sisters on us."

Bernard had developed a painful case of jungle rot on one leg, one arm, and parts of his back. He joked, "All I can say is: I do get my PhD the hard way—an insidious thing, as soon as you hit a trail, you've got it, that and leeches."

By August 9, the fungus was hurting so badly that he sought hospital treatment. His groin was raw and every step caused burning pain. Bernard started the necessary treatment. "The general idea is to rip open the pores where the fungus is lodged, and then kill the stuff inside. This is done by first shaving the body hair in the area affected, then using a nylon finger brush on the sore area until it breaks. Then taking some cotton and rubbing the entire area with a solution combining salicylic acid, benzoic acid, iodine, sulfuric ether, and pure alcohol. Together, you ought to be able to melt metal with it." He said he was too big to cry but it would have been a relief.

While at the hospital he had seen French soldiers with devastating wounds which he described in agonizing detail. Some were men who had entered the army in 1939 and never stopped fighting. He was deeply moved by their suffering.

As he recovered from his afflictions, he wrote me a letter in which he explained why his work was so important: "From the general point of view this place is a hotbed and a more likely spot to start a general war than ten Koreas. Any knowledge we get out of it soon might help a few bigger people than you and I keep things on an even keel, and I happen to be one of the guys trained to present such knowledge intelligibly." Even then he saw that Vietnam could explode into an international disaster, that Westerners didn't understand the situation, and that he might be able to help avert the disaster. He closed by telling me, "Keep your chin up. It isn't that long! And we'll soon be together for a very, very long time."

A few days later, still sick with a cold and fever, he took a plane to Saigon and reported: "Arrived in Saigon. Doesn't look like there's a war on at all." Saigon was a city of broad avenues, beautiful gardens, Parisian shops, food stores with refrigeration, and an abundance of cars. It was so far removed from any sign of war that he found it eerie. People he met were incredulous that he had voluntarily gone to the North. Although Bernard liked Saigon, he found life there superficial. Rich Vietnamese lived in the center of the city, while 800,000 Chinese huddled in nearby Cholon, on less land than the 50,000 Europeans in Saigon.

On August 24, he wrote:

This day was loaded with excitement, I must say. Spent a full 2 hours with the President of Viet-Nam who was a 'dear.'

He's a nice, old but very active man with a crew cut whose own family is a nice example of the tragedy that goes on here. 2 of his 3 sons were killed (chopped to bits in a scientific slow way) by the Viet-Minh. His last son is the V-Nam Commander-in-Chief. But, the husband of his oldest daughter ironically is surgeon-general *for* the Viet-*Minh*. The President, too, spent years in a Jap concentration camp. But you should see him! He's outspokenly for Vnam independence and certainly no French puppet, though he's realist enough to know that V.N. can't stand alone yet.

The French high commissioner of Vietnam introduced Bernard to his top staffers and instructed them to assist him with his work. The Vietnamese minister of information, Dr. Le Van Hoach, invited Bernard to fly with him to Tay Ninh, capital of the Cao Dai, one of the politico-religious sects of Vietnam that insisted they be treated as independent entities. Some of the sects had their own armies and some sided with the Communists. To keep them on the non-Communist side, some of their leaders were taken into the Vietnamese central government. Dr. Hoach was such a man, a member of the powerful Cao Dai, which was a mixture of Buddhism, Catholicism, and other religions and honored such saints as Jesus, Buddha, Joan of Arc, Victor Hugo, and Lenin. They had their own "Pope" and Bernard was going to meet him.

Dr. Hoach surprised Bernard by flying his own plane, a four-seater Ryan Navion. They soared over flooded rice paddies, huge forests, rubber plantations, beautiful villages, and then, rising up 3,400 feet in the middle of the plain, the Sacred Mountain. Beyond it they could see the spires of the Cathedral of Tay Ninh, the Holy See.

The Pope of the Cao Dai was in the garden of the papal retreat, observing construction of a swimming pool. Dr. Hoach excused himself and Bernard stayed with the Pope for three hours. "The man had a piercing intelligence and his approach to things is very realistic. I learned more about Indochina than I'd learned before in 3¹/₂ months. To think that he was sitting there with me talking about the need for French help after he'd spent 5 years in French banishment in Madagascar. The man was fascinating and I can see why 2 million people think he's the next thing to God himself—and that includes a lot of educated Europeans." Bernard said the cathedral itself was worth the trip, decorated as it was with rococo swirls, dragons, flowered clouds, and geometric patterns in contrasting and often garish colors.

In the meantime, I was falling in love with San Francisco, its beauty and friendly ambiance, the vistas from atop the hills, the golden sunsets. Across the Golden Gate Bridge, the mountains, eucalyptus trees, and redwood trees were an exotic vision. I enjoyed the temperate climate, the variety of cultures, the weekend trips to Yosemite. Restaurants were inexpensive and the food was sublime. The satirist Mort Sahl was performing at the hungry i nightclub with his welcome attacks on Senator Joe McCarthy and his caustic comments on President Eisenhower and Vice President Nixon. There was so much to do and see. I wrote Bernard that perhaps he should come there, instead of returning to Syracuse, and we could live together and get to know each other better before deciding about marriage. Bernard wrote back that perhaps we should get married in San Francisco, and enclosed his cartoon of a man and woman in striped prison garb, linked by a ball and chain, who faced two road signs—one that said "Alcatraz," the other "Marriage."

He wrote that he was leaving on another combat operation but he could not say when and where. "Don't worry, kiddo, in case you don't get a letter for 5–6 days." Another risk-taking adventure, I thought. Did he really need this for his research? Or was it the old thrill of facing danger? His next letter was sent from Siem Reap, Cambodia, and dated October 6.

"They have again parachuted thousands of men into Lao Kay, so as to cut off the flow of supplies coming from China, just as they did in Langson in July. However, there, they were only 80 miles from safety and in LK, they're 120 to Laichau (and that's NO safety) or 300 mi. through Red-hot territory back to the perimeter of Hanoi. Well, all we can do now is hope for the best."

He described the wonders of Angkor, the lost city of the Khmer Empire, which had been rescued from the jungle and patiently restored by French archeologists. He said the temple walls are covered with delicately chiseled frescoes that are as much as 1,200 years old. "The whole thing makes it a stone symphony. Deadly silence. It always looks deserted because people are so puny compared with it."

He said that the previous evening he had watched a small number of French troops in their isolated outpost, presenting arms, exchanging salutes, "going through the whole rigamarole [sic] as unconcerned as ever, as if their goose wasn't cooked whenever some little jerk here felt that the time was ripe. . . . It'd be ridiculous if it weren't so pathetic."

He also told me he had an interview with Prince Norodom Sihanouk, Cambodia's chief of state, but gave no details, perhaps because he considered the meeting sensitive. Later both of us would get to know the prince better when we lived in Cambodia for a year.

Before dawn the next day Bernard left on a fast convoy consisting of three jeeps, eight men, two Browning automatic rifles, "and everybody else with tommyguns." Under the cover of darkness they made their way to Phnom Penh. He arrived exhausted after sixteen hours in a truck, having been delayed by eleven blown-out tires among the three vehicles.

In Phnom Penh he was treated royally under orders from the French high commissioner. He wrote to me that "I am spoiled rotten forever, living immoral with luxury." What he mistook in the dark the day before as the guest house of the French high commissioner turned out to be the commissioner's residence itself, so he wound up staying a few doors down in the same corridor. The commissioner dropped in that night—in pajamas,

Bernard in briefs—to add a dedication to a book he'd written and presented to Bernard earlier during their formal audience. Built in 1944, the place was luxurious, with enormous rooms and much pink marble. A houseboy served him coffee in bed and took care of his laundry. A chauffeured car was at his disposal and turbaned Moroccan sentries guarded this epitome of colonialism.

The next morning he left for Saigon in an unescorted vehicle, relying on speed for a safe return. He had a date the next evening with an airline hostess—"just for dancing" he assured me—at a nightclub. As it turned out, the girl had to work that night and was in Haiphong, a thousand miles away. "So you're happy?" he wrote. I told myself that had it been more than a date for dancing, he would not have mentioned it.

As his departure from Vietnam drew near, Bernard wrote to me, "Mixed feelings about leaving? Sure. With all my bookish air and with my highly peaceable education, I nevertheless enjoy a good tough scrape, just to prove to myself that I'm no sissy. I guess that I've been trying to prove a point to myself ever since my parents died."

I thought that was a profound piece of self-analysis, suggesting why he had become such a rare combination of intellectual and warrior.

As he packed to leave, Bernard sacrificed nearly all his earthly belongings in order to take his files and records with him on the plane. He took with him barely a change of shirts. On October 16, while flying above East Pakistan on the way to Calcutta, he wrote to me: "I've left Indochina, just about as hale as I got there, and somewhat the wiser." If he was hale, it was in spite of having lost a tooth and suffering both jungle rot and bouts of dysentery. He spent his last days saying goodbye to many new friends, thanking them for the help that was so generously given him. He departed carrying his hand luggage, a little airline bag plus his transistor radio, typewriter, camera, the gadget bag I had given him, and a 'Tai hat that measured three and a half feet in diameter. Having shipped his long pants by boat, Bernard was wearing his khaki tropical shorts when he finally arrived in an autumnal Paris.

6

THE YELLOW BAMBOO AND THE PRUNE TREE

DOROTHY FALL

Two years after his departure to study in the United States, Bernard was back in Paris to visit his sister Lisette as well as his aunt Marcelle and her husband, Auguste Biret, the couple he had lived with briefly before his mother took him and Lisette to Nice. Marcelle and Auguste now operated Librairie Biret, a popular bookstore on the Champs-Elysées. On November 19, the family celebrated Bernard's twenty-seventh birthday—twenty-seven years in which he had known more drama, heartbreak, and achievement than most people do in a lifetime.

The city was lovely that fall of 1953. The trees were magnificent in their autumn colors. "Wish I could walk with you down the avenues," he wrote. Instead, he enjoyed Paris with Lisette. They walked in the Tuileries Royal Gardens, where they had played as children, and along the Left Bank, exploring open-air bookstands, some with "genuine phony old books selling for exorbitant prices to gullible foreigners."

Bernard went with Auguste to visit his uncle's family, farmers in a village in Brittany. The ride through the countryside was calm, with the rolling hills and windmills, and the two men enjoyed the opportunity to gossip and tell stories. Arriving at the farmhouse they were greeted by Auguste's family, nineteen of them, "plus some odd dogs." It had rained for three days, Bernard wrote me, and "we sunk ankle-deep into the mud and cow dung as soon as we stepped out of the car. After we got through kissing each other on the cheeks (I'm known and referred to as l'Indochinois) we were fed a little snack that lasted three hours with a half-dozen wines that had to be tasted and commented upon." Next Bernard journeyed to Vienna and delivered two speeches, which earned him eighty dollars, as well as a chance to be with his beloved Uncle Franz and Aunt Hilde.

He wrote to me constantly, letters full of his declarations of love, but I remained uneasy, trying to sort things out. I was angry that instead of returning quickly to my arms from Indochina, he would spend another six weeks in Europe. If he loved me so much why didn't he rush back? Of course, he had work to do in Paris, where the Indochina war was the subject of heated debate. He attended conferences on the war and met with the French secretary of state for Indochina, the colonial minister, and the Vietnamese high commissioner in France. Unexpectedly, getting his visa became a problem, which frustrated us both. On November 23, after several visits to the U.S. Embassy, and concerns that something was being drummed up about his past, Bernard finally received his visa. "I'm *too happy* for words to know that I'm *not un-American.*" The delay had been due to an economy move which had reduced the embassy staff, and it caused Bernard to miss his boat.

Finally, on December 8, Bernard sailed for the United States. He arrived in New York, where he visited the United Nations, the Institute of Pacific Relations, and the French Consulate General, then returned to Syracuse to report to his professors and to deposit all the treasures of his Indochina research. I didn't rush to join him. I wasn't anxious to trade San Francisco for the gray Rochester winter, so I procrastinated, hoping he would come for a visit. I dreamed of persuading him to settle down with me there.

Given my reluctance to return east, Bernard hopped an airplane to San Francisco with every intention of bringing me back. After a seven-month separation, I did not feel entirely comfortable with him. He seemed a stranger. For his part, Bernard's first order of business was to present me with a lovely ring, one with a basket weave in white gold holding a diamond. It was lovely, a symbol of his commitment. I was living in my brother's apartment, which he had just vacated to move to San Jose. We had a week to readjust to each other and to share our growing happiness at once more being together.

Still, my efforts to persuade Bernard to remain in San Francisco were unsuccessful. It was soon clear that I would return east with him. The three-day train trip was dreary but we savored the intimacy of it. After an overnight stop in Chicago, we boarded the New York Central Railroad for the last lap towards home—our separate homes until our marriage. Unlike today's world of cohabitation, it was not considered respectable for unmarried couples to live together. I left the train in Rochester and Bernard continued on to Syracuse.

Helped by the recommendation of Syracuse professor Donald Bishop, Bernard had been offered an assistantship at Cornell University. He would lecture on Indochina and teach a graduate course, Government and Politics of Vietnam. Bernard was thrilled to be teaching such a course at this beautiful and rich university. In Ithaca he would be close to Syracuse and his mentor and academic advisor, Dr. Wladyslaw Kulski, while he wrote his doctoral dissertation.

Professor Kulski and Bernard had both arrived at Syracuse University in the fall of 1951. As a Polish diplomat, Kulski had negotiated the treaty with Great Britain that led to that country's declaration of war on Nazi Germany. He was a professor of political science and a recognized expert on Soviet foreign policy and Communism. Bernard became Kulski's first graduate student at Syracuse. The two men had in common their European backgrounds and having studied in Paris. Kulski, his wife Antoinette, who had been a dentist in Poland, and Bernard became close friends. They conversed in French and Bernard viewed the couple as a second family. After Bernard and I met, the Kulskis would include me in the gatherings of graduate students frequently held in their home. These were evenings filled with warmth, congeniality, and humor. They kept close tabs on us. Antoinette said that I was Bernard's Cinderella and he was my Prince Charming.

In January 1954, soon after his return to America, Bernard went to Washington to brief officials at the French Embassy on Indochina. In return, they offered him new research material. It was an early example of his growing repute. He simply knew things that few others knew.

While we awaited our marriage, I lived with my parents and worked as a freelance designer for Harry Leffler, my previous employer. My parents were not entirely pleased with my choice of husband. My mother feared that I would be taken off to France, never to be seen again. She made plans for a Jewish wedding, but Bernard wanted to be married by a justice of the peace. "In France, one is legally married in the mayor's office," he declared. "I refuse to be married in a religious ceremony first." I respected his position but what could I tell my parents? They would not understand.

This had become a delicate matter. Bernard no longer thought of himself as Jewish, but for me to marry out of my faith (such as it was) was unacceptable to my parents, and I could not hurt them. Finally, under pressure from me, Bernard conceded that he was Jewish. This victim of the Holocaust, instead of embracing his religion, rejected it. "It was the Jewish Council in Nice that gave the names to the French police, who came after us, who did the bidding of the Nazis," he told me angrily. Another time, he said with great emotion, "I don't want my children raised as Jews. I don't want anyone coming after them the next time." Those remarks, I thought, were another glimpse into the pain that lived beneath his tough exterior.

Finally we agreed to be married in a civil ceremony in New York City with just us and our friends, one that would be a secret from my family. After that, he said we could go through the religious ceremony, which he considered meaningless.

I agreed, although I was fearful that our scheme would be found out. Two wedding dates were set. The first was February 20, and the second was February 28, when my parents had planned a religious wedding, or at least one with a rabbi officiating.

On February 19, we slipped off to New York. The following morning, Bernard and I were married by a justice of the peace in Manhattan's City Hall. A party followed at the apartment of Bill Benenson, a friend of the Birets. He was an art collector who spent several months a year in Paris, where he frequented the family bookstore. My roommate Iris was there along with Jean Brandes, Bernard's friend from Nuremberg, and a young Vietnamese acquaintance, Nguyen Thai.

The following Saturday, the religious wedding took place at a hotel in Rochester. The guests included relatives I rarely saw and a few of my friends, including Iris and Betty. I had bought a light blue taffeta dress—strapless, with a skimpy bolero jacket. My sister Mary, my matron of honor, insisted on sewing lace along the edge of the jacket to cover my shoulders. Since my parents never attended religious services, Bernard thought it hypocritical to have a rabbi perform the service, but he decided to be a good sport and enjoy the festivities.

In Ithaca, we settled into a three-room flat over a food market at 324 College Avenue. From the kitchen windows we enjoyed a view of the hills beyond the town. Spectacular black thunderheads, presaging a storm, would roll across the valley. In spring and summer, vibrant rose and blazing vermilion sunrises would forecast the joyful optimism of the coming day.

Bernard's papers and files soon overflowed his desk, which was in reality a seven-foot door and filled half of our tiny living room. The door remained his desk, the same one I am using fifty years later. My Vietnamese love scrolls hung on each side of the living room archway leading to the bedroom. Like many students in those days, we had bookshelves made of bricks and boards throughout the apartment. In addition to working on his dissertation and teaching, Bernard had started writing articles for *Pacific Affairs*, a publication of the Institute of Public Affairs (IPR); for *Wehrwissen-Chaftliche Rundschau*, a German military publication; for *Ost-Probleme*, a United States Information Agency publication in Germany; for *Far Eastern Survey*; and for *The Nation*.

Soon after his return, Bernard wrote an article that appeared in the March 6, 1954, issue of *The Nation*, two months before the French defeat at Dien Bien Phu. He began by quoting a French colonel:

What we have here is a sort of *gouvernement crepusculaire*—a twilight government. In our own area we control the cities and major roads from daybreak till nightfall. Thereafter the Vietminh has the country to itself to levy taxes, attack our posts, and execute the 'Vietnamese traitors,' that is, the Nationalists who still profess to believe in victory for our side.

Bernard said that after seven years of bitter fighting, and huge expenditures by both France and the United States, the French and the Vietminh had reached a military stalemate. With peace talks upcoming, "a face-saving victory that would make negotiation palatable has eluded [French commander] General Navarre for the past six months, and the military situation, while by no means desperate, was never more humiliating than at this moment."[1]

The French could neither win militarily nor simply withdraw, he said: "Thus negotiations offer the only solution, and the first step . . . must be a cease-fire." He recognized that the United States would be tempted to intervene if the French faltered, but added that a Communist regime pressured into neutrality by U.S. foreign aid (and its fear of Chinese domination) could be acceptable to the United States, which already coexisted with North Korea and Communist China, as well as the Soviet Union and its satellites. The answer, he concluded, was a far-sighted policy, not "a few additional plane-loads of napalm."

The article reflected both the perceptions of a reporter who had been in the field and a scholar who understood the historical and diplomatic realities. It would be difficult for any rational person, fifty years later, to disagree with the views Bernard expressed, but for the time being he was a voice in the wilderness. Every U.S. administration from Truman's to Nixon's was obsessed with "stopping Communism" in the jungles of Vietnam.

I was pleased to find that my graphic design skills were in demand in Ithaca. I was hired by the Grange League Federation Exchange (GLF), a major agricultural cooperative, to design such materials as brochures for farmers and farm organizations. It was a pleasant job, enhanced by my early-morning walk to work, which took me across the footbridge over Six Mile Creek.

In the evenings I would return home to a husband immersed in his writing and obsessed by Vietnam. His research documents spread around him, he wrote incessantly. Dinner conversation was about Vietnam and the dissertation, or we simply each read while we ate.

It was a pleasant time but a serious problem soon arose. Having arrived back from Indochina in December 1953, Bernard was told he must have his dissertation completed six months

Bernard writing his dissertation, Ithaca, 1954.

later, in May 1954. Such a deadline put him under tremendous pressure. Dr. Kulski, to whom he was so devoted, was his advisor. A letter from him awaited Bernard on our arrival in Ithaca. Kulski had sent back, unread, the first portion of the thesis that Bernard had sent him.

Kulski's irritation was understandable, since Bernard had written the material on onionskin paper, typed on both sides with no margin for comments. He was not so much being rude as seeking, as was his habit, to economize on paper and postage. Unfortunately, Bernard had ended his letter with, "Please return texts soon so that I can make suggested changes in time." Kulski responded, "Finally, do avoid in the future the inopportune observations of the type I have found in your letter. . . . The texts will be returned each time according to my own time-table; please note that you are not my only student and not the only one to submit a thesis." In no university in America or Europe, the professor added, did the student "impose his time-limits on the faculty."

Bernard realized his errors and sent a letter of apology. "It is, of course, understood that I shall re-type and re-submit in draft form any corrections you require. I can but apologize for my remark on the time element, which was not at all meant to give my work any special priority over that of my fellow candidates or over your heavy work and study load, and will endeavor to adhere to all such rules as there are, so as to facilitate your task to the utmost."

The situation worsened. Dr. Kulski sent countless demands for changes in the work, many of which Bernard considered petty. Kulski's area of expertise was Soviet foreign policy and he often wanted Bernard to make comparisons with the Soviet system. Bernard would go to Syracuse for a conference, then would return dejected over their disagreements.

In late March, Bernard confided in Professor Donald Bishop, chairman of the International Relations Program, about these conflicts. Dr. Bishop suggested that Bernard raise the question directly with the advisor. To Bernard's chagrin, he added, "We are assuming that you as a near-PhD are quite mature and, therefore, able to do a thorough scholarly piece of research in your chosen field. If you are not this mature, you should not be working at this level of scholarship, and if you are I suggest that you buckle down on your research project, push it forward as rapidly as you and your advisor are able to do, and complete it to the very best of your ability."[2]

Bernard found this insulting. Moreover, he thought Bishop had spoken to Dr. Kulski, who became ever more hostile. Amid this turmoil, Bernard struggled to finish his dissertation, which eventually became more than a thousand pages long.

Some of his dissertation was typed by Ann Gregory, whose husband, Gene, a teaching fellow at Cornell, had been a press officer at the American Embassy in Saigon in 1950–53. She had been with Gene in Vietnam. Even when he was serving in Vietnam, Gene had been opposed to American support of the French and he opposed American intervention. Gene and Bernard met several times a week to talk. Ann, who also knew a lot about Vietnam, offered to type Bernard's dissertation. The venture ended badly when they disagreed about the payment. The Gregorys later returned to Vietnam, where Gene and others started an English-language newspaper, the *Times of Vietnam*.

The dissertation deadline was extended to December 1954. Kulski continued to make numerous demands for changes. Bernard responded politely, but he was in agony, trying to do his best work but unable to please his advisor. At one point, when he was suffering from a middle ear infection and throwing up, I thought his condition was caused by stress over the situation.

Kulski's comments were mixed. He wrote:

> While I have read those pages with great pleasure because they are well balanced and written with a sense of moderation, I cannot say the same about pages 770–788, which reflect a highly emotional mood. Certain sentences are insulting both in intention and in style. I seriously wonder whether it is proper for a foreign student at an American university to talk in these terms about American policy. Mind you, this is not the matter of your opinions which I do not intend to censor or modify but of the form in which you express your opinions. I would advise you to read those 18 pages as though you were an American (Mrs. Fall may help you in the evaluation) and then devote some thought to my observations. If you agree with me after second reading, write anew the same pages, expressing the same views but in a courteous manner.

I assume Bernard complied. He always said that he was well aware that he was a guest in this country. He tried not to directly criticize the U.S. government, although the factual evidence he presented often read like criticism.

When Bernard completed his thesis he did not include the professor in his acknowledgments. This resulted in a handwritten note, which said in part: "I have read with interest your acknowledgments. They measure up to your usual courtesy. Sincerely yours, W. W. Kulski" Clearly, he was angry that Bernard had not mentioned him, and did not understand the pain Bernard felt in his behavior.

Finally the dissertation was approved.

In an effort for reconciliation, Bernard sent a Christmas gift to Professor Kulski, who returned it several weeks later, without explanation. Angry and hurt, Bernard wrote a scathing letter to his one-time friend and mentor:

> It was very obvious that my sending you a card and gift meant that I wanted to make amends for whatever slight I may have done you, and a truly 'great person' would have picked up things from there. However, you seemingly find great pleasure in the series of petty persecutions, and fits of displeasure and rudeness that have marked your and another professor's relations with me since my return from abroad. . . .
>
> For a very young man, it is always a terrible thing to see one of his idols shattered—to find out that the giant happens to rest on clay feet. Thus, all this hurts me as much as losing a cherished member of my family, and that is why I did not fight back, but swallowed my pride for ten long months, fighting with your picayunish corrections in my thesis, with your personal insults and snide remarks ("this is not journalism," etc.). . . .
>
> Oh, what a great victory of a powerful professor over a little student! 'Petitesse d'esprit' doesn't sound as well in English as it does in French, but nothing else fits what you have displayed towards me.
>
> Therefore, let me thank you for all the *good* things you did to me, and I may assure you that I still think of you as one of my great professors and guides in the scholastic field.

This long-ago tempest in an academic teacup is of interest now only insofar as it casts light on Bernard's character. One assumes that a diplomat-turned-professor will display a degree of self-importance. The problem was that Bernard was in no regard a typical graduate student. He had survived the Holocaust, armed encounters with the German army, and the war zone in Vietnam. He was a proud, angry, thin-skinned, and passionate man. It was not his nature to turn the other cheek or sidestep a fight. Moreover, while he was writing his thesis he was also writing for national magazines, emerging as an expert who might soon rival or surpass his professor. I wish that Bernard, in this situation and others, could have been more of a diplomat, but the fierce pride he displayed in his conflict with his professor was the same pride that drove him to become the great journalist and scholar that he was.

In December 1956, when we were living in Washington, a mutual friend wrote to Bernard saying that the Kulskis were coming to Washington for a semester of research on Russia. He said Professor Kulski greatly regretted "the misunderstanding" between them and was anxious to resume their friendship. The two men did meet, and were cordial, but they could never recapture the happy, carefree relationship of the early days at Syracuse.

After Bernard's death, Dr. Kulski wrote of him in the *Syracuse University Alumni News* of June 1967: "Shortly before his last visit to Vietnam he mailed a copy of his most recent book, *Hell in a Very Small Place: The Siege of Dien Bien Phu*. This was his masterpiece, a brilliant contribution to military writing. His feelings on Vietnam were reflected discreetly in the dedication: 'To Professor W. W. Kulski, my dear teacher and example, this story of a battle which was to be an end but which, unfortunately was only a beginning, with respectful affection, Bernard Fall.'" The dedication was written in French with the dateline "Saigon, Noël 1966." In a sense, they were finally reconciled.

Despite the conflict with Kulski, Bernard had in 1954 produced a thousand-page document that reflected his extraordinary understanding of Vietnam. The first and shortest section, at 238 pages, was *The Viet-Minh Regime*, which Cornell University would later publish in 1956 in conjunction with the Institute of

Pacific Affairs; eventually it was published in French as well. This section detailed every aspect of the Vietminh: the workers' party, education, trade unions, the armed forces, propaganda techniques, foreign relations, even religion. It was the fullest account available of the Communist rebels who had defeated the French army—for the battle of Dien Bien Phu had occurred in May 1954, as Bernard worked on his thesis. No one in the Western world knew more about this extraordinary movement than Bernard and few suspected that these Vietnamese Communists would grow even more important as America volunteered to finish the job the French had failed to accomplish.

The second volume, at 767 pages, was *the State of Vietnam*. In it, Bernard examined the entire country. Writing just after the French defeat, Bernard addressed the two new countries that were emerging, the Communists in the north, led by Ho Chi Minh, and the French-supported Bao Dai regime in the South. He looked at their economies, politics, and resources, and at the possibility of a political settlement that could bring peace to the country. The third volume, *Vietnam: International Aspects*, examined French and American policy towards Vietnam, as well as how the conflict looked from Moscow and Great Britain.

When these three volumes were bound, I created a cover for each. The first was all red with a yellow star representing the flag of the Vietminh. The second was in yellow, with three thin red stripes, the flag of the Bao Dai regime. The third was half red, half yellow, with an outline of the map of Vietnam, the colors divided at the 17th parallel, as proclaimed by the Geneva cease-fire.

In the future, of course, Bernard would write often about Dien Bien Phu, most notably in his last and greatest book, *Hell in a Very Small Place*.

With the dissertation finally behind us, we left for France on the *Liberté* on February 5, 1955. To work in the United States would require a change in Bernard's visa, which could only be arranged in France. Lisette happened to be in New York and saw us off at the dock. She had arrived a month earlier on the *Liberté* and had befriended the bursar, so she was able to get our tiny room upgraded to a comfortable second-class stateroom.

This was my first trip to Europe. I would finally meet Bernard's family and see the Librairie Biret. After a week-long crossing, and my introduction to French cuisine, Auguste was waiting in Le Havre and drove us to Paris. The family's elegant house in Neuilly was of pink stone, with gray shutters and ornate black grill work, and its sleeping gardens promised floral and edible bounty in season. Bernard and I were given the small bedrooms that he and Lisette had used after the war. As our visit progressed, I began to see that some in the family viewed me as an unsophisticated American. My French was often corrected by Marcelle, and my use of a knife and fork was also found wanting. Of course, when I ventured out into Paris, I also encountered the French disdain for Americans. Years later, when I related this to Auguste's sister in Brittany, she said, "How could this be? Everyone knows that it was the Americans who saved us from the Germans." But this attitude was not universal.

Bernard spent his time doing research in the French military archives and seeing friends and contacts in Paris. Sometimes we met them and their wives for dinner. Claude Bourdet was founder and editor of *L'Observateur* for which Bernard would soon write. Philippe Devillers, respected author of *Histoire du Vietnam de 1940–52*, became a friend, and Roger Lévy, erudite scholar of the Centre d'Études de Politique Étrangère later wrote the preface to the French edition of *Hell In a Very Small Place*. In March, Bernard gave a talk at the Centre, "American Politics and Vietnam." Paul Mus of the Collège de France, who had a distinguished academic career both at the Collège de France and at Yale, had lived in Vietnam and wrote books about subjects ranging from Buddhism to Cambodia to Vietnam. Nguyen Dê was a Vietnamese statesman we had known in Washington. We visited Rémy Malot and his wife at Fontainebleau, as well as Henri Pohoryles, another comrade from the war.

We journeyed to Vienna, where I met Bernard's Aunt Hilde and Uncle Franz and their adorable daughter, Gertrud. I was introduced to the opera and the Prater, Vienna's large amusement park with the giant Ferris wheel that I knew from the movie *The Third Man*. We returned through Germany, with stops at Bernard's old haunts. Munich in March 1955 was still showing the scars of the war. Bernard took me out to Dachau, so I could experience this reminder of the horrors of the Holocaust. The camp was terribly moving, even years after the killing had stopped. I felt uncomfortable in Germany but Bernard showed no emotion. He simply wanted everyone to see the horror of the Holocaust for themselves. We also stopped in Bastogne to retrace a key battle of World War II, then visited Verdun and saw the beginning of the Maginot Line. Such visits were important to Bernard as a student of war.

We sailed home on the ocean liner *United States* on April 19 and proceeded to New Haven. Bernard had accepted a job with the Human Relations Area Files (HRAF), a nonprofit research organization headquartered in New Haven and affiliated with Yale University. Its mission was to collect, organize, and distribute information of significance on societies, cultures, and social behavior. But when Bernard reported to the HRAF office at Yale, he was told that he had been reassigned. "Don't unpack," he told me. "We are to report to their branch in Washington." I was thrilled.

I had been to Washington only once, in 1950, when I was a college sophomore. To escape my dorm for the weekend, I forged a letter from my mother. A boy and I had planned to hitchhike from Syracuse to Cornell University, an hour away, but our first ride was driving to Washington, and we decided to make the long trip with him.

It was after midnight when the driver dropped us near the Lincoln Memorial. I remember my awe as we climbed the stairs to stand before the great man, bathed in light and gazing down at us. We went outside in the still, black night and sat on the stairs, moved by this dramatic introduction to the wondrous city. We walked to the Jefferson Memorial, the Capitol, and the Supreme Court building. We explored the city all night before hitchhiking back to Syracuse in the cold March wind. I arrived before my Sunday evening curfew.

Now, no longer a hitchhiker, grown and married to a fascinating man, I was ready to return to the city where I would spend the rest of my life.

7

WASHINGTON

BERNARD'S job at WAHRAF, the Washington branch of the Human Relations Area Files, started with high hopes in the spring of 1955 and ended badly eighteen months later. The problem was that Bernard, who probably knew more about Indochina than anyone else in the Western world, and had been hired to write about it, found himself being told what to write by people who knew little or nothing about the region. The miracle was that he lasted there as long as he did.

Bernard had at various times spoken of teaching at a university or working for the United Nations or some other international organization. But none of those jobs had come through and the offer from HRAF sounded promising. It was a research organization set up to produce handbooks for the Psychological Warfare Division of the United States Army. It was housed in a prefabricated building at American University in northwest Washington. Books were planned on countries in which the military might become involved, including Vietnam, Burma, Cambodia, and Laos. The focus of each book would be on the country's culture, history, ethnic groups, religion, social structure, foreign relations, economy, and more. Each book would bring together information from many sources; in theory, a military man could read it and have at least a start toward understanding that country.

An Iran handbook was in the works, and Bernard was part of a team to produce one on Vietnam. An outline for these handbooks, which the writers were expected to follow, was provided by the Defense Department. A monograph prepared at the University of Chicago explained the format. As to content, the writers were to make use of the files from the Human Relations Area Files. Two directors, both anthropologists, made final decisions on the handbooks, and insisted that the staff strictly follow the guidelines provided. A military officer was in overall charge.

We arrived in Washington as the Vietnam team was being organized. David J. Steinberg headed it. He was an economist who had worked in London with the Marshall Plan and then for the Department of Commerce. He had never been to Vietnam. Bernard was the Vietnam expert and political scientist and wrote some history as well. Other members of the group, including an anthropologist, a political scientist, a historian, an economist, a sociologist, and a member of the military, would write chapters on their area of specialization.

"Because of his expertise, his audacity, and his personality, Bernard came on like gangbusters," David Steinberg recalled for me, years later. "He was this aggressive Frenchman, not happy with those who did not agree with him. Bernard was a special personality with whom none of us had ever had to deal before. He certainly knew his stuff, and he insisted that you do your homework, that you do your research."

David added, "There was no animosity. The relationship was never hostile. We developed a very good, very constructive relationship, and we all evolved. Bernard himself evolved. Our military participant, Colonel Van Way, had this cooperative spirit. Bernard sat opposite him and eventually learned how to criticize constructively. Van Way, with whom Bernard had a warm relationship, played a significant role in Bernard's transformation, and we all developed an affection and respect for Bernard."

David also noted, "There were two things that were hallmarks on how close you were to Bernard Fall. One is you don't call him Bernie. The other is the way you spell Viet-Nam." He insisted on that spelling, with the two words hyphenated.

Ralph Greenhouse, an anthropologist who worked with Bernard on the Cambodia handbook, recalled Bernard's "contagious energy, which he infused in others, . . . his energy and exuberance and a great sense of humor. He was rather charming, a schmoozer, an excellent networker, quick to engage others. He had a lot to say about everybody else's chapters. And we, in turn, criticized some things we read in *his* drafts, some wording we thought ought to be improved upon."

The staff found the HRAF files outdated, sparse, and useless. In preparing the Vietnam handbook, there was little outside material available except in French. Bernard was the only person on the staff fluent in the language, which increased his importance in the project.

After the Vietnam handbook was complete, Bernard joined the team that was starting one on Cambodia. Despite occasional friction, an esprit de corps developed among the group, even extending to a social life that included picnicking, hiking in the Shenandoah Mountains, and parties with spouses invited. On one occasion, Bernard showed the group films he had borrowed from the Army on Nazi atrocities. He often showed these films to friends and students. He thought they were the best way to make people understand the reality of Nazism. The films were somewhat subversive in Washington, at a time when our government mainly wanted to forget about the Nazis and concentrate on our ties to West Germany.

One evening in May 1956, while having dinner at the home of one of Bernard's colleagues, we met Paul Blackstock, a military intelligence specialist at the Pentagon. He asked Bernard where he was employed and Bernard told him. Blackstock replied, "I hear they have a French spy working there." After a pause, Bernard replied, "*I'm* the French spy." They laughed and in time Paul became our good friend.

In spite of the congeniality of most members of the project, they shared increasingly low morale, thanks to its directors, the anthropologists. When Bernard and other writers deviated from the format, conflicts arose. Moreover, the directors wanted to cover areas the staff had not agreed upon, because data wasn't available. To fill these gaps, the directors wanted the writers to take liberties with the research materials and to reach conclusions that might not be accurate.

There were many disputes over these questionable practices. Bernard wanted to go with *his* data, which he knew was correct. The directors sent back chapters as unacceptable, demanding changes that Bernard and others found dishonest. Sometimes, those not complying were fired. Finally, Bernard stormed into one director's office and told him that he refused to put in materials that were not up to his standards. The director stood up and shouted, "I don't give a damn about your standards!" Bernard was outraged. The next day, he submitted his letter of resignation:

Dear Colonel Hutchinson:

I hereby wish to tender my resignation from WAHRAF, to take effect after my accumulated leave, on or about November 15, 1956.

There is an old Army saying with which I am sure you are familiar: to wit, that if too many of a unit's effectives are on company punishment, this does not reflect so much upon the men's lack of discipline as upon the poor leadership of the subordinate staff commanders. . . . The non-military directing members of the organization must bear fullest responsibility for the ever-increasing turnover of personnel and the low morale and efficiency resulting therefrom.

As a non-specialist in the research field, you have felt compelled to rely upon what you call your "technical staff" to direct the destinies of your personnel policy. I hereby charge that your so-called "technical staff" has greatly abused its delegated powers so as to disrupt, through indiscriminate dismissals camouflaged as "resignations," the performance level of this organization to the point where its primary mission is in jeopardy. . . . I feel compelled, in view of the professional reputation which I enjoy, to disassociate myself from the organization now that I feel that its standards are no longer compatible with the goals it set out to attain. . . .

I have enjoyed working with you and Colonel John, as well as with my colleagues. I have full confidence in the need, in terms of national defense, for the successful accomplishment of WAHRAF's mission. However, I am equally convinced that this can no longer be successfully done under the present circumstances. I sincerely hope that my resignation may convey to you the earnestness of my feelings in the matter.

Very truly yours
Bernard B. Fall

When Bernard joined the project, it was with the understanding that the handbooks were exclusively for use by the Army and would not be commercially published. However, in 1959, three years after Bernard left the program, the Cambodian handbook was commercially published by the HRAF Press. Bernard and other staff members were cited on the title page as authors, although the published book was not the one they had written. Many aspects of the handbook had been revised by people not on the original team. Bernard was appalled. At his insistence a disclaimer was inserted stating that he did not participate in the revision and was not responsible for modifications in the book.

There were also plans to publish the Vietnam handbook commercially and Bernard made clear to David Steinberg that he strongly objected. He was preparing his own book, *The Two Viet-Nams*. Much of the material in the Vietnam handbook was *his*, and he didn't want it to compete with his own book, especially since he had been promised this could not happen. As it turned out, the Vietnam book was never published. It was simply sent to the Army's Office of Psychological Warfare, in line with the

Bernard and Dorothy with the infamous Jeepster.

original agreement. As I discussed this era with David Steinberg, he took out his copy of Bernard's *The Two Viet-Nams* in which Bernard had inscribed: "To 'DJ' Steinberg, sad survivor of earlier Asian endeavors, this sad tale of missed opportunities and exploded myths. Christmas, 1964."

On our arrival in Washington, Bernard bought another Jeepster. He seemed to have an emotional attachment to the vehicles that went back to his army days. This one was not new and its linkage would sometimes get stuck. If I had stopped for a red light, and the car refused to move, I had to jump out, open the hood, and pull the jammed link, a simple but annoying procedure. This was a time when most Americans drove big comfortable sedans. Eventually, after our first baby was born, Bernard agreed that drafty plastic windows were no longer suitable, and we bought a huge 1955 Chevrolet with automatic transmission.

I found a job with Kal Ehrlich and Merrick, an advertising agency located in the *Washington Star* building. Newspaper advertising was monotonous and non-creative. I compensated by attending painting classes in the evening at American University, where my work improved thanks to an inspiring professor, Joe Summerford.

Bernard suggested I look into the U.S. Information Agency, which produced a variety of anti-Communist publications for overseas consumption. Art director Will Anderson was impressed with my portfolio but told me a job would be impossible because of various bureaucratic hiring rules. However, he got around the rules by hiring me as a temporary employee. Even then, I would have to go through the process of getting a security clearance. That took a year, and at one point my next-door neighbor told me how an FBI agent, with his foot in her door, questioned her about Bernard and me, asking whether we had wild parties and tossed lots of liquor bottles in our trash.

The temporary job evolved into permanent status in June 1956 when I joined the staff of *Amerika Illustrated*, a new Russian-language magazine, which arose out of a cultural affairs agreement with the Soviet Union. It was exciting to help produce this gorgeous magazine, which was somewhat modeled on *Life*. We tried hard to give the Russian people a realistic understanding of American life. We showed the benefits of our capitalist system— our most popular issue in Russia showed America's new cars— but we also showed a country in turmoil in the sixties, with articles about the civil rights and anti-war movements.

For the next sixteen years, I would be a graphic designer there. I was given the flexibility to work part-time when my children were young, and twice allowed to take a year of unpaid leave to follow my husband to the Far East. Later, I returned full-time as deputy art director. Knowing that I had a secure government job was important to Bernard. It meant I could support myself should something befall him.

Following his resignation from WAHRAF, Bernard took a job with the Systems Analysis Corporation, where he was engaged in administrative operations and management studies for private corporations and government agencies. Still hoping to find work in lesser developed areas in Asia or Africa, Bernard applied to other international organizations and to the U.S. Agency for International Development, but nothing satisfactory was forthcoming.

Bernard's writings were making him increasingly well known. Diplomats sought Bernard's opinions and he was glad to share them. A young political officer at the French Embassy, Jacques Andreani, and his wife, Huguette, became our friends. Jacques had been against the French war in Indochina. When I spoke with him years later, he said it had been terrible what France did.

According to Jacques, de Gaulle told Kennedy, "'Be careful of Indochina. If you go there with your troops, it will be a lot of trouble.' Kennedy thought there was no way to equate the situation [with that] of France. This was a colonial power trying to retain colonial prerogatives." Kennedy said that the United States was intent on bringing democracy to Vietnam "so that all the bad things that happened to the French in Indochina could not happen to the Americans, that the situation was totally different. Kennedy had a great vision, in principle, about the role of America." Jacques thought that Kennedy should best have heeded de Gaulle's warning. How different history would have been if he had.

Jacques recalled fondly his conversations with Bernard as a young diplomat. "I picked his brains. He had to do something meaningful with his gifts. It was very important for him to do this." Jacques returned to Washington in 1989 as the French ambassador.

Not long after we arrived in Washington, Bernard expressed his pride in his wartime service by joining the French War Veterans, the *Anciens Combattants Français*. Bernard attended meetings on the first Monday of each month and in time became president of the group. There were ceremonies on Veterans' Day, and they marched on Memorial Day and sponsored a Bastille Day Ball and an annual Christmas party for the children. My favorite of their activities was an annual couscous event at the home of one of the Jacob brothers, originally from the French colony of Algeria. Owners of the French Market in Georgetown, they introduced Washington to the pleasures of French food. We sat at long tables on their property in Potomac, Maryland, feasting and having a delightful celebration with our families.

Vietnam was never far from Bernard's thoughts and an unexpected opportunity to return there soon presented itself. Early in 1957 William Holland, director of the Institute of Pacific Relations, commissioned Bernard to present a report on the foreign policy of Vietnam since the Geneva cease-fire of 1954 to the thirteenth International Conference of Pacific Institutes to be held in Lahore, Pakistan, from February 5 to 14, 1958. Delegations from various member countries would attend and papers would be presented by scholars from many countries.

Bernard never doubted that he must write this important report on the basis of fresh, first-hand experience—meaning a

French veterans at the Jeanne d'Arc monument in Washington's Meridian Hill Park on Memorial Day. Left to right: Jean Jacob (holding American flag), Pierre Feron, group president Bernard saluting, French Ambassador Charles Lucet, and French Consul Roger London.

second trip to Vietnam. The institute did not propose to pay for such a trip and he could not afford to pay his own way, as he had as a graduate student in 1953. However, he had developed a close relationship with the Vietnamese Embassy and with Ambassador Tran Van Chuong, a charming diplomat whose daughter, Madame Nhu, was married to President Ngo Dinh Diem's brother and would soon become world famous. In February 1957 Bernard wrote to the ambassador and reminded him of an earlier conversation.

"During the course of our conversation you had the kindness to express to me the interest of your government in all research having the objective and destined to make better known to the world the problems and successes of the new Viet-Nam." He described the importance of the International Conference of Pacific Institutes and the significance of its reports, which would subsequently be published in book form.

Bernard described his first trip to Vietnam in 1953, during the war, and added, "The Viet-Nam that I know thus, ravaged by war, is no longer the Viet-Nam of today. It would be an injustice to the work accomplished by Viet-Nam since 1954 if I permitted myself to write about it based on second-hand reports and my own recollections during the time of war." He explained that the institute could not pay his research costs, and pointed out that he now had family responsibilities that would prevent his going to Vietnam with personal funds. But he was willing to devote the summer months to such a trip if the South Vietnamese government would help meet the costs of his mission.

He pointed out that he was "an independent researcher whose reputation is established in France as well as in the United States" and whose books and articles would give "important weight" to what he wrote. "As for my sentiments towards free Viet-Nam, you, Excellence, know that better than anyone." He added that he had recently been "personally attacked by Radio Hanoi for my writings on the situation in North Viet-Nam."

Bernard's letter was a success. Through the efforts of Ambassador Tran Van Chuong, the government in Saigon agreed to pay Bernard's travel costs and part of his expenses. Soon he would be off again.

8

THE PURPLE ORCHID

AT THE invitation of the South Vietnamese government, Bernard returned to Vietnam for a three-and-a-half-month visit during the summer of 1957. When he departed on his first trip, in 1953, I had been a lovesick girl consoling herself in San Francisco. This time, when he left in early June, I was at the beginning of the sixth month of my first pregnancy, and fearful that he would not return in time for the birth of our child.

I wasn't happy about his leaving, but I would not ask him not to go. I accepted the trip as essential to his work. But I also realized he would not have allowed himself to be thwarted. I was dedicated to him and considered his work more important than my own needs. I called Vietnam his mistress. He sometimes called it a bad love affair.

He stopped first in California to visit my brother Morris, his wife Skyle, and baby Tony, and then took off across the Pacific. Along the way Bernard sent me beautiful picture postcards, green valleys from the island of Oahu, Ginza Street with its vibrant neon lights from Tokyo, the scenic blue panorama of Kowloon facing Victoria City from Hong Kong. I found them painful to look at.

We exchanged many letters during his trip but they were different from those we exchanged in 1953 when we were still trying to see if we loved each other enough to marry. This time they dealt with the mundane tasks of maintaining a household, the mail I had forwarded to him, the challenge of keeping our Jeepster running, and the progress of my pregnancy.

Bernard must have felt some guilt for leaving me. Before he left he made an arrangement with a florist. Every few weeks, a box would arrive at my office containing a purple orchid and a card. Although I scoffed at the garish flower, I pinned it to my bosom as a memento from my absent husband. I hated having him gone, and it didn't help when friends and coworkers teased me about his being away at this delicate time.

His absence pained me but it was also a challenge. I was without a husband but not without a social life. Invitations to interesting parties poured in: to the Laotian Embassy for their national day, for example, and to a coveted cocktail party at the home of French Minister Robert Valeur—I wrote to Bernard that I would wear one of his orchids there. Friends invited me to dinner and I entertained them. I felt wanted for myself, not just an appendage to my increasingly famous and outspoken husband. As a married, pregnant woman, I felt that I could be flirtatious without being threatening. I wrote Bernard that I was "well taken care of" and he responded: "You seem to be having quite a time all around, more than when I am there!" I found that leisurely Sundays alone could be quite enjoyable.

Of course, my social life was not all that I had to occupy me. *Amerika Illustrated* was in full swing. Because of our six-month lead time, it was July when we sent off our December issue to be printed in Beirut. We then held a Christmas party in July, and a pretty wild one at that. We were proud of our beautiful magazine, and for me the work was exciting and fulfilling. Bernard's absence also provided more time for my own art. I formed an ad hoc class in landscape painting with two of the women from WAHRAF, Marilyn Heilprin and Lucy Kramer. We met at various sites around the city on hot Saturday mornings. One of my favorites was under Key Bridge, near Georgetown, where my cubist, semi-abstract water colors examined a series of bridges and the interplay of their arches.

Meanwhile, Bernard was far away, on a trip that was important for him, and possibly for the world if he could help policymakers understand the reality of Vietnam. Despite the fact that

Dorothy, painting and pregnant, waiting for Bernard to come home, 1957.

the Vietnamese government made his trip possible, he would not deviate from the truth of his findings. His study would cover the aftermath of the war, the partition of the country and the departure of the French, the entry of other countries to fill the vacuum, and the role of South Vietnam on the world stage. He would have to interview a vast array of people and travel extensively. Bernard arrived in Saigon on June 18 and quickly began seeing officials of the Diem administration and the National Assembly. He wrote to a friend in France: "I am once more in my favorite hunting ground, that is, so to say, political research."

On June 19 he met with his French contact, Colonel Guiol, who had spent nearly two decades in Vietnam. Bernard went with him and his wife to Cap St. Jacques, a popular beach resort, where he wrote me a vivid description of the trip:

> The Vietnamese countryside was its usual glorious self, with its rice-thatch huts, its many-hued rice fields, the brown buffaloes, and the big billowy clouds under a deep blue sky. From time to time we passed villages that looked more orderly than others and were huddled around a more or less elaborate church. Each house had in front of it a small wooden cross: Catholic refugees from North Vietnam. Subconsciously I keep looking over the roadsides in the usual wide and wary sweeps of wartimes—but there's nothing more dangerous in sight than a buffalo suddenly emerging from the underbrush. The [French military] watchtowers, now showing the wear and tear of the war years and of neighboring scavengers eager to use their bricks for building materials, are unmanned. The country's at peace at last . . . but for how long?

He said that a few miles from Cap St. Jacques was the "vastest army camp I ever saw . . . abandoned. It is France's latest boondoggle before she left Indochina. Hoping until the last that President Diem would allow them to keep a SEATO [Southeast Asia

Treaty Organization] base at Cap St. Jacques, the French had spent 3 billion francs since 1954 concentrating in this little cape all that an army needed for its upkeep over an indefinite period . . . now it is all dead and showing the early signs of tropical decay."

On June 25 he had meetings with USIA staff and with U.S. economic officers, because the economy of South Vietnam was a focus of this trip. Bernard remarked that the Americans are as nice as ever and "want to go home p.d.q. No colonialists they."

Bernard had an appointment with Ngo Dinh Nhu, brother and political advisor of President Diem. "Nhu is quite handsome with his steel gray hair and slim figure and seems a very intelligent man. I rather not say more here." In fact, they had discussed Vietnamese foreign policy, including the great question of what the Americans were going to do.

He continued with some first hand reporting: "Yesterday did the Saigon docks from wharf No. 14, under a blazing sun, and it was damn well worth it. My feelings as a U.S. taxpayer are more raw. Nearly all the merchandise I saw bore the two clasped hands on a U.S. shield of the Mutual Security Program (official figures have U.S. aid at 90% of total trade!!!) and the stuff so imported is in incredible condition thanks to local stupidity and mismanagement. I personally saw six brand new Ford trucks (1957–2 ton) crushed because somebody had unloaded on top of them a cargo of cement bags." He would later write in detail about the corruption and incompetence he found in both Vietnam and Laos.

July 7 was celebrated as the day President Diem had come to power in 1954. Diem chose the seventh day of the seventh month of 1957 because the number seven has historically been considered sacred and revered in the East. "The city is ornate with huge paintings of the same scowl in true democratic style. Everybody received an invitation to the events." Bernard awoke at six to attend the inauguration of the third year of the reign of President Diem. "It was impressive with the ambassadors right behind Diem and me sitting about ten feet away."

Ngo Dinh Diem had been appointed prime minister of South Vietnam by Emperor Bao Dai, Vietnam's head of state, following the withdrawal of the French. Diem demanded full political and military power and became president through a rigged election; he actually claimed more votes than there were voters. He had dictatorial powers and his rule was puritanical, nepotistic, and pro-Catholic. His brother Nhu was his closest advisor and Madame Nhu became increasingly outspoken. Diem forged a close relationship with the United States, which gave him strong support until 1963, when he was deemed to have outlived his usefulness and he and his brother were killed in a military coup that the United States sanctioned.

In mid-July, Bernard wrote to me of making a new friend and seeing two old friends. The new friend was François Sully, a young French reporter for *Time* who would later join *Newsweek*. Bernard and François had much in common. They had both fought in the Resistance and then with the French army. Both were critical of the Vietnamese government's claims of success. Both were accused of cynicism, as Frenchmen whose country

Ngo Dinh Diem, July 7, 1957.

lost the war in Indochina and thus automatically assumed that the United States could not succeed. Neither was content to write about the war from the safety of his desk, but went out into the field to see for themselves, to talk with the soldiers, not the generals. For Sully, as for Bernard, Vietnam was a calling, a passion and compassion.[1] Diem would later have him expelled from the country for writing too honestly about the situation there.

The old friends were Gene and Ann Gregory, whom we had known in Ithaca. They had proceeded to Saigon where Gene and others started the English-language *Times of Vietnam*. Within a year the *Times* went from a weekly to a daily newspaper and Gene was a political player with easy access to President Diem. His newspaper's articles were strongly pro-Diem and sometimes critical of the United States and American journalists. Ann had become Madame Nhu's confidante and the *Times of Vietnam* became a mouthpiece for her vitriol. Madame Nhu became known as the Dragon Lady, given to shrill speeches that castigated anyone critical of her family's regime. When I spoke with the Gregorys in Ho Chi Minh City in 2000, I was incredulous when Gene told me, "Poor Madame Nhu. She was very quiet. Vietnamese women were not supposed to be outspoken. President Diem [a bachelor] urged her to be his hostess." Madame Nhu never needed any urging to seize the spotlight.

Bernard told me that two Vietnamese friends with government connections had warned him that Gene and Ann Gregory were highly critical of him. He wrote, "I want you to know this so that you can take proper action with U.S. authorities in case anything at all befalls me here." In the context of Saigon in 1957, with the Diem dictatorship fighting to maintain power and hostile to all critics, his fears did not seem unwarranted. Saigon was a beautiful city, but beneath the surface a violent and dangerous one. Bernard also heard that Ann was spreading the rumor that he was a French agent. Soon enough, that charge would turn up in his FBI file.[2]

Although Bernard wrote to me regularly, he did not send the

kind of detailed, candid accounts he had in 1953, because the Diem regime read letters and confiscated whatever was unacceptable to them. To avoid Diem's censors, Bernard and I regularly sent our letters via French army mail, in care of Colonel Guiol, which took longer than civilian mail but provided privacy. Even then he was discreet: "If my letters are somewhat dull (and they are) this is due because there is no longer a war on and because the things that are most interesting, of course, are my conversations with many people, and those I can't put into my letters. . . . Under the colonialists the only censorship consideration was military security while now it is thought orthodoxy."

In one letter, he told me he had a "terrific break." The French army had given him their secret file on the death marches the Vietminh imposed on French prisoners of war after Dien Bien Phu. He called this "the most harrowing thing I've seen since Dachau, pictures of hundreds of guys, with their detailed stories. In your present state I'll spare you the details—it even turns my stomach over what the Commies have done to our men. And it is kept secret for fear it'd upset the delicate apple cart in certain situations. Like hell—I'm gonna get some of this out and politics be damned."

On July 23 he wrote, "Another week and I'm practically on my way back. It wasn't too bad, I hope, Darling. I think a great deal about you and make great resolutions. Regarding being a good husband and father till the wanderlust gets me again. Next time, I'll take you along." Actually, it would be another seven weeks before his return. Another time, he wrote, "May as well make this as interesting as possible before I get back to wails, diapers, and bottles." In fact, he was a Frenchman, and diapers and bottles never loomed large in his life.

In August, he sent this account of one of his trips:

Trip to Nha Trang was interesting in its very lack of excitement, not exciting because there is no war. Who would have thought three years ago of taking a train trip to Nha Trang.

Then, the trip was via the 'Raffales,' armored trains equipped with radio, artillery, mortars, even light tanks with a heavy supply of spare rails and bridging equipment which zoom through with supply and passenger trains in between. In order to avoid Viet Minh ambushes, the departure date, even the days, were never announced in advance. You just sat near the railroad station and then made for the train after a few days' sitting, when one of the 'Raffales' made a try for it. And often they didn't make it. Nha Trang itself is a very ugly town located at a most beautiful beach, whose horizon is dotted with small islands with all sorts of fantastic shapes. The water is absolutely limpid and swimming is ideal, like in Nassau. Had requested permission to go into the Moi plateau with one of their patrol units. Seems like everything there is just as calm as when I was in the north in 1953. So there's something to be seen here.

He meant that in 1953, the situation had also looked good and the north was calm, but in reality it was infested with the Communist enemy. Nha Trang became a major military base during the American war in Vietnam.

Bernard was asked to speak to the Saigon Rotary Club and wrote on August 9 that his appearance was a triumph: "I was consecrated a social success here. The Rotary is a big thing here with the French, the Vietnamese, the U.S. and the Chinese. . . . My subject was, 'A French professor in the U.S.' Several Vietnamese cabinet members were there, the head of the French cultural mission, head of USOM (ICA Mission), and the chiefs of most of the big businesses.

"You know me—I kept things relaxed and, I think, fairly interesting. I did not knock the U.S. (on the contrary) but did not skirt witch-hunting or racial discrimination either, and ended on a note on French cultural influence which cheered the French without hurting anybody else."

Bernard's letters in August showed how extensively he was

traveling. He spent several days in Cambodia and then visited the Cai-San refugee settlement project at the western edge of South Vietnam, near the city of Rach Gia. This involved a four-hour trip across southern Vietnam in a Willys station wagon, past rich green rice fields and occasional water buffaloes.

Bernard wrote to me that he had been the first foreigner to travel with a South Vietnam army division in an operations area, up near the line that divided North and South Vietnam. Or, as he put it, "Smack on the 17th parallel facing the commies." He wrote of a trip to a refugee camp: "We embarked in outboard-engine boats and went to visit some of the villages escorted by one boat of tommy-gun-toting policemen just in case. Wonderful feeling to go down these canals with the breeze in one's face. Left for where the primitive tribes are. Tonight I'm freezing [at] 2000 feet altitude at Dalat. Lake, golf course wonderful, (comfortable) hotels. Feels like France. A must for you. I'm really made here, and were it not for you and the baby would like to keep on fighting."

When he had spoken to the Rotary Club in Saigon, Bernard had met the head of the powerful Terres Rouges rubber plantations, which he called "the biggest money earner of Viet-Nam." The man invited Bernard to fly to one of the plantations in his private plane the following weekend. Bernard was glad to do so, for it would add to his understanding of the Vietnamese economy. Bernard had a deep-seated dislike of colonial exploitation, which he felt that such an operation represented, but he was nonetheless highly impressed by his tour of the plateau Eaux.

By mid-August I felt terribly alone. The baby was due on September 21 and Bernard had arranged to return on September 16. I didn't want to go through childbirth by myself and I thought he was cutting it far too close. The baby could, after all, arrive early. Moreover, he was planning to stop in France on the way home.

Having had no previous experience with newborn babies, I took a one month course, "Baby and Child Care," at the Red Cross. There were two-hour classes twice a week. I was saddened to see that all the other women in the class were accompanied by their husbands. They taught us how to hold, feed, burp, change, and bathe a baby—for the bath, they taught us an ingenious hold that I passed on to my own daughters when they became mothers. By then, my baby was moving and kicking more and more, and I was sorry that Bernard was not there to share in this amazing experience. He had made clear what he wanted, of course—a son!

I was surprised and pleased when he wrote of being offered a job in Cambodia. He had been asked to teach at the Public Administration School in Phnom Penh. "Looks fascinating. Phnom Penh was lovely after the other places. At least it looks alive. Job would be for 1958–60 so that we finally have time to get the boy (!) growing before we leave and transplant him (her). I'm really enthused for the first time in 3 months. The next year will be a good one for all three of us. Yes, you're going on a trip next year, 95% certain—Cambodia. . . . Salary $12–14,000 plus house and trip for all of us. Two year contract renewable."

My response was entirely positive. "I would love it. I am excited already. Your experiences sound wonderful and I am so envious. Would love to travel around with you. Will you still love me even if I am roly poly?" He wrote back, "Cambodia job is 'in,' unless the whole country folds up."

On August 26 Bernard sent me a candid, handwritten letter from Vientiane, Laos: "Economically, the country is totally corrupted. What goes on in any other place in Indochina and the Far East is absolute kid's play in comparison to Laos. They're throwing the U.S. dollars around as if the damn things were going out of fashion. Fantastic bribes are paid and accepted. . . . The chief of the import commission was to be fired for notorious incapacity and bribery. The week before his departure from office, he signed import licenses for forty million dollars of goods on which he took five percent commission."

In Vientiane, Bernard met Col. Jean Deuve, who had led a Franco-Lao guerilla war against the Japanese during 1945. Now he was an advisor to the prime minister of Laos, on Laotian security and intelligence, and one of the best-informed men in

Laos. Deuve gave him first-hand information about the situation in Laos that was far more candid that the official line.

Deuve introduced him to the Laotian intelligence officials working on Pathet Lao subversion, Vietminh activities in Laos, and Chinese propaganda along the northern border of Laos. Because Bernard had Deuve's blessing, these people gave him honest opinions about the misuse of American aid, all of which confirmed what Bernard had found elsewhere.

It was only after Bernard's return that I got the full story of what he learned that summer. When Bernard had arrived in South Vietnam, he was told by government officials that the situation had vastly improved since the country was partitioned. President Ngo Dinh Diem was said to be in full control of the South. But Bernard kept finding evidence to the contrary. He was particularly intrigued by obituaries he kept reading in the South Vietnamese press about the deaths of village chiefs. He thought there were too many, at least one a day, reported killed by "unknown elements" or "bandits."

He discovered that in one year there had been 452 dead village officials. He made a map of where they had died and another map of reported guerrilla incidents occurring at the same time. It became clear that the killings of village chiefs were in exactly the same areas where there were Communist cells operating and frequent attacks by pro-Communist guerrilla units. All this was happening while Vietnam was supposedly at peace and Diem was supposedly in full control. In fact, Bernard saw that Saigon was encircled by villages whose murdered leaders had been replaced by Communists.

He went to see the minister of the interior, and said, "Your Excellency, you are in trouble in Vietnam. Do you know that?"

"Yes, I know that," the minister replied.

"Did you tell President Ngo Dinh Diem?" Bernard asked.

"Nobody can tell President Diem that we are in trouble," the minister said. "He believes we are doing fine."

Bernard asked, "Do the Americans know?"

The minister replied that he did not think so.

When Bernard showed the man his maps, the official pulled out his own map that showed known Communist cells inside Vietnam. His map showed an area of Communist control just one-fifth of the size that Bernard's had defined. It was increasingly clear to Bernard that Vietnam was in the process of being lost, whether or not the Diem regime or its American sponsors chose to admit it. The cease-fire and the partition of the country had not stopped the Communist revolution in Vietnam; it had simply ended one phase of it and begun another.

Bernard also made use of data that the International Control Commission was receiving from North Vietnamese authorities about guerrilla incidents in South Vietnam. This data suggested close coordination between Vietminh agents and guerrilla fighters in the south and Ho Chi Minh's regime in the north.

Bernard's reporting on the killings of the village chiefs, and the conclusions he drew from them, was much like his work in 1953 when he found that the French-backed Vietnamese government was not collecting taxes or assigning teachers in the countryside it claimed to control. He was using the same technique that his friend I. F. Stone applied back in Washington: If you knew what you were looking for, you could often find priceless information hidden in official documents.

Bernard came to think that his discovery of the murder of the village chiefs was crucial to understanding the political reality of South Vietnam under Diem. In a 1966 article he elaborated on the political meaning of the killings:

And in June, 1956, the South Vietnamese government made perhaps its most fateful decision. In defiance of one of the most hallowed Vietnamese traditions, according to which the power of the central authorities stops at the bamboo hedge of the village, the Saigon administration abolished by a stroke of the pen elected village chiefs and village councils and replaced them by appointive members. In doing this, Diem outdid anything that either the North Vietnamese Communist regime or the French colonial administration ever attempted. . . . In South Vietnam, elected village chiefs were replaced by centrally-appointed individuals who, in many cases, were not even native to the village and who, as insecurity grew, preferred to live in the nearby district town. This broke all normal feedback between the 80 percent of the population which lives in village units of about 2000 people, and the South Vietnamese government.[3]

Diem thus gave the Vietcong a priceless opportunity to replace unpopular, unelected village leaders with their own people, and he also made a mockery of his—and American—talk of bringing democracy to Vietnam. Diem had killed democracy.

Bernard felt that his second Indochina trip had been highly productive and he was anxious to start writing about it. His one failure had been that North Vietnamese officials had refused to admit him to their country. He blamed this on continuing hostility between France and North Vietnam. He noted that in Laos he had met three French typists who had been waiting four months for visas from North Vietnam. He was therefore consoled that his inability to enter the country was at least "not a personal grudge of the Viet-Minh against me."

Bernard left Vietnam the first week of September, stopped in Vienna to see his Aunt Hilde and Uncle Franz, then in Paris to see family and conduct interviews, and finally arrived in Washington on the afternoon of September 16, five days before our baby's due date. He must have felt guilty because he brought many gifts, and said he was surprised I wasn't bigger. The next day I went into labor. Nicole Françoise, a beautiful and healthy seven pound, four ounce girl, was born two days later, September 18. My first words to Bernard after the delivery were, "I must have held my breath until you arrived home."

He marked the baby's arrival by giving me a wristwatch with a solid gold bracelet. When I thanked him he said, "It would have been diamonds if it had been a boy."

9

SPEAKING TRUTH TO POWER

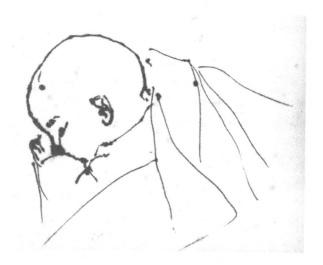

Bᴇʀɴᴀʀᴅ was an adoring father—playing with the baby, photographing her, and admiring her progress. I had given little thought to returning to work, but I had found my job with *Amerika Illustrated* magazine exciting and Bernard suggested that I ask USIA about the possibility of working half-time. To my delight, my request was granted.

In the fall of 1957, along with his teaching and lecturing, Bernard wrote *The International Position of South Viet-Nam, 1954–58*, the report commissioned by the Institute of Pacific Relations.

His 120-page report examined the aftermath of the French Indochina War, the divided Vietnam, and South Vietnam's economy, politics, and place in international affairs. In early February of 1958, Bernard went to Lahore, Pakistan, for the thirteenth International Conference of Pacific Institutes, where his report was well received.

In his acknowledgments, Bernard gave thanks for the "friendly cooperation of Vietnamese, French, and American officials in and outside Viet-Nam." He particularly thanked Ambassador Tran Van Chuong and officials of the Republic of Vietnam, who had underwritten part of the cost of his trip. The ambassador was pleased with Bernard's report and asked for additional copies to send to Saigon. All this would soon change.

The May 31, 1958, issue of *The Nation* contained Bernard's article "Will South Vietnam Be Next?" which was bitterly resented by the Diem regime and those in this country who saw Diem as a bulwark against the spread of Communism in Vietnam.

The article began: "On July 11, 1957, a group of armed men machine-gunned to death seventeen occupants of a bar in Chau-Doc, South Vietnam." Bernard listed five more examples of guerrilla violence against civilians, village chiefs, Vietnamese security police, and even American soldiers. These attacks, he said, were culled from hundreds of such incidents reported in the South Vietnamese press during the past six months. "They clearly express a trend which has been developing over the past year and one which is hidden from the casual foreign observer."

He continued: "In spite of a most generous measure of American financial aid (more than a billion dollars in the past four years) and political support, the South Vietnamese Government of President Ngo Dinh Diem is faced today with growing insecurity in the countryside and an economic crisis which threatens to wipe out most of the benefits" the country was reaping from U.S. aid. "Without this aid, South Vietnam would, beyond a doubt, have collapsed long ago."

Bernard noted that more than $200 million out of about $250 million a year in U.S. aid went to support the South Vietnamese army and security forces, and that more than a thousand members of a U.S. military assistance group were there training the Vietnamese forces. He said that the Vietnamese economy was falling apart, the government's land reform program was bogged down, corruption was rampant, and the South Vietnamese and their American allies often did not like or understand one another.

He continued:

As to politics, warning is due against any starry-eyed illusions about 'democracy' in South Vietnam. President Ngo Dinh Diem was elected by a 98.2 percent vote and opposition journalists in Saigon, as reported recently in the *New York Times,* tend to 'vanish' and their newspapers to be wrecked by well-coached mobs. . . . These are the hard facts, and they are not very pretty. But they must be revealed now, while it is not yet too late to change course. The change may not be undertaken in Saigon, but must be carried out in Washington in the face of probable opposition by the well-established 'Vietnamese lobby.' The United States cannot afford yet another defeat in Asia without losing whatever remains of Asian confidence in the West's ability to understand and cope with Oriental political, economic, and social problems.

Bernard closed with a pointed warning that the United States, France, and other nations could not afford to take a "devil take the hindmost" attitude toward the people of Southeast Asia: "For in this case the hindmost are the landless farmer and the jobless worker. And they made up the Communist shock troops who defeated the French at Dien Bien Phu."[1]

Here, as so often when I read Bernard's writings from the 1950s and early 1960s, I want to cry out "Why didn't they listen?" If one young scholar could go to Vietnam and see the corruption and ineptitude of the Diem regime, why couldn't the U.S. government and its intelligence agents understand that? The answer of course is that most of them didn't want to understand it. In the just-ended McCarthy era, politicians had been traumatized by the cry of "Who lost China?" Now others feared being accused of "losing" Vietnam. As if it was theirs to lose. The French experience made clear the dangers of a war in the jungles of Indochina, but American politicians and military leaders assumed that we were tougher and stronger than the French, that we could never be defeated by little men in black pajamas. So we marched on, into the quagmire.

For the most part, Bernard's article was greeted not with understanding but with outrage. He was labeled a pessimist, a crank, a French agent. As he once noted, he was "the unwelcome bearer of ill tidings." *The Nation* was swamped with an avalanche of letters from the Diem propaganda machine, accusing Bernard of being an unreconstructed French colonialist, saying that he did not know what he was talking about. The State Department also attempted to discredit him, because its own credibility was threatened.

Virtually the only thing Bernard was not accused of was being pro-Communist. He was more dangerous than that—he was pro-fact, pro-truth.

Incredibly, in Saigon, the Diem regime, apparently working with the U.S. Embassy, was able to kill Bernard's appointment as a professor to the Royal School of Administration in Cambodia. Officials said he had become "controversial."

Bernard was told by a friend in the State Department not to request a visa to Vietnam because it would be refused. His relationship with Ambassador Tran Van Chuong deteriorated, and he was persona non grata with others at the Vietnamese Embassy. He was unhappy about all the hostility that arose from his insistence on revealing the truth about South Vietnam in the face of Washington's blind commitment to the Diem regime.

About this time the FBI accelerated its scrutiny of Bernard, with reports that spoke of his "activities on behalf of the French government" and called him "a possible propaganda agent for the French government." Years later, after a long legal fight, I obtained parts of Bernard's FBI file.[2]

Bernard's file contained the usual gossip and speculation. Anyone could say anything about you and the FBI would add it to the file. After one of Bernard's speeches, State Department officials complained that he "irresponsibly criticized the United States Aid Program in Vietnam." The irony was that, beginning in 1959, Bernard's views were increasingly sought by the U.S. military. The reviews military men gave him were mixed. One FBI document quoted a colonel who had attended a lecture and said Bernard's criticisms of the U.S. military-assistance program were "completely erroneous." Yet the FBI file also quoted a retired Army officer familiar with Bernard's books and articles saying that "Dr. Fall is an expert and forthright observer of Communist tactics in that part of the world, a man who does not hesitate to voice his opinions, chips falling where they may, and without doubt *a strong anti-Communist.*"

For the next seven years, Bernard's movements were documented, our mail was inspected, our phone was tapped, our house was watched, and people who I thought were friends reported details of our life to the FBI.

In January 1959, Brig. Gen. J. B. Sweet, USA (Ret.), a senior editor of the Stackpole Company, formerly the Military Service Publishing Company, wrote to Bernard that the company was favorably impressed with his proposal for a book. In fact, he enclosed a contract for *Street Without Joy: The Indochina War, 1946–54.*

General Sweet wrote, "I frankly believe you are capable in this book of doing two things: (1) produce a work that will be both enlightening and entertaining; and (2) by your analysis of the Southeast Asia situation and the Communists, especially as we may be affected, challenge the thinking people of the U.S. and of the West generally."

The title Bernard had chosen for his book was in French *La Rue Sans Joie*, Street Without Joy. That was what French soldiers had called a desolate and dangerous stretch of the north-south coastal highway 1, between the cities of Hue and Quang Tri, where many Frenchmen had died in Vietminh attacks. Like Heartbreak Ridge in Korea, or the Trail of Tears traveled by American Indians, it was one of those terribly sad names that arise spontaneously from those who have suffered great pain.

Bernard's life had prepared him to write this book. His years in the French Resistance taught him about guerrilla warfare. In the French army he learned the camaraderie of a soldier fighting for a just cause and gained respect for the military. He had studied Vietnam and in 1953 had accompanied the French army on operations against the Vietminh. His first-hand experience would be augmented by research in the French army historical records, including unit diaries and operation plans, and the detailed letters he wrote to me in 1953 were a record he could draw on. He would show dispassionately how the Vietminh outfought, and how Gen. Vo Nguyen Giap outmaneuvered, the French.

Bernard naturally wanted to make a third trip to Indochina to research his book. This was made possible by a fellowship from the Southeast Asia Treaty Organization (SEATO) to write a report called "Problems of Communist Subversion and Infiltration in Certain Territories in the SEATO Area." Bernard made plans to spend the summer of 1959 in Thailand and Laos, even though he suspected he would not be allowed into South Vietnam.

I was not overjoyed by this new trip, but his offer of a trip to Europe helped pacify me. The three of us left for Paris on June 3 and upon arrival found that France had changed. President Charles de Gaulle, in his effort to revitalize the country, had urged that his countrymen be more civil to foreigners, and I did find that people were much more pleasant on this trip. Bernard, unconcerned about his countrymen's manners, was busy studying

French army historical records. We proceeded to Nice, where we met with Sœur Emmanuelle, now quite old but happy to see Bernard and his family. By June 23, he was off alone to Bangkok, with stops in Rome and Tel Aviv. He admired the Israelis and sometimes wrote about their wars. He proceeded to the Galilee border, Nazareth, Tiberius, Beersheba, and the desert. With his friend Col. Alex Zielony, former Israeli military attaché in Washington, he visited soldier-pioneer settlements twenty-five yards from the Syrian border.

Nicole and I proceeded to Rome and then to Venice. We swam at the Lido and chased pigeons in St. Mark's Square. In our windowless room on the edge of the square, the nights were full of loud sounds of motorcyclists and revelers enjoying the beauty and excitement.

Dorothy, Nicole, and Bernard in Nice, 1959.

When we arrived back home in Virginia, letters were arriving from Bernard in Thailand. He was busy interviewing officials there, but he still wanted to get to Vietnam for research and interviews. Bernard's 1958 article on Vietnam had not offended the French as it had the Americans and South Vietnamese—the French had learned from hard experience that what Bernard said was true. The French Embassy offered to intercede in his behalf. Bernard was delighted: "They're really wonderful. It feels good to be backed up. Speaking of backing up, the Vietnamese have lost none of their vindictiveness: believe it or not, the Hon. U. Alexis Johnson, U.S. ambassador here, went specifically to see the French ambassador to tell him that the Vietnamese notified him that they wouldn't give me a visa. The French ambassador here, while being perfectly polite about it, told him that this was strictly a French-Vietnamese affair and he couldn't possibly see what business it was of the U.S. Embassy in Thailand. Frankly, I'm really puzzled. . . . I must have tread [*sic*] on some mighty sensitive toes. But I'm making a point here of being polite and nice, to make no cracks whatever (it's hard, but I'll try)."

He added: "Viet-Minh agents near Saigon attacked and killed two U.S. officers, wounding others—and *now* Washington announces that '*SVN censorship is hiding the facts*'!!! The s.o.b's. I truly feel sorry for the two Army guys who had to get killed because of Diem's propaganda—but I stand vindicated in full."

While in Thailand, Bernard's research into insurgencies led him to the south of the country where Malaysian rebels were causing trouble in border areas. He also learned that the Vietminh were infiltrating northeast Thailand and Cambodia and he went there, to the contested areas. In Ubol, Thailand, he stayed with the French bishop, a patriarch of six feet two, with a beard down to his belly. Bernard had met one of his priests, Brother Guidon, when he visited Lai Chau in 1953. They talked about all the "guys" and Bernard wrote: "This is always bad for morale, and then I had a mass said for all those who didn't quite make it. . . . Hell, one may not have religion, but it was impressive." Bernard said the mass left him close to tears.

Determined to get into Vietnam, Bernard found that the country's visa regulations provided that, in direct transit, one could stay in the country for forty-eight hours without a visa. He arranged his air travel to Laos via Saigon, so he could stay from Friday to Sunday afternoon. French officials in Bangkok notified their embassy in Saigon by coded message and arranged for the military attaché to pick Bernard up at the airport and keep a close eye on him. He wrote, "I know it's a risk but one I've got to take: I'm only sorry that we have come to a pass where a citizen of a friendly country has to be protected in an 'allied' country."

When Bernard arrived in Laos after his short, furtive visit to Vietnam, he was angry and bitter. He had spent forty-eight hours

In Ubol. Bernard (second from left) stands with Brother Guidon (in black) and three other priests.

feeling hunted, being whisked about in closed limousines, not being able to phone friends for fear of having the call tapped and endangering them. Before he arrived he thought the whole thing was a joke and he could clear it up by just appearing. But when he saw the precautions that his French allies were taking he was quickly sobered. He was seen to the airplane by a French army major in civilian clothes and the chief of French intelligence, and met at the Saigon airport by the French deputy military attaché. "I could see that I was really hated . . . and all that just for having said the truth as honestly as I saw it."

By contrast, the Lao were helpful. The government gave him important documentation for his report. He was invited to dinners with the French ambassador and the military, and was asked to address the Rotary Club with the American and British ambassadors on hand. He spoke with a key U.S. military attaché who had been one of his students when he lectured at the Strategic Intelligence School.

He was staying with his friend Pierre-Bernard Lafont. They had met when Lafont parachuted into southern France in 1944. Now, he was an expert on the ethnic minorities of Indochina with the École Française d'Extrême Orient. Bernard had seen Lafont in Lai Chau in 1953. His little daughter Dominique, whom Bernard found adorable, only made him miss his own Nicole more. But he had to complete his mission, which was to find out what was really happening with regard to the Communist insurgency in Laos.

When I wrote Bernard regarding my concern about what I was reading in the newspapers about violence in Laos, he wrote back: "As to the fighting that has broken out here, don't believe everything the newspapers say. . . . Frankly, nobody really knows what's happening."

As he said, the situation was extremely unsettled. After years of skirmishes between pro-Communist Pathet Lao rebels and the Royal Laotian army, an agreement had supposedly been reached. The two factions were to be integrated into the Lao army.

Instead, because of mutual mistrust, the integration did not take place and the Laotian rebellion of 1959 began. There was general insecurity while Bernard was there in August, with small attacks in almost every province and larger attacks against Lao army posts in Samneua and along the route to the capital of Vientiane.

Bernard wrote to me: "Well, I might as well tell you—as you'll find out sooner or later: I was in combat again in Samneua." Bernard had flown five combat missions to Samneua in a single engine plane. He said that Samneua province was surrounded on three sides by the North Vietnamese army. He included his hand drawn-map of the region and said angrily:

> Now the bastards have fun gnawing away at the province, and, as usual, we're in the position of having to hold onto ground not of our choosing. The Lao general (Amkha) is a great guy, the only Christian general in the army, about 45, a major in the French regular army; his deputy, Col. Khong Vongnuarith, is also an ex-regular. They're as competent as they come. I've seen Khong jump into a jeep at 11 p.m. with three guys and their carbines, going after a purported enemy patrol [that had] infiltrated . . . our airfield.

He described a harrowing flight in an overloaded plane carrying four tons of heavy equipment. One Air Laos plane had been shot at by some Vietnamese machine guns east of the run-

Bernard with Gen. Amkha Soukhavong.

135

way, so they took off in the opposite direction and nearly crashed. Bernard, who had been sitting in the copilot's seat, wrote, "Dorothy, for the first time in a long time I felt something like real terror." I hated to see him in danger, but I hoped it might encourage him to avoid such situations in the future.

He went on to describe dramatic scenes of fighting: Radio calls coming in, pleading for reinforcements and ammunition. Méo villagers waving at Bernard's plane from the top of their hill as they peeled off to drop rice bags and other provisions. The message from a Méo chief: "We can hold out until noon; do something for us." And ugly scenes as civilian administrative chiefs fled for the safety and comfort of Vientiane, what Bernard called the "don't give damishness of the whole thing."

Continuing his study of the insurgency, Bernard visited every Royal Lao army outpost along the border between Laos and North Vietnam, plus he paid visits to the Communist China border between North Vietnam and Burma. He believed the major problem was the complete collapse of the Lao civil government and the lack of leadership in the army. The government could not control corruption and the army was reluctant to fire on other Laotians. He gave the example of the escape of the Second Pathet Lao Battalion when encircled by five Royal Lao army battalions. According to Bernard, the Lao army commander-in-chief was present but did nothing to prevent the escape. He said that the U.S. position was that the Pathet Lao had cleverly avoided detection, while French officers said the Pathet Lao were simply *allowed* to escape.

Bernard maintained that there were only 1500 rebel troops fighting against the government. He said that small numbers of Pathet Lao troops were conducting a form of psychological warfare against government troops. The Pathet Lao would fire machine gun bursts during the night, designed to prevent ill-trained government troops from sleeping. After several nights of this, the government troops were too rattled to continue resistance. The outpost commander, in order to save face, would then invent an attack by a Pathet Lao battalion and withdraw his men from the area.

Bernard felt that the Western powers were losing the hill tribes to Communism by default. He saw Laos at the same stage as China in 1948, poised to fall. He thought the solution might be a UN trusteeship over the mountain areas, if that could be arranged.

As there came to be more and more calls for U.S. military intervention in South Vietnam, Bernard became a hero to those who thought that would be a huge mistake. He was friendly with Senator William Fulbright of Arkansas, who became a thoughtful and outspoken opponent of the war. Bernard had a special admiration for the senator, since he had first come to America with the assistance of a Fulbright grant. Bernard once told me, as he prepared to go back to Vietnam, "Should anything untoward happen to me, go to see him," meaning Fulbright.

Before one of Senator Fulbright's Senate hearings on Vietnam, Bernard sent him a letter to express his views. Citing articles by himself and others, he expressed his belief that the situation in South Vietnam was worsening. He pointed out that 425 local officials were being killed each year by Communist terrorists:

> It must be evident to anyone even remotely connected with public administration that this Communist plot to undermine the South Vietnamese local administration is more dangerous to the internal stability of the country than the badly deteriorated economy (look at the economic statistics of the last three years) alone would warrant. Put simply, if the Communist terrorists kill two village mayors in succession, the third will be either a Communist, or someone who will do their bidding to stay alive. And that is exactly what is happening right now—all soothing reports to the contrary.

With a touch of bitterness, he concluded:

Yet persons who voice such fears have come under sharpest attack—even vilification—by local interest groups and even officials unwilling to see, as the saying goes, beautiful theories destroyed by harsh facts.

Bernard would spend the rest of his life trying to deploy harsh facts to defeat the flawed theories that guided American policy toward Vietnam.

10

HOWARD UNIVERSITY

IN SEPTEMBER 1956, Bernard became a part-time lecturer in government at Howard University, the prestigious black university in Washington, and a year later he accepted a full-time teaching position there. He loved the school and made it his base for the rest of his life.

It was an exciting time at Howard. In those days, the great white American universities hired very few black professors, which meant that top black universities like Howard had faculties made up of black scholars and intellectuals who today would have the top Ivy League schools competing for their services. Howard students could study literature with the poet Sterling Brown and the novelist Toni Morrison, or philosophy with Eugene C. Holmes. Harold Lewis taught the classics, as did Frank Snowden, dean of the school of liberal arts, author of a classic book on black people in ancient civilizations. Leo Hansberry was the early specialist in ancient tropical Africa. Sociology professor E. Franklin Frazier had just published *Black Bourgeoisie*, which created a storm of controversy by arguing that America's black leadership had failed to inspire the masses to build a strong black community.

Howard had also produced such major leaders as Supreme Court Justice Thurgood Marshall and United States Senator Edward Brooke. Ralph Bunche was professor of political science from 1928 to 1946; he resigned to join the United Nations, where he rose to undersecretary and eventually won the Nobel Peace Prize.

Although Howard is often thought of as a university for the black elite, the university had students of all races and backgrounds. Many came from Africa or the Caribbean islands. Some were the first in their families to go to college. Others, like Ed Brooke in the 1930s, were Washington residents who lived at home. Some were veterans of the Korean War, taking advantage of the G.I. Bill. Some came from the American South where segregation was constant and harsh; others had not known persecution and for them it was a shock to arrive in Washington, a Southern city still segregated in most regards. The white artist Lila Asher, who taught at the university for thirty-five years, recalls, "Howard was the only place in Washington, D.C., where color didn't matter."

Bernard enjoyed university life and had great affection for his colleagues. His position allowed time for his own writing and outside lecturing and left the summer months free for travel. Marc Raskin once told me that he believed Bernard taught at Howard to champion an oppressed people. I replied that Bernard always protested that he had no ideological reason for teaching there, but chose Howard because it offered him the best salary. Marc said, "He *would* say that."

When I corresponded with French Col. Jean Deuve, he recalled asking Bernard, when they first met in Laos, what he was teaching at Howard. Bernard replied, partly in jest, *"Nous fabriquons de futurs révolutionnaires!"* ("We are forging future revolutionaries!") That was an exaggeration, but when I spoke with many of Bernard's students I found there was some truth in it. Bernard had strong feelings about wars of liberation and he was glad to impart them to young people who were often part of the American civil rights revolution.

Bernard saw himself as a scholar who was dedicated to scholarship, research, integrity, and commitment. He was thrilled when in 1958 he was appointed to the Ralph Bunche Chair in International Relations. In those days, the department of government was small, consisting of Emmett (Sam) Dorsey, its chairman, Vincent Brown, Robert Martin, and Bernard. The department, eventually renamed political science, grew, in ten years, from four professors to fifteen. Sam Dorsey and Bernard became close. Sam was a towering black man with a booming voice who had a PhD from American University. He was tough and opinionated, and he was controversial, for his left-wing politics and for having visited the Soviet Union in the '30s. He became a target of right-wingers during the McCarthy era.

I spoke with several of Bernard's former students about their memories of him. Acklyn Lynch, who came from Trinidad, recalled the Howard faculty around 1960 as including everything from Communists on the left to conservatives on the right who came out of the black bourgeoisie. The students, too, held wildly divergent views, from activism to apathy. Lynch, now a retired professor of political economy and culture, took three courses with Bernard. He recalled Bernard as fearless. "Those of us who were in the civil rights movement, we did it through him. We became activists because he planted the seed."

Lynch recalled a particular course with Bernard:

> He was dealing with the struggle for independence, and the debates that were going on in the United Nations along the question of independence at the time. He took three revolutionary struggles and he dealt with them: Vietnam, Algeria, and the Congo. It was 1960–61. Lumumba had died; the Vietnamese struggle was still going on. The Algerian struggle was still going on. It was as a result of Fall that we got introduced to a number of people attached to the Algerian movement. We heard about Frantz Fanon, Jean Paul Sartre. We began to see Albert Camus, Patrice Lumumba, Giap in Vietnam, Ho Chi Minh. We dealt with the whole notion of the art of war.

Lynch told me that in 1961 he was president of the International Students Organization and Bernard was its advisor. They put together a United Nations Security conference at Howard that brought speakers from around the country to focus on colonialism, the Algerian revolution, Vietnam, disarmament and peace, and the UN position on struggles for independence. He recalled that Bernard twice took students to the UN, and both times arranged for them to meet with Ambassador Ralph Bunche.

Lynch spoke of Bernard's influence on the civil rights movement:

> The students of Howard University had a deep and profound sense of the *national* struggle here for civil rights. So it was

Bernard Fall who added a dimension to that by helping us to understand what that *international* struggle was and its relationship, not just to the national will of the people of Vietnam, or the national will of the people of Algeria or the Congo, or Ghana, but its relationship to race. Race and class were things that he understood. He didn't come to us as an ideologue. He came to us more as a pragmatic intellectual or journalistic intellectual. You had to have your facts. But he never dismissed you for your ideological position. Rather, he encouraged you to expand your ideological position, with a critique to it. The only thing he was opposed to was fascism. It was natural for him. He was always a freedom fighter.

Frank Savage, a student who went on to success in banking and global investment, recalled of Bernard:

In 1958, I was a political science major and an economics minor, but I had not decided where I wanted to focus my activities. In the first semester of my junior year, I took a course in international relations, taught by your late husband. He was such an exciting lecturer and he got me so excited about the field of international work. He opened up my eyes. Remember, this was in 1958 and Ghana had become the first African nation to get its independence. I will never forget us talking about that event. A light bulb went off: 'International relations. That's what I want to do. And Africa is where I want to focus. I think that all these countries are ultimately going to get their independence. The United States will have to have people who understand Africa and African culture and politics. That's what I'm going to do.' At the time, the only profession I could even think about was in the foreign service.

My life's work came together in his class. The only thing that I didn't know at that time was where I would take this. . . . Ultimately, I got my masters at SAIS. Rather than going

143

into the foreign service I went into business. I joined Citibank in the International Division—the Middle East and Africa Division. That was the beginning of my international career. Even today I'm heavily involved in international work. I trace it all back to Dr. Fall. In 1964 everything was opening up and I was one of the few African Americans ready to take advantage of those opportunities.

Frank Savage served on Howard's board of trustees for ten years, seven of those years as chairman. In 2002, his gift of five million dollars became the largest individual gift in the university's history.

Stokely Carmichael rejected scholarships from several white universities to enter Howard in 1960. He was already known as a charismatic leader of the civil rights movement. Later, in his book, *Ready for Revolution*, he said of white professors at Howard in the early 1960s:

The white Americans, at least some of them, may have been chased to Howard either by McCarthyism, or, again, may have elected to serve there out of principle. . . . One professor, a Frenchman, a political scientist, published the earliest clear analysis of the looming disaster fueled by American arrogance and ignorance in Vietnam. His name was Bernard Fall. . . . Before most people in the States even knew where Vietnam was—way back in the Kennedy administration— this Frenchman was writing about the Vietnamese's twenty-five-year struggle for independence from the French. I'll never forget a lecture he gave on the battle of Dien Bien Phu and the contempt of the French generals for the 'primitive and backward' peasant army. They always referred to the Vietnamese commander as 'schoolteacher Giap' because that had been the general's profession before he studied war and took up arms to liberate his people.[1]

Marie Murray, a graduate student in 1960, went on to be a foreign service officer. She recalls of Bernard's classes: "He was a tough teacher who expected a lot academically. It helped. It challenged us in different ways." She found Bernard a cheerful, upbeat person, but recalls that he had "a sort of fatalist attitude about" his trips to Vietnam. "He used to joke that there would be a Fall Hall if he didn't quite make it."

Claude Mathews, an NBC producer and lawyer, took Bernard's graduate course on Southeast Asia. In 1965, at Bernard's prompting, he applied to a program that sent graduate students to spend the summer in Vietnam. He was soon one of twenty-five graduate students from all over the United States assigned to various provinces in Vietnam. Mathews lived in the village of Hoi An with the USAID representative to Quang Nam province. He moved around the province looking at USAID projects and talking to people.

At the end of their tour, the students were brought in for a news conference at the Joint U.S. Public Affairs Office. Reporters asked if they thought the war could be won. Students from Harvard, Yale, and Princeton—everyone said yes. Except Mathews, who said, "No, I don't think we can really win this war. We're making the same mistakes the French made. I think we're going to wind up with the same result." An Associated Press story said, "All of the graduate students endorsed the war except one—Claude Mathews, a Negro from Howard University."

When Mathews returned to school, he found that Bernard was delighted. "He was really pleased. He said, 'Yeah, they didn't pull the wool over *your* eyes.'"

Hanes Walton, now a professor at the University of Michigan, took two graduate courses with Bernard between 1964 and 1966.

Howard did not have a program on Southeast Asian affairs. It was just Dr. Fall teaching classes in it. It was absolutely fascinating because these were real area studies on the topic

145

at that time. Vietnam was the absolute hottest international event going on at [that] moment. The information that he taught us about guerrilla warfare was just unbelievable—the precision and the way in which a guerrilla war was fought, how it was won, how it succeeded, and how it failed. . . .

I remember one lecture where he came in and told us about Senator Goldwater's argument that we needed to use low-yield nuclear weapons. Fall pointed out how silly and disturbing that kind of proposal was: that what you needed in Vietnam was more armor, tanks, and all that stuff. He would just take these arguments apart. At the University of Michigan, when I teach foreign affairs and defense policy, I almost always start with telling people that they should read Bernard Fall's books. You learned from his lectures just how bad these policy experts were on Vietnam. [They] really hadn't thought it through when they committed the country and its resources. Your husband understood that we were literally uninformed about this part of the world.

Bernard's students with Nicole and Elisabeth at the annual garden party at the Fall home, circa 1965.

While Bernard was at Howard, I would see his students each spring at the garden party we gave for them at our home. I always enjoyed the students, but it wasn't until I began seeking them out years later, for this book, that I realized what a profound influence Bernard had on many of them. Bernard is best remembered for his keen knowledge of and writings on Vietnam, but his teaching may have been an equal achievement.

11

STREET WITHOUT JOY

FOLLOWING Bernard's return from his 1959 trip to Thailand, Vietnam, and Laos, he resumed his teaching duties even as he began work on *Street Without Joy*. It was a cooperative effort—at his request, I became a military illustrator. While Bernard wrote, I produced drawings and finished his maps, adding type for locations and battles, and filling in shading to differentiate or emphasize important areas. *Night Patrol*, showing French soldiers with rifles ready, traversing a tall grass area, served as the frontispiece. In the third edition of the book, the drawing was on the cover. Other art included the canyon-like, silent valley of Chan-Muong, Vietminh troops in battle, tanks on the road, airplanes bombing a village, and an interpretive diagram of the Vietminh tunnel hideouts. Some drawings came from photographs, others from my imagination. My drawing of Ho Chi Minh surrounded by his people carrying the Vietminh flag, inspired by a photograph, set the tone.

Our second daughter, Elisabeth Anne, was born three weeks early, on August 19, 1960. Four days after leaving the hospital, I was back at my drafting table, working on the cover. Again it was in red and yellow, the colors of Vietnam, with a photo of men on tanks moving through abstract shapes of color.

Bernard continued to face hostility in some governmental circles. In 1960, he was selected to go to Laos as a field advisor

Nicole is introduced to her new sister, Elisabeth, 1960.

for the United Nations. As we were making preparations for an exciting year in Laos, a friend at the State Department warned Bernard of opposition to his selection. Soon his appointment was canceled. Bernard was disappointed and angry that his honesty was being punished by the government.

As *Street Without Joy* progressed, Bernard consulted with Marshall Andrews, a veteran of both world wars and Korea, who was serving as a military analyst at the Operations Research Office. Andrews, the author of *Disaster Through Air Power*, not only advised Bernard on *Street Without Joy*, but wrote a compelling foreword for it, in which he said:

> The sort of war fought by the French in Indochina may well be a model for those to which U.S. Forces most likely may be committed in the future. . . . The United States Army is no more indoctrinated and trained for that sort of war than were the French in Indochina.[1]

Or, as Bernard put it in a memorable passage from the book:

> In the monsoon jungles of Southeast Asia, there is no cheap substitute for the most expensive commodity of them all— the well-trained combat infantryman; not the "divisional training camps" so dear to the Korean war, but the patiently trained jungle fighter who will stay in the jungle—not on the edges of it—and who will out-stay the enemy, if need be.[2]

Bernard knew from the French experience how difficult it was to find Westerners who could be that sort of jungle fighter.

Street Without Joy was published in mid-April 1961 and was dedicated, *"To those who died there."*

Like most authors, Bernard did not think his book was adequately promoted or that it received the attention it deserved. But six weeks after publication, Tillman Durdin, who covered

Marshall Andrews wrote the foreword to Street Without Joy.

the Indochina War for the *New York Times*, published a major review in the *Times Book Review*. He said in part:

> What makes Mr. Fall's book important today is his portrayal of the Indochina conflict as a major example of the new kind of warfare waged by revolutionary forces that enjoy the advantages of what he calls "an active sanctuary.". . . Americans who want to understand the in-fighting and the odds we would have to face if we got involved in a new Indochina war would do well to read Mr. Fall.[3]

Philip Foisie, the first foreign editor of the *Washington Post*, in his review in the *Post*, declared that "the United States and the free world generally are traveling down their own street without joy in the whole of Southeast Asia and in many other parts of the world." Foisie, who was Secretary of State Dean Rusk's brother-in-law, concluded: "Whatever one may think of the views of this controversial young Cassandra, whose warnings of disaster in recent years are well known in Washington, it must be admitted that events in Southeast Asia have placed the burden of proof on his critics. Certainly, this book should be widely read."[4]

As both these reviews suggest, history might have been much different if officials of the Kennedy administration, which had just taken office—and suffered a huge setback with the ill-advised Bay of Pigs invasion in Cuba—had studied Bernard's warnings about the dangers of a land war in Indochina. But several years passed before *Street Without Joy* became required reading for U.S. Army officers going to Vietnam, and its lessons were never heeded at the top levels of the White House.

Or, as Gen. Colin Powell wrote many years later, in his book *My American Journey:*

> I recently reread Bernard Fall's book on Vietnam, *Street With-out Joy*. Fall makes painfully clear that we had almost no understanding of what we had gotten ourselves into. I cannot help thinking that if President Kennedy or President Johnson had spent a quiet weekend at Camp David reading that perceptive book, they would have returned to the White House Monday morning and immediately started to figure out a way to extricate us from the quicksand of Vietnam.[5]

One person who did act as a result of reading *Street Without Joy* was a soldier, Ron Ridenhour, who later became an award-winning journalist. In 1969 Ridenhour wrote a letter to Congress and the Pentagon in which he exposed for the first time the horrifying massacre and coverup of My Lai. Ridenhour was not with his old company when the barbarism took place but was told the story by many of the men who had participated in the massacre. When asked why he and he alone spoke out, Ridenhour replied, "I had read Bernard Fall's *Street Without Joy* on the boat going over to Vietnam and it gave me a historical perspective that few of my peers seemed to have." He told the truth.

With the publication of *Street Without Joy*, Bernard's reputation continued to grow. Requests for articles and speaking engagements, particularly from the military, accelerated. He was a charismatic speaker, captivating his audience with his charm, the depth of his knowledge, and his blunt, unsparing analysis. He spoke wonderfully idiomatic English; he would say things like, "The French really got clobbered at Dien Bien Phu." Still, his message—that there were limits on the ability of Western nations to impose their will on Southeast Asia—often fell on deaf ears.

With Bernard's growing celebrity came new friends. P. J. Honey, a British scholar on North Vietnam, contacted Bernard about writing an article for the *China Quarterly*. We later visited Honey and his wife at their home on the outskirts of London. Paddy, as he was known, arranged for Bernard to be interviewed on the BBC. The two men became friends but soon disagreed on Vietnam.

Bernard first met with I. F. Stone in September 1959, when the independent journalist invited him for lunch at the Hay

At a book party for Street Without Joy, *1961.*

Adams hotel, across from the White House. They were a wonderful pair, two men obsessed with revealing the truth. Izzy Stone, as he was known, was a short, cherubic older man, a maverick who wore inch-thick glasses and, since he was hard of hearing, a small microphone around his neck for others to talk into. Even with these impediments, Izzy saw and heard much that others could not. Bernard found in him a senior colleague who understood his findings and his methods. Although one was considered an investigative reporter and the other a scholar, they had similar methods of research—delving into publicly available documents to find the revealing facts with which to dispute or debunk the conventional wisdom. Each was utterly uncompromising. At first, Bernard goaded Izzy about going to Vietnam to get the real picture of what was happening, and Izzy eventually did go.

I. F. Stone's Weekly was produced with Izzy's devoted wife, Esther, who handled the production and business side of things. Esther and I had great rapport as the wives of men with strong opinions and large egos. We sat in the background while our husbands held center stage. In later years, when we lunched together, Esther finally voiced complaints about how Izzy's work took precedence over his family, how he had left her alone with little children to go off to Israel in the days of the Jewish underground. I told Esther how I sat and listened to Bernard unquestioningly, feeling invisible, because Bernard had told me not to contradict him in public.

We became friends with the Stones before Izzy became as accepted as he was later. In the uptight 1950s, Washington was a more conservative place and McCarthyism still echoed through the corridors of power. In those days, Izzy was suspect as a radical, a troublemaker, perhaps some sort of subversive. Esther later told me that she was moved when Bernard introduced Izzy as *his friend*. In the 1960s, the times caught up with him, and he became more widely respected and beloved by many.

After we moved from Hollin Hills, Virginia, back to Washington in late 1963, we lived only a few blocks from the Stones. Bernard and I would drop by their house, perhaps with some juicy documents for Izzy. Esther would greet us cheerfully as she addressed thousands of copies of the *Weekly* to send out to their faithful readers. Ten years later, the *Weekly* would have seventy thousand subscribers and Izzy was a cult hero.

Bernard had a storehouse of little-known documents about and from North Vietnam, often ordered from the Chiao Liu Publication Service in Hong Kong. They had titles such as *Souvenirs from Militants*, by Vo Nguyen Giap, and *Prison Diary Poems of Ho Chi Minh*. Chiao Liu also gave him a subscription to the Democratic Republic of Vietnam's *Vietnam Advance*. Vietnam News Service, in Rangoon, Burma, an agency of North Vietnam, regularly sent him *Viet-Nam Information Bulletin*. They first contacted Bernard in 1956 to request two copies of *The Viet-Minh Regime*. A listing of new material arrived bi-monthly from the Foreign Language Publishing House in Hanoi. Daily reports from the U.S. government's Foreign Broadcast Information Service were invaluable, as were research materials from France. All these were grist for Bernard's scholarship, no matter how much he upset the FBI.

When writing an article, Bernard would gather his reference materials around him and just start typing. Once a page came out of the typewriter, he was finished. There was no second draft. At the end of the day, he might correct a word here, capitalize another there, or put in a comma. Then off it went—to the *New York Times*, to *The Nation*, to the *New Republic*, or to many other publications. It was a phenomenal output. His thinking was sufficiently well organized that, when writing a book, he might dictate parts of it into a tape recorder.

In addition to his books, articles, and book reviews, Bernard had a voluminous correspondence. He wrote many letters to the editor, on Vietnam issues and other topics as well, including guerrilla warfare in other Third World countries, the Algerian war, World War II, and Nuremberg. Even as a graduate student, he had written letters to the *New York Times*, sometimes on esoteric points, but always on issues that he wanted to clarify or imprecisions that he felt obliged to rectify.

Bernard always substantiated his writings and always answered critics. If he was proven wrong, he admitted it. In his second revised edition of *The Two Viet-Nams*, he states in the preface, "I am also grateful to such scholarly critics as P. J. Honey and I. Milton Sacks who drew my attention to inadvertent errors or shortcomings in previous editions." Both were men with whom Bernard often strongly disagreed, but facts were facts.

Bernard learned that the Rockefeller Foundation had introduced a program of grants to scholars "with emphasis on research on emergent problems of foreign policy, diplomatic analysis and history, and theoretical studies in international relations." He applied for and received such a grant for "a study of the foreign policies of Laos, Cambodia and the two regimes of Viet-Nam." The ten-thousand-dollar grant would support us for the 1961–62 academic year, and Bernard proposed that all four of us spend it in Indochina.

He assumed that we could not reside in Vietnam, so Bernard decided on its neighbor, Cambodia. Finally, I would experience his world firsthand. Although I felt some trepidation in taking two young children to an unknown place, I was eager for the adventure. We would spend the first three months in Paris, where Bernard would do research for *The Two Viet-Nams* and also meet with the translator for the French edition of *Street Without Joy*, Serge Ouvaroff, with whom he developed a warm relationship.

USIA could not grant me a leave of absence for the year, so I resigned with the understanding that I would be rehired upon my return.

Just before our departure, Bernard received a letter from the director of the U.S. Military Assistance Institute that was dramatically different from the criticisms then often aimed at him by agencies of government:

August 18, 1961

My dear Dr. Fall:

It is with considerable regret that I send this certificate of appreciation to you since it means that the students of the Military Assistance Institute shall not have the good fortune to sit in on your presentations on matters pertaining to Laos, Cambodia, and Vietnam. Your discussions of the political and military situations in these countries have been most instructive and, in many instances, far in advance of your contemporaries. That your views have been corroborated in time is evidence of your deep interest in Southeast Asia and your tireless efforts to secure the facts and data as they are, and not as one wishes them to be.

We look forward to the day of your return to the Military Assistance Institute, and wish you God's speed.

Sincerely yours,

Henry G. Newton

Brigadier General (Ret.)

Director

Military leaders sent Bernard many other letters like this over the years. He kept the most impressive of them in a spiral note-book. Military leaders respected Bernard because he was a realist and they had to be realists, too, or men would die. It was politicians who often found reality inconvenient.

We left for Paris on September 2, 1961. Elisabeth was just a year old, not yet walking, a fair-skinned, chubby baby with large gray-blue eyes and light-brown curls, who still had to be carried. Four-year-old Nicole was a contrast with big brown eyes and a mass of dark brown curls. As usual, the children and I were in one row on the airplane. Bernard sat elsewhere, perhaps so he could read.

Paris was glorious that fall. September and October were sunny and warm. We found a ground-floor, two-bedroom apartment in Neuilly, not far from the Biret house. The kitchen had a stone sink which seemed to be of eighteenth-century vintage. An English student became our babysitter, allowing me to attend life-drawing sessions at the Atelier de la Grande Chaumière. Nicole was enrolled in a nursery school with its requisite *tablier*, a smock to cover her clothes, so that all children started off equal. My morning walk to deposit her there was a delight as I inspected, in passing, the *charcuterie* and *epicerie* and bought bread at the *boulangerie*. Women were already out doing their daily marketing, many dressed in high heels and fashionable suits.

We rented a diminutive Fiat, which just held the four of us. Paris contributed immeasurably to my driving skills. The Étoile with its twelve radiating avenues, which I frequently navigated to get to Neuilly, would have challenged a race-car driver.

While we were in Paris, Bernard was unexpectedly summoned by the Cadillac Gage Company of Warren, Michigan, for consultation on the design of their "Commando," a small jungle warfare vehicle. They contacted him after reading *Street Without Joy*. He wrote to me that he was sent for because "the guys here saw my book on *every* MAAG officers' desk in Vietnam, who say it is 'the Bible.'" Thus impressed, company officials wanted his advice on the needs of armored vehicles in jungle warfare. Bernard was there for about five days and consulted with engineers and executives. Bernard told them that the prototype they had was completely inadequate and it was quickly scrapped. His suggestions to incorporate more belly armor, as a protection against land mines, and interior cooling for the occupants were later incorporated into the plans for the vehicle.

Meanwhile, the FBI was snooping about, alarmed that Bernard might have glimpsed classified information at Cadillac Gage. When I later obtained Bernard's FBI file, I learned that company officials assured them that no classified data had been available to Bernard's prying eyes.[6]

Bernard preceded me to the Far East to take care of our living accommodations. After a stop in Vienna, he went via Moscow to Uzbekistan. It was his habit, with each trip to the Far East, to explore new countries. In Bangkok, he stayed temporarily with Lloyd Burlingham, our friend from WAHRAF days.

I took off with the two girls on December 3 with a one-week stop in Israel to meet two aunts, my mother's sisters, and their children. When my mother and her sister Clara had gone to America, three of her sisters had chosen to live in what was then Palestine. With the children remaining in Natanya with Aunt Devorah, I toured the country with my Aunt Sara. In Haifa, I met new cousins and my mother's stepmother, a very old woman by then, a moving and remarkable experience.

Finally, we flew Air France to Bangkok. We rested for a few days at Lloyd's home and then set off to Cambodia, where a new adventure would unfold.

12

CAMBODIA

Bᴇʀɴᴀʀᴅ met us at the Pochentong airport in Phnom Penh on December 12, 1961. This would be our home until the following August, while Bernard worked on his Rockefeller Foundation project.

Cambodia in those days was a never-never land with a rich mix of cultures and an aura of tranquility. It was a mysterious country with a legacy of the ancient Khmer civilization that had produced one of the wonders of the world, the temple city of Angkor. I marveled at the exoticism of the city. Palm trees lined the boulevards of Phnom Penh, and flowers and green grass decorated the central islands of its broad avenues. As a bonus, the French colonizers had left behind their culinary genius in many fine restaurants.

The city offered large, beautiful playgrounds for children. A quiet walk led up to the Wat Phnom, the highest point in the city, with its dome-shaped Buddhist shrines, or stupas. Surrounded by a lush park, it provided a place for contemplation and a taste of total serenity. Exploring beyond the city, we encountered dirt roads and people living in thatch-roofed huts on stilts. It was normal to see an elephant walking with its caretaker or leading a funeral procession down the road. Monkeys would jump down from trees in hopes of being fed, but they were vicious and one was wise to avoid them. There were vibrant emerald-green rice fields and tranquil villages. The sugar palms, their fronds whirling atop the long, curved trunks of the trees, were a visual delight and would inspire images for my art.

Buddhism is a peaceful religion, and you felt that in the people, in the air, as you moved along the city streets. The sweet smell of the purple frangipani covering garden walls and the flaming, six feet tall poinsettia in the gardens were balm to my soul. December's coolness was a surprise. The months would change along with the heat and the monsoon rains; the latter would not last long but would inundate the streets as high as the car doors.

The Cambodians did not seem impoverished. There was no begging. We found an abundance of fresh food. This was a land of bountiful exports of rice, sugar cane, fish, and spices. It was an under-populated country with only part of the arable land under cultivation. They were a fun-loving people, happy with each other. No one could imagine the horror that would begin there only thirteen years later.

The country revolved around Prince Norodom Sihanouk, the

former king, who had abdicated the throne to his father in 1955, demoting himself so that he could take a political role in his country. As head of state, he walked a fine line between the East and West. He clung to neutrality to protect his country from joining Vietnam and Laos in the expanding war, a choice that outraged many in Washington. Americans at the embassy in Phnom Penh scorned him and mimicked his high-pitched voice and French repartee. They denounced him as a fool or a crypto-Communist. But his policy of neutralism was working. I respected that and could excuse his eccentricities and even enjoy them.

Sihanouk was a master showman, a dynamic personality who constantly worked the diplomatic community. Foreign ambassadors were persuaded to join him in digging trenches or trying their hands as bricklayers in his Manual Labor campaign. This set an example which was meant to encourage workers to return to the rural areas they had left in search of an easier life in the city. The prince played the saxophone and wrote plays in which he starred with his beautiful wife Monique. He put on volleyball games that were command performances for the diplomatic and military communities. All would come, all would play, and the prince's team would always win. Afterwards he entertained the participants at the Royal Palace.

Shortly after his arrival, Bernard had an audience with Prince Sihanouk that lasted an hour and a half. He told me that he was "extremely impressed with the enormous amount of sense Sihanouk made—more than any other politician in Southeast Asia." They hit it off so well that Bernard was invited by the prince to accompany him on trips, and I gladly went along, to see more of this fascinating country.

Sihanouk worked hard to take care of his people. They were like his children. The Cambodians loved him and throngs came running whenever he appeared, to touch him and to receive the money handed out by his aides. On one of his trips, a helicopter hovered overhead dropping brightly-colored bolts of cotton cloth, patterned with a symbolic Khmer temple in a jungle setting with palm trees. People eagerly caught them as they fell. I too scooped one up and years later collaged sections of the cloth into my paper-pulp paintings.

Because Bernard was teaching a course at the Cambodian Royal School of Administration, we were entitled to an apartment in the Bâtiment des Experts, which housed primarily UN advisors and journalists. It provided a basic but enjoyable existence. The long, narrow cement building was built on stilt-like pylons to keep it above the monsoon flooding. Our living room ran the width of the building, and at either end were immense balcony sized openings. These exposed us to the rains and monsoon winds and formed a sort of wind tunnel that could only partially be diminished by closing the ill-fitting louvered shutters. We essentially lived in open air. There was no hot water, but it was easy enough to heat some to wash my hair. The kitchen was also exposed to the outside and offered easy access to our resident rat, which we would sometimes glimpse scampering to its hiding place in the cupboard. Even with air conditioners for the enclosed bedrooms, we slept under mosquito netting. Many evenings, a bat would enter one end of the living room, fly through, and disappear. Later, I would find it perched upside down, on a ledge outside the girls' bedroom. It looked so innocent that I soon forgot about the old wives' tale that a bat's wings could get tangled in your hair.

From our third-floor haven, a lovely garden spread out below. It was a central courtyard surrounded by American-occupied buildings with their own generator. When the electricity would go off all over town, as it frequently did, often just before a dinner party, we would prevail upon our American friends for ice and related needs. We ate dinner by candle light, and our cook had no problem creating her delicacies in the tiny charcoal stove.

With daughters aged one and four, I soon hired two servants, an affordable luxury in Cambodia that gave me time for my art. We found two Vietnamese women, Thi Hai, the cook and house-

keeper, and Thi Ba, the nanny. Thi Hai was a good cook and followed my instructions with regard to boiling water, cooking meat
well done, and washing vegetables to be eaten raw in permanga-
nate. We didn't get sick, except for an unrelated kidney infection
that Bernard developed near the end of our stay.

We were unconnected to any organizations, did not have a
lot of money, and lived on the local economy. We had access to
no American commissary where we could buy products from
the United States. This was not a hardship but an adventure, as
we dined on local fish, the freshest vegetables, and exotic fruits,
including exquisite mangoes in season. Bread, a legacy from the
French, was fresh and crunchy even with the baked-in bugs that
lived in the flour. I asked an Army wife to purchase some cereal
for me from the commissary, for our girls, but she said that was
against the rules, so I sent to Hong Kong for corn flakes, which
arrived somewhat stale.

There was no problem getting around town, as there were
always cyclo drivers waiting outside the building. Cyclos were
one-passenger vehicles, built on a bicycle frame, with the passenger sitting up front and the driver behind pedaling. We eventually bought a Citroën Deux Chevaux from a young Canadian
couple who were leaving the country. Fresh from operating a
little Fiat in Paris, I had no trouble coping with this car, peculiar
as it was, and we needed it for trips outside the city.

Charles Meyer, a Frenchman, was Sihanouk's foreign policy
advisor. A gentle man with a dark mustache and serious de-
meanor, he offered access to the inner workings of Sihanouk's
government, and he and Bernard quickly became friends. They
shared a love of Indochina and savored long political discussions. Some at the U.S. Embassy whispered that Charles had been
sent by the French to keep an eye on the prince, a charge that
infuriated him.

His Chinese wife Sika and her sister Lika greeted me warmly
and introduced me to the city. They showed me the ropes—the
things that I, as a foreigner, needed to understand to navigate

At Pich Nil, Prince Sihanouk's hideaway in the Cambodian mountains.
Left to right: the prince, Dorothy, Bernard, unidentified woman,
Sika Meyer, and writer Donald Lancaster. Photo courtesy of Charles Meyer.

the native culture. For example, before I attended a special evening event, Sika took me to her Chinese hairdresser. When we received our bills, Sika explained that as a foreigner I would pay more. Thus, as an American "long nose," I learned about Cambodia's double standard.

Charles Meyer arranged some graphic design assignments for me. In addition to illustrations for a book on Cambodia, I found myself designing campaign posters for Prince Sihanouk. He was running for reelection, and the posters illustrated the progress he had brought to Cambodia. I was delighted to see my posters hanging all over Phnom Penh and thus, as American artist incognito, to be playing a role in the Cambodian election. The Prince won the election as easily as he won the volleyball games.

Phnom Penh was a city of intrigue, a meeting place for people from all parts of the world with often conflicting interests. Our arrival caused alarm within the American Embassy. What was the abrasive, controversial Bernard Fall, a French agent, doing in Phnom Penh? In this small post, there was a panic about this outspoken Frenchman who questioned U.S. support of South Vietnam at a time when the U.S. was pouring billions of dollars into its anti-Communist crusade there. What did he want? One of our friends at the embassy told us that, at a specially called meeting, the embassy's public affairs officer warned: "He may not be on our side."[1] That was true enough—Bernard was not on anyone's side. People were told to keep him at a distance. An old poem was updated to, "We do not like you, Dr. Fall, for reasons that we can't recall." Nervous American officials assumed that Bernard was working for the French or for Sihanouk. He certainly did not share the embassy view that Sihanouk was a temperamental, narcissistic, troublesome despot.

For a while we *were* shunned. But some people from the American Embassy befriended us. Tom Hirschfeld, second man in the political section, and his wife, Hana, sought us out. They were of European background and enjoyed sharing ideas and ignoring official edicts. Years later, Tom told me, "Bernard was the only one writing about the Vietnamese as if they were human and had national aspirations of their own. This was a view that, during the days of the Cold War, was unacceptable. There was a Gallic flavor to Bernard's stuff. He was acutely aware of the French experience and he gave it, like any Frenchman, a lot of weight. The effect of that with American officials was, 'So what. If the French can't do it, why does that mean that we can't?'"

Avoided by most U.S. foreign service people, Bernard befriended the military, with whom he always had rapport, although some of them were guarded in their contact with him. Most were advisors to the Cambodian army, serving in MAAG, the Military

Assistance Advisory Group. Soon after I arrived, Lt. Col. Ray Gertie and his wife, Rita, invited us to their house for Christmas dinner. Bernard had met Ray in Washington when the officer attended one of his lectures before leaving for his assignment to Cambodia. Although official policy was to avoid Fall, Gertie felt that what he did in his own home was his own affair. It was a friendship that lasted many years.[2]

On several occasions, Prince Sihanouk invited us to dinner at the Royal Palace. The invitation sometimes arrived late in the afternoon for a command appearance that evening. Before we bought our car, we went by cyclo. Two drivers would greet us at the bottom of the landing. Bernard got into one cyclo and I into the other, carefully sitting back into the chair so as not to wrinkle our best clothes. Arriving at the Palace, we were an incongruous sight descending from these jerrybuilt vehicles in our finery, while others emerged from chauffeured limousines. The first dinner we attended at the Royal Palace was honoring a visit by David Rockefeller, which was fitting since Bernard was there on a Rockefeller Foundation grant. Another dinner honored former Secretary of State Dean Acheson, who was presenting Cambodia's case in the Temple Preah Vihar dispute before the World Court in the Hague. The temple, situated on the border between Cambodia and Thailand, had been occupied by Thailand in 1953. The case was later settled in Cambodia's favor.

It was a sumptuous feast consisting of fine French wines and an elaborate selection of French dishes. There were many toasts, and dinner was followed by a performance of the Royal Cambodian dancers. They wore splendid, gold-encrusted costumes and elaborate headdresses. Beautiful, delicate women performed as celestial creatures, half-woman, half-bird. One dance portrayed goddesses and an evil deity wielding an ax. His defeat portrayed evil defeated by purity and innocence. Finally we left as we had come, by cyclo.

To connect with his people and to show foreign diplomats his country, the prince made inspection trips throughout Cambodia, inviting members of the diplomatic corps and journalists to accompany him. Thus, we were able to see remote parts of the country that were best reached by private plane. In those Cold War days, Communist and non-Communist countries did not often associate with one another, but on these trips diplomats from both camps were side by side, including the envoys from North Vietnam and Red China. We traveled in World War II vintage DC-3s (Bernard and I always flew in separate planes, out of concern for our children), and always breathed easier upon landing.

The first places we visited were Kompong Cham, Battambang, and Stung Treng near the Laotian border. The diplomats were shown newly constructed hospitals, schools, and playgrounds, and local crafts. Sihanouk greeted the throngs who came to touch him while his aides distributed money. Ethnic minorities lived in these remote regions and Sihanouk sought to convince them that they were Cambodians.

One day we made a day trip to Ratanakiri province, bordering Vietnam. The traveling party included twelve ambassadors, other diplomats, journalists, and Sihanouk's own entourage. We departed at 7:30 a.m. and flew to Lomphat, a lovely spot where we cooled off in a lake. From there, we flew through a terrifying thunderstorm to Labansiek, where Jeeps took us to the village. The roads had been newly hacked out of the forest for the prince's visit. Clouds of clay dust, churned up by the car wheels, began to settle on our clothes and faces as we perspired in the tropical sun. The ambassadors' light-colored suits turned terra cotta red. The Czech ambassador turned to a colleague and said, "Don't look now, but the American ambassador, he is all red." Of course, by "red" he also meant Communist.

As we traveled by Jeep from the market to the military plantation, to the hospital, to schools, and to other destinations, we were a bedraggled, dusty crowd, except for Sihanouk, who rode in a closed limousine. Our schedule called for our return to Phnom Penh after lunch at four thirty, but at two we still had two more villages to visit. It was at six, after an aperitif at a waterfall and too late for some of the captive ambassadors to get back for their own embassy receptions in distant Phnom Penh, that we sat down to a sumptuous lunch of French food and fine wines. We departed for Phnom Penh at nine.

It was an idyllic life. Bernard taught his courses at the Royal School of Administration, in addition to the challenge of writing articles, keeping up his vast correspondence, and meeting with people seeking his views. As 1962 began, publisher Frederick Praeger was waiting for the manuscript for *The Two Viet-Nams*, which Bernard was finishing, along with a profile of the North Vietnamese General Giap for an English translation of the general's book *People's War, People's Army*. Praeger, originally from Vienna, regarded Bernard as a compatriot. He wrote to Bernard: "When I consider our heritage and Viennese background, I cannot help finding the world funny with you staying in the jungles of Cambodia and me grinding out books on Communism, on East Asia, on guerrilla warfare, etc., at a steadily increasing pace. When you come back we must drink a special toast to Taborstrasse." (Taborstrasse is the main street of the Jewish section of Vienna. Bernard lived on Taborstrasse as a child. Perhaps Praeger lived there too.)

Bernard's first article for the *New Republic*—the first of many—was written that winter in Phnom Penh and published in the spring. Instead of publishing it under his name, it was signed "Z." This harked back to George Kennan's historic "X" article, published in *Foreign Affairs* in 1947, which proposed a policy of "containment" toward the Soviet Union. Kennan was a diplomat and writer whom Bernard greatly admired, but I think the main reason Bernard published the article anonymously had to do with security. Not his own—he never worried about himself—but concerns that the article would further antagonize the dictator in South Vietnam at a time when his family was unprotected in nearby Phnom Penh. Of course, among those who followed the Vietnam issue closely, there wasn't much doubt about who "Z" was.

The *New Republic* article was bluntly titled "The War in Vietnam: We Have Not Been Told the Whole Truth." It was a hard-hitting statement on the deteriorating situation in South Vietnam, the false information being put out by our government, the influential pro-Diem lobby in the United States, and how many journalists unquestioningly supported the official line. Bernard warned that the situation in South Vietnam had become, early in 1962, "what North Vietnam had become in the tragic spring of 1954: a lacework of fortified villages and army posts completely surrounded by a population that is either deliberately hostile, or at least terrorized by an efficient network of Communist guerillas into cooperating with them. . . ."

He quoted an American Army colonel saying "this is a brutal, grubby, dirty method of fighting," after spending twelve fruitless days chasing after an elusive Vietcong unit, and he noted that it was a war "whose killing rate has been increasing steadily. At first there was a steady trickle of about 30–50 dead a month in 1957–58. Late in 1959, the figure had increased to 10 a day, and in the spring of 1960 a figure of 25 a day was openly admitted in the press." (Unlike U.S. officials, who spoke only of American casualties, Bernard was always concerned with Vietnamese deaths as well.)

He added that major magazines like *Time* "fell for the 'Bastion-of-the-Free-World line," and that "those few journalists or scholars who sought to buck the trend soon found themselves the target of an equally well organized whisper and letter-writing campaign on the part of [the] Ngo Dinh Diem regime's lobby, the American Friends of Vietnam, whose first honorary president was General Donovan of OSS fame."[3]

The article challenged what the Kennedy administration and most of the media were telling the American public, but it did not have nearly the impact as one Bernard wrote later in 1962 when he became the first Western journalist in years to interview Ho Chi Minh—and proceeded to write about him in that most mainstream, apple-pie of American magazines, the *Saturday Evening Post*.

Nicole attended a French school; a bus picked her up and returned her. Our apartment had no telephone to disturb us; communication was by messenger. With few household duties, I had time to paint. I would go out into the street, a pad of paper under my arm and sketching materials in hand, up to the Wat Phnom or down to the river to draw the ferry or the melon boats or the village on the other side of the muddy water. As soon as I sat down to draw, a crowd of young people would suddenly gather round to see the spectacle of a Caucasian lady and her art.

Sometimes I had a painting partner, George Ann Gillespie, the elegant wife of a MAAG colonel. She was showing her art at the United States Information Service library, where I hoped to exhibit once I had enough works. It was a simple, thatched-roofed building on the embassy grounds. Once George Ann and I went out to a village in the countryside, where we painted portraits of the children. On occasion, I took Nicole along on painting trips and she, too, sketched the countryside.

Now and then our daily routine was broken by some festival or ceremony. An important one, attended by the royal family and all members of the government, as well as the diplomatic corps, was the "Ploughing of the Sacred Furrow." It was held in a large park festooned with colored banners, and marked the beginning of the agricultural year. Many people dressed in traditional Khmer costume. The ceremony began with a member of the royal family walking with a plough behind a beautifully decorated ox and followed by a princess sowing grain. Then two oxen were led to a row of silver platters, each containing a different item: rice, corn, beans (signifying an abundance of food), grass, water (signifying sufficient rain), and sugar cane. Whatever the oxen chose to nibble predicted what crops would prosper that season.

Another ceremony, the Fête de Genie, was a Chinese ritual outlawed in other countries. Men dressed in glistening red and gold paraded by, carried on wooden contraptions. One man was piercing his tongue with his sword. He licked gold papers that were then distributed to outstretched hands in the crowd: the blood of this genie was supposed to drive away evil. Another man had long bamboo stakes coming out of his cheeks, piercing one side clearly through and out the other, forming an X. One woman passed by in a trance. Others waved knives. All were dressed in red, to signify blood. The ceremony filled me with terror.

Bernard remained persona non grata in South Vietnam. From Saigon, Malcolm Browne of the Associated Press wrote to Bernard that *Street Without Joy* was banned in South Vietnam. The Diem Regime was unhappy that a number of correspondents had visited Phnom Penh to seek Bernard's views. His friend François Sully of *Newsweek* had come in January and later quoted Bernard in an article. By then, the *Times of Vietnam* regularly attacked any journalist critical of the Diem regime. In August 1962, our old friend Gene Gregory, editor of the *Times of Vietnam*, denounced a *Newsweek* article by Sully and called Bernard a "phony military analyst, better known as a café strategist who spent a few months in Vietnam in 1953." Sully had quoted Bernard as saying the common soldier in South Vietnam "doesn't have an ideology worth fighting for" and that "there would be no victory in South Vietnam until political deficiencies were corrected."

Our August departure was approaching and I hoped to have an exhibit at the USIS library. Tom Hirschfeld arranged for me to meet with the head of the U.S. Information Service, Darrell Price, but no invitation was issued and finally Bernard said, "If the Americans don't want to show your work, why don't I ask the French?" He pointed out that the French had a grand cultural center, the Maison de France, which would be a much better place to exhibit than the isolated, rather shabby USIS library. The French were happy to sponsor my exhibit. Perhaps with Charles Meyer's intervention, the Cambodian Ministry of Information became the cosponsor. A week later, Tom called to say that USIS would, after all, give me a show, but it was too late to change my plans. I don't know if USIS didn't want to sponsor my show, or was just slow, but either way they lost some good publicity. Large posters appeared all over town that announced, in French and Khmer, my show *"Impressions du Cambodge."*

The Maison de France was filled with my impressions of the country. I felt that our time in Cambodia had inspired a breakthrough in my work. The country was such a visual feast for a painter. I had gone into the villages, drawing the smiling, curious children, the huts on stilts, the water buffaloes cooling off in a muddy pond. I had portraits on display. I showed the river and the melon boats, the green-skinned, plump fruit piled high under the circular roofs, the fields in colors from yellow chartreuse to thalo to dark green to blue, and the ducks and chickens and pigs in their sties. There were women planting rice, moving in unison in the brightly colored paddy, in their dark clothes.

I was delighted with the exhibition. Ambassadors, diplomats, and friends attended. Sihanouk did not attend but requested a private showing a few days later. He spent an hour studying my impressions of his country and bought six works.

A little later, he gave a farewell luncheon for us, thanked Bernard for his "intensive research on the contemporary political situation in Southeast Asia," and urged us to return soon. Finally, on August 21, 1962, we started home. Our Cambodian interlude had taken place during a time that can never return, with a people who will never be the same. The mass slaughter inflicted by the Pol Pot regime in the late 1970s was unimaginable then. Of course, neither could we imagine that we Americans would be fighting in Vietnam for another dozen years.

While we were in Cambodia, in addition to his work on the Rockefeller report, Bernard had published his initial *New Republic* article on Vietnam as well as another piece there on the situation in Laos, which he felt that U.S. meddling had pushed from neutralism into chaos. But the most important journalistic outcome of our stay in Cambodia—one of the most important articles he ever wrote—was published in the *Saturday Evening Post*

Prince Sihanouk visiting Dorothy's exhibit, August 1962.
He bought this oil painting.

on November 24, 1962, and told of his visit to North Vietnam and his exclusive interview with its leader, Ho Chi Minh.

No Western journalist had been to North Vietnam since the departure of the French eight years earlier. Bernard urgently wanted to go there, to interview its Communist leaders and to see how the country had changed, under their rule, since his 1953 trip. Early in 1962 he had written to the Foreign Ministry in Hanoi, requesting permission to visit.

Five months later, in early July, a telegram arrived. It said simply: "PERMISSION GRANTED WIRE DATE ARRIVAL HANOI." Bernard was thrilled. To get to Hanoi, he flew to Vientiane, Laos, and boarded an old Boeing Stratoliner of World War II vintage. His visit lasted from July 10 to July 24 and its highlight was an interview with Ho Chi Minh. That journalistic coup enabled Bernard, upon his return, to sell his article to the prestigious *Saturday Evening Post*.

Unsurprisingly, he opened his interview with Ho:

"'It took us eight years of bitter fighting to defeat you French in Indochina,' said the slightly built, grandfatherly man with the wispy goatee. 'Now the South Vietnamese regime of Ngo Dinh Diem is well armed and helped by ten thousand Americans. The Americans are much stronger than the French, though they know us less well. It may perhaps take ten years to do it, but our heroic compatriots in the South will defeat them in the end.'"

A little later in the article, Bernard again quoted the seventy-two-year-old Vietnamese leader, whom he described as "looking very spry": "'I think the Americans greatly underestimate the determination of the Vietnamese people. The Vietnamese people always have shown great determination when they were faced with a foreign invader.'"

Bernard is perhaps best remembered as a historian and analyst, but the *Post* article showed what a fine reporter he could be, as he captured the beauty and energy of this new nation he was visiting as well as its politics. He wrote this about his arrival by air:

> I thought for a while that the land looked much as it had when I had known it in the days of French rule. In the Red River Delta I could see dark green patches where tree-lined villages nestle between the rice fields of lush light green. But something had changed even here. Some fields are no longer small, handkerchief-like squares but are far larger than before, with no dikes to interrupt their expanse. They belong to the new collective farms. Communism has already left its mark on the landscape. And as we came in for a landing I noticed the brutal reds of new tile roofs and the glaring whites of factory walls where there once had been nothing but farmland or French forts.

Having described his meeting with Ho and others in "official Hanoi," he added, "There is another Hanoi, full of the bustle of any Asian city, with children swarming around, street merchants peddling duck eggs, and lines forming in front of movie houses. I saw one food queue too—people lined up to buy the Vietnamese equivalent of Popsicles." He also related that when he was dining, almost alone, in the huge dining room of what had once been the elegant Metropole Hotel, "the public-address system—perhaps in my honor—switched from a propaganda speech to a scratched record of Glenn Miller's 'In the Mood.'" Bernard was astonished, because that was one of the songs he most fondly remembered from his time with the American GIs in 1944–45.

His article also examined the nation's economy: "In contrast to China, the industrialization of North Vietnam is relatively easy, for it is a nation a little smaller than Missouri with a population of 17 million. A few modern machine-tool plants, for example, can change it from a machine-importing to a machine-exporting country." He concluded, "The country is functioning, and developing at a very rapid rate."

Bernard also described his talks with Premier Pham Van Dong, who spoke scornfully of South Vietnam's President Diem: "Monsieur Diem's position is quite difficult. He is unpopular, and the more unpopular he is the more American aid he will require to stay in power. And the more American aid he receives, the more he will look like a puppet of the Americans and the less likely he is to win popular support."

Bernard said that sounded like a vicious circle, then: "The premier's eyes showed a humorous gleam as he said that it was more than 'vicious.' 'It is really more like a descending spiral.'"

Bernard closed the article with a call for a negotiated peace to avoid a potentially disastrous war:

> I believe we could press more effectively for some kind of truce settlement on terms that would definitely not be 'surrender.' We could demand the immediate end of guerrilla fighting in the South and a far more effective international inspection system to police the truce. We may not achieve such a settlement, but I feel very strongly that we have no reason to fear it. And we must clearly realize that the alternative means the bloodshed and misery of a long and prob-

ably inconclusive guerrilla war—a war which Ho Chi Minh
is well prepared to fight.

On a lighter note, Bernard described how he had given Ho a
copy of his newly published *Street Without Joy* and mentioned
that it contained a drawing of Ho by his wife. "Where? Where?"
Ho demanded. "Let me see it." He studied the drawing and announced that he liked it. Then he took a bouquet of flowers
from a nearby vase and handed them to Bernard. "Tell her for
me that the drawing is very good and give her the bouquet and
kiss her on both cheeks for me."[4]

Bernard did just that on his return to Phnom Penh, making
me one of the few American women to have been kissed by Ho
Chi Minh, even by proxy.

*Bernard interviewing North Vietnamese Premier Pham Van Dong
in Hanoi, July 1962.*

13

THE OMEN

Fʀᴏᴍ Phnom Penh, we flew to Australia via Bangkok. I stayed in Sydney while Bernard visited the commando center in Brisbane and spoke at the Australian army's survival school. Our hotel room offered a spectacular view of the harbor, which I sketched, and we toured the Taronga Park Zoo, where the girls adored the koala bears.

We flew next to Tahiti, which Bernard had dreamed of since he read *Mutiny on the Bounty* when he was nine. Our visit began badly. No one had told us that I, as an American, needed a visa to enter Tahiti. They sent us to police headquarters, where Bernard began to argue my case. "Just a minute," the Tahitian official said. "If you are French, then your wife is French. Therefore, she doesn't need a visa."

After that, Tahiti was paradise. Bernard later told an interviewer that the island had truly lived up to the image he'd carried around since childhood of fair maidens and swaying palms: "It was really true! It was a beautiful island with thoroughly friendly people, and we actually had a real palm-thatch hut on the beach not far from where Gauguin used to paint, there on the lagoon." Soon he was talking about buying some land. He always wanted to live on an island. Why not the island of his dreams? Fortunately we caught our plane before he could sign anything.

Back home, as 1963 arrived, we entered a busy and complex time in our lives. Part of my post-Cambodian readjustment was living without the luxury of Thi Hai to cook and Thi Ba to help with the children. Bernard suggested that we import a French au pair to help with the children. He said his sister Lisette would find a young woman who wanted to learn English. It turned out to be an ideal arrangement with successive au pairs. Nicole and Elisabeth learned to speak French, while the French girls learned English. It also eased my return to my half-time job at USIA.

To reacquaint Nicole with her native land, we took her on a trip to a nearby farm. She gazed at grazing horses and cows, but was looking around impatiently.

"What's the matter?" I asked

"But where are the elephants?" she asked.

Bernard and I missed the elephants too.

The Kennedy administration continued to expand the U.S. presence in Vietnam and Bernard was increasingly called upon to write and speak about it. Actually, he often turned down lucrative speaking engagements because he preferred to write, and articles reached more people. As his celebrity increased, so did the hostility from some elements of the U.S. government.

On December 7, just two weeks after Bernard's *Saturday Evening Post* article appeared, Chalmers Wood, director of the State Department's Vietnam Working Group, sent a letter to Ambassador Fritz Nolting in Vietnam in which he said, "I hope to get to the *Saturday Evening Post* people about the two poor articles in their November 24 issue. Bernard Fall's recommendations certainly follow very close to the neutralist, crypto-Communist line. I don't think that he is a Communist, but his emotions have been so long wrapped up in Viet-Nam that his judgement is false."[1]

A friend who worked at the State Department showed Bernard a memo by Joseph Mendenhall of the department's Far East Bureau, saying that Bernard should not be allowed to lecture at State. He later saw others circulated by both Wood and Mendenhall that sought to discredit him. In his most sardonic manner, Bernard later dedicated his *Viet-Nam Witness* to Joseph A. Mendenhall and Chalmers B. Wood.

The Two Viet-Nams was published in 1963 and dedicated *"To the valiant and long suffering Vietnamese—North and South."* In it, Bernard said: "This is a book in praise of no one. I have written it not to plead a cause or to propound a pet theory, but simply to attempt to bring some understanding to the plight of a valiant people that happens to find itself, no doubt much against its will, at one of the focal points of a world-wide struggle."[2]

The Kennedy era was at its peak. I was proud to see Jackie take Paris by storm. It was exciting to watch her bring style, sophistication, and a love of the arts to the White House and to the country.

But despite my enthusiasm for the New Frontier, Attorney General Robert Kennedy ordered our phone tapped.[3]

Bernard's increasing fame, based in part on his interview with Ho, was reflected on January 2 when he was interviewed on the *Today Show* about his visit to North Vietnam. His days were filled with lectures, often to U.S. military audiences despite the State Department's grumbling. All this was in addition to teaching at

Howard. When taking a break, he would romp with the girls. With his teaching schedule he was often at home when the children returned from school.

All the while, Bernard wrote. Living with him was living with Vietnam. But I would not complain. With the children, my work, the household, and my art I, too, was fully engaged.

For his *Great Battles Series*, Hanson Baldwin, the author and distinguished military affairs writer for the *New York Times*, asked Bernard to write a book on the battle of Dien Bien Phu. Bernard gladly accepted. In the summer of 1963 we went to Paris where Bernard began his research. He had received authorization from the French ministry to consult the newly released files of Dien Bien Phu at the archives of the Service Historique de l'Armée.

From Paris, the four of us traveled to Algiers, where Bernard interviewed Algerian officers who fought with the French and Vietnamese at Dien Bien Phu. France, as a colonial power, had often enlisted soldiers from its colonies to help fight its wars. Bernard found that the Algerian soldiers' experience in Vietnam trained them for their own fight for independence. As prisoners of the Vietminh, some had been indoctrinated into revolutionary doctrine.

Our arrival in Algiers was one of my most terrifying travel experiences, as a horde of men almost overran us wanting to carry our luggage to the taxi. Even with Bernard next to me, I felt extremely vulnerable with our little girls in hand. Our plans were for a brief visit, but one officer Bernard needed to see was in another city and would not return for a day. Bernard persuaded me to take the girls and go on to Tunis without him. A nightmare of cancelled hotel reservations ensued, and did not end until Bernard finally met us in Naples. All was well as we left Naples, and traveled along Italy's Amalfi coast with a stop at Positano, where the children played happily on the beach.

In Vietnam, the Catholic Diem was repressing Buddhists, despite American objections. The Buddhists retaliated by orga-

nizing rallies and hunger strikes. Foreign journalists were notified and the events were well covered. The culmination was the
self-immolation of an elderly monk, which took place at a busy
intersection in Saigon. Malcolm Browne's photograph of the
burning monk was seen throughout the world. Madame Nhu
referred to the tragedy as a "barbecue." She told one interviewer,
"Let them burn, and we shall clap our hands."[4]

In the fall of 1963, Madame Ngo Dinh Nhu was traveling in
the United States with her eighteen-year-old daughter, trying to
rally support for the regime of her brother-in-law, Ngo Dinh
Diem. Through her father, Tran Van Chuong, Bernard invited
her to come to Howard University to speak. Tran Van Chuong
had resigned as ambassador because he disapproved of Diem's
persecution of the Buddhists. I imagine Bernard issued the invitation because he thought Madame Nhu's appearance would be
a coup for the university and for him. He knew he was high on
her government's black list. She greeted Bernard with, "You are
an enemy of my country." Bernard responded, "No, Madame, I
am a critic of your government."

Bernard presents a copy of the Two Viet-Nams *to Mâdame Nhu
and her daughter, who visited Howard University in October 1963.*

She spoke for about fifteen minutes, followed by a forty-five minute question-and-answer period, which Bernard moderated. He felt that her appearance went smoothly, although demonstrators outside rocked her empty automobile. She was in California when her husband and his brother, President Diem, were assassinated. General Duong Van "Big" Minh took over the government and Madame Nhu was told not to come back. It would have meant her death. She continued around the United States, blaming the CIA and the Kennedys for the fatal coup. She charged, "Mr. Henry Cabot Lodge and Robert Kennedy have on their hands the blood of the Vietnamese patriots."[5] Bernard said at the time that no one should imagine that the removal of Diem was going to win the war.

Throughout the fall of 1963 we were on the lookout for a house in Washington. Bernard found the commute to Howard from Virginia grueling and it was a long drive in for Washington dinner parties in the evening. After months of looking, our real estate agent showed us a house she knew we would like, a contemporary design much like our house in Virginia, but more spacious and better built. It was more expensive than we had planned, but we decided to buy it.

About then, Bernard began to have back pains. The first doctor he saw said he had a muscular problem. The second said that the pain was probably due to stress and gave Bernard a tranquilizer, which he threw away.

On November 20, the day after his thirty-seventh birthday, still suffering from back pains, urinary problems, and dizziness, Bernard sought help from Dr. Norman Paul, whom we met through French friends. Dr. Paul tapped Bernard's back and said, "Your kidneys are full." Both kidneys had ceased to function. Bernard was rushed to George Washington University Hospital. The ureters were blocked and Bernard was in the final stages of uremic poisoning. The kidneys had to be drained immediately. Tubes were inserted into both kidneys to release the urine.

I was in despair. How could this happen to a robust man of

thirty-seven? It was a nightmare. Three days later, as I rode up the hospital elevator to see Bernard, I heard the news that President Kennedy had been shot. The world was coming apart.

Between November and January, Bernard had four major operations. The second determined that Bernard's blockage was caused by a rare disorder called retroperitoneal fibrosis, a growth of fibrous tissue in the back of the abdomen. The tissue grows and envelops the ureters, squeezing them shut so that the urine does not leave the kidneys to enter the bladder. The urine backs up into the kidneys and gradually destroys them. In surgery, the fibrous mass was cut away from the ureters, but both kidneys were damaged. There was little hope for the left kidney and it was eventually removed. Kidney transplants had not yet been developed.

Bernard remained in the hospital for two months. Even in the hospital he continued fielding calls, working on papers, having visitors. He had his typewriter with him and continued pounding out articles and answering mail. As the medical bills kept piling up, far exceeding our insurance coverage, Howard University did us the magnificent kindness of keeping Bernard on teaching status so he would continue to draw his salary.

We had signed the contract on the house in Washington. The closing was to be in a few weeks. From his hospital bed Bernard said, "I want you and the children to move into the house. I want to come home from the hospital to my new home."

Although totally inexperienced in business matters, I handled the settlement. I studied the paperwork scrupulously. Since we already had our own insurance, I caught the duplicate charge on the settlement sheet. There were other questionable items. I was developing an armor that I would need to cope with the future.

On December 20, with Bernard still in the hospital, I had all the furniture and belongings moved to our new home. Annick, our au pair, and I packed Bernard's library of a thousand books. Gradually, the paintings and relics of our trips, the Buddhas, the ceramic warriors from Cheng Mai, the Japanese scroll, statues of the Vietnamese elders, the Cambodian burial cloth, all were hung on the walls or placed on shelves; the Lurçat tapestry of a flying ram hung over the sofa. It was glorious how everything had a place, and visually belonged in the house.

At Bernard's request, our friend Herbert Stein Schneider provided a huge Christmas tree for the holiday season. It fit nicely beside our double chimney and almost touched the cathedral ceiling. The girls and I did our best to enjoy Christmas, but with Bernard's absence it was very sad.

On January 12, Bernard came home from the hospital. The girls were excited about Papa's arrival at this house they had quickly come to love. Bernard was greeted by a blazing fire I had built in the fireplace. His books were still in cartons in the basement waiting for shelves to be constructed. Although Bernard's right kidney was functioning, urine from the left one emptied into a tube and bag coming out his side. It was my job to change

Lisette, Uncle Auguste, Bernard, and Aunt Marcelle in France, 1964.

the dressing, to clean the blood and pus around the tube and replace the dressing. On one occasion, I was momentarily called away before the bandage that held the tube in place was affixed. In my absence, the tube slipped out. An ambulance took Bernard to the hospital to have it reinserted. I felt terribly guilty. Eventually, when the ureters were recovered and the kidney functioning, the tube was removed.

Bernard went to France during two weeks in May both to see his family and to get a second opinion about the removal of his left kidney, but the experts there agreed with the Washington doctors. Bernard carried out more research at the French army files for his book on Dien Bien Phu. It was good that he had time with his aunt Marcelle, for she died five months later.

On June 20, 1964, Bernard entered George Washington University Hospital for removal of his left kidney. Three weeks later he danced with me until 1 a.m. at the French Veterans' Bastille Day Ball.

But his ordeal was not over. The following year, his colon was constricted because the fibrous tissue was still growing. In an exploratory operation on March 2 the tissue was snipped away and there were no more symptoms, but Bernard felt that he did not have long to live. It was an omen. Bernard had always attributed his mental and physical energy to his "machine," his rugged body. Now he feared that his machine was failing him. He felt that his days were numbered. He only worked harder. In the three years left to him he wrote dozens of articles and his most important book.

14

SURVEILLANCE

THE FBI surveillance of Bernard picked up in earnest in 1963. We became aware of it in stages. First, there were hints of it in odd sounds on our telephone, mail that was late, and men who sat in parked cars outside our house for hours. Friends in government told us of interviews by the FBI and of high-level efforts to discredit Bernard.

I first tried in 1979 to obtain Bernard's FBI file. After several years, a totally blacked-out copy, and an unsuccessful appeal to the courts, I gave up. Then in 1995, I saw in the paper that President Clinton had ordered the FBI to be more forthcoming with such files. I tried again and this time, after five years of negotiations, was given some two thousand pages of documents that of course had many names and facts blacked out. The story these documents tell is outrageous. It was clear how extensive and intrusive the government snooping had been.

One early memo—the FBI blacked out the date—said that back in 1959, "Office of Naval Intelligence advised that subject [Bernard] had been a guest speaker before a class of the Military Assistance Institute during which subject unjustly criticized the Military Assistance Advisory Group in Viet-Nam." Despite this unjust criticism, the memo noted that "subject was described as a strong anticommunist."

This early 1963 memo ended with an "observation": "Regardless of the fact that the subject is employed as a professor at Howard University, Washington, D.C., in view of the allegations received, it is felt we should intensify our investigation. In this regard, it is believed WFO [Washington Field Office] should determine if misur [a microphone] and tesur [a phone tap] can be instituted on the subject's residence and WFO should employ spot fisurs [physical surveillance] of subject where warranted, not on the campus of Howard University, to determine his activities."

All this, the memo concluded, was "to determine if he is engaged in intelligence activities for the French Intelligence Service." In other words, they were afraid that this very public man, who spoke to U.S. military training programs and wrote for the *Saturday Evening Post*, was a French spy. If so, he was the most conspicuous spy in history.

In those days, J. Edgar Hoover sent letters to the attorney general to obtain approval for both "misur" and "tesur" surveillance. The attorney general from early 1961 to early 1964 was Robert Kennedy.

A July 1963 memo said: "We are instructing Washington Field Office (WFO) to conduct surveys for a microphone (misur) and technical (tesur) surveillance coverage of subject's residence and to utilize physical surveillance (fisur) of subject where warranted." Subsequent memos promised to "conduct spot check fisurs [physical surveillance, i.e., watching our home]," as well as making "attempts to develop neighborhood and other sources against subject," carrying out a new mail cover, and searching through our trash. An August 30, 1963, memo said that while it was "technically not feasible" to install a microphone in our house, the phone tap would be possible. A later memo reported that as of 11:00 a.m. on September 18, "tesur" [a phone tap] on our house in Virginia was "effective" and "maximum security assured." Other memos discussed obtaining a picture of Bernard, a sample of his handwriting, and "results of Civil Service investigation of subject's wife."

One memo revealed that back in May 1958 the FBI had discussed a mail cover, when we were living in a large apartment building at 4000 Massachusetts Avenue, N.W. However, mail there was delivered in bulk and not "broken down" until later. Thus, because of "possible embarrassment" the request was denied for the time being.

A September 1963 memo noted that Bernard and I were flying Air France to Algeria (for his interviews of Dien Bien Phu veterans), and noted that "because it was a government-run airline, any inquiry at Air France at this time could not be made discreetly."

A memo in October of 1963 noted that one of the FBI's informants was talking to Bernard on the phone when "there was a distinctive sound of interference on the line. FALL commented: 'That is the FBI cutting in. They are changing tapes. I am joking, I hope.'" The memo continued, in the FBI's inimitable deadpan style: "No particular significance is attributed to these comments other than an alertness on FALL's part that he should maintain guarded telephonic communications."

As this suggests, we were not oblivious to the snooping, although it became more clear later. At the time, I wondered why the wife of a navy officer who lived nearby would come tripping in at all hours of the day to see what we were doing, although I suspected it was to flirt with Bernard. Later I thought she was one of the "neighborhood sources" the FBI had recruited. Our daughter Elisabeth remembers that after we moved into Washington in Christmas of 1963, when she came home from school she would often see a blue car with a man sitting in it parked diagonally across the street from our house. He would sit there for hours.

An October 1963 memo advised that "a confidential informant, who has furnished reliable information in the past"—a favorite FBI phrase—had reported that Bernard "has been invited to lunch with Senator George McGovern on Friday, October 18, 1963, to discuss South Viet-Nam." Another October memo listed the mail Bernard had received in August and September, much of it from various U.S. government agencies sending him books and information he had requested.

The memos make clear FBI Director J. Edgar Hoover's direct involvement in the surveillance. Late in 1963, Hoover sent a memo to the agent in charge of the Washington Field Office that began: "Pursuant to your request there are enclosed Photostats of uncertified income tax returns of the subject and his wife for the years 1958 through 1962." The memo ended by saying the tax returns had been obtained from the IRS "to determine if there is any indication he was receiving [blacked out] in the United States." Probably they hoped to prove that Bernard was being paid by the French government. Or maybe they just wanted to make sure he was paying his taxes, with an eye to prosecution if he was not.

A memo from Hoover to his Washington office in December of 1963, when the girls and I moved to our new home in northwest Washington—Bernard was in the hospital—gave permission to install a phone tap there and to find out if a microphone could also be installed. A few weeks later the Washington office reported: "Subject's new home is constantly occupied by his wife, two small daughters, and a French maid who has a room in the home. One additional maid (probably part time) has recently been seen. [The "French maid" was our au pair. The other "maid" cleaned the house once a week.] To date secure access cannot be obtained to premises. It is possible that after subject has rested at home and returns to work, WFO, with aid of tesur [the phone tap] recently instituted on subject, can secure access to his home. If such conditions are found at a future date, Bureau will be advised and request submitted for a survey provided status of case then justifies same."

Bernard's sharp tongue gave the FBI plenty of spicy quotes to contemplate. Another memo that fall quotes Bernard telling an informant, with regard to an article by pro-war columnist Joseph Alsop, that Alsop is "the same stupid ass he always was." Alsop was famous among the younger reporters in Vietnam for visiting the country briefly, hobnobbing with generals, and writing about his trips "to the front," when one central point of the war was that it was what the French called "la guerre sans fronts"— a war without fronts.

Other FBI memos in the spring of 1964 quoted Bernard's criticisms of Secretary of Defense Robert McNamara, the former Ford president whose analytical genius was supposed to assure victory in Vietnam. In one public appearance, Bernard said that McNamara could return from his occasional trips to Vietnam "without making a fool of himself every time" but had not yet done so, because he never managed to learn anything when he was there. Another time, the FBI quoted Bernard as saying that McNamara and other top officials "do not know the kind of war we are in, what our goals are, or what 'victory' is." Truer words were rarely spoken.

Another report quoted Bernard telling an audience that McNamara had "covered himself with shame in Viet-Nam. . . . McNamara perhaps thinks he is not lying since he probably believes that, up until now, we have been winning in Viet-Nam." Another memo quoted Bernard as saying that McNamara "swallowed a lot of nonsense and now has a rude awakening." Years later, McNamara was viewed by some as a tragic figure for his role in the Vietnam disaster. It's a shame that he and others didn't listen to Bernard when it might have helped them grasp the reality they faced.

A June 11, 1964, memo quotes an informant, apparently a friend of Bernard's, reporting what Bernard had told him about his upcoming operation on his kidneys. The memo says that FBI agents, parked on our block, had seen the informant enter our house at 3:07 p.m. Then, "Fall had been seen just prior to this washing cars in front of his residence and to enter same at 2:46 p.m." Ah, the secret agent, trying to blend into his environment by washing his car.

As the surveillance became obvious, I sometimes felt like a character in a spy novel. Someone was after us. I was careful about what I said on the telephone. When I got into my car and put the key in the ignition, my paranoia would kick in and I would wonder if the car might explode.

FBI agents attended Bernard's lectures around the country, reporting breathlessly on opinions and criticisms that he proudly expressed in articles and many other lectures. Even at Howard, Bernard and his students believed that FBI agents sat in on his classes. Given the FBI's history of racism, they must have thought Howard a hotbed of Communist activity. Former graduate student Hanes Walton recalled for me that in his evening class on the politics of Southeast Asia, "Dr. Fall would always have these people from the CIA or State Department and he would point them out to us. Dr. Fall would say, 'I see we have people from the CIA.' They would look embarrassed. There were anywhere from three to five of them. It was a frequent occurrence. They were white and they really stood out in the class where all the students were African American or from Africa." Actually, they were probably FBI, not CIA.

One memo stated that we sometimes entertained diplomats from the French Embassy, which of course was true. Another said that in my work at USIA I should not have access to classified material. I didn't, of course—we didn't deal in secrets.

An official of the U.S. Agency for International Development, whom we had known in Cambodia, asked Bernard to have lunch with him and another AID official who was going to Vietnam. The idea was for Bernard to brief the man about what he might expect there. The three of them had a friendly lunch in a crowded restaurant. A few days later, our friend had a visit from three FBI agents who knew all about the lunch and exactly what had been discussed. One reason for such an exercise is intimidation. It would not encourage a government employee to have lunch with Bernard.

It apparently was a matter of great concern to the FBI that, even as they snooped on Bernard, high-ranking military officers continued to regard him as an expert on counterinsurgency and to invite him to speak to Army personnel. They seemed to think this raised questions about the loyalties of the military officers involved. On February 11, 1964, the agent in charge of the Washington field office sent Hoover a memo saying: "The Bureau is requested to consider requesting G-2, Army Intelligence, to interview [blacked out] and [blacked out] to determine the nature and purpose of their contacts with subject [Bernard]. It should be determined by G-2 whether or not these officers have access to classified [blacked out] information in their present assignments and if they have furnished any information to subject which would be considered classified or which could be used by subject in his lectures or writings to the detriment of the United States."

The memo closed by saying it was classified SECRET because "disclosure of the Bureau's investigative interest in French intelligence activities could result in serious harm to the national defense interest."

This is a classic example of guilt-by-association at Hoover's

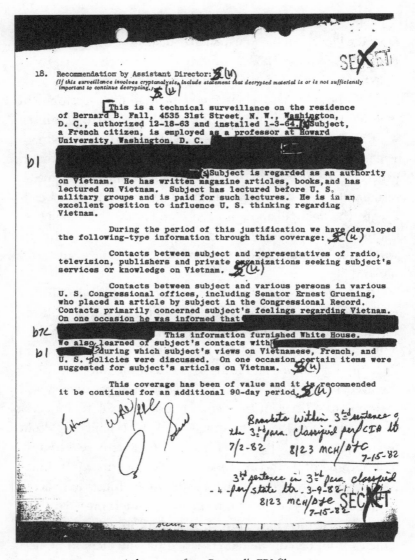

A document from Bernard's FBI file.

FBI. Unable to find anything on Bernard, they proposed to investigate the military officers who had invited him to lecture.

An FBI memo from April of 1964 made clear how the FBI and senior military officials conspired to cut Bernard off from the commanders who wanted to make use of his knowledge. It

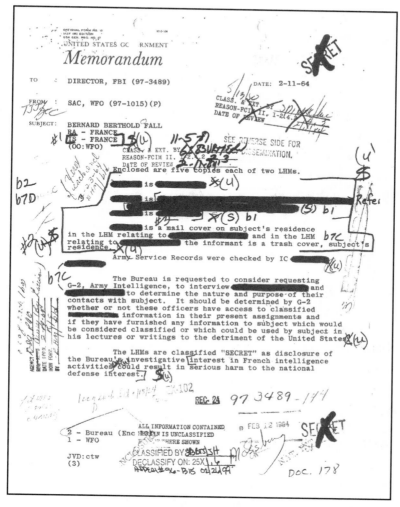

Another document from Bernard's FBI file.

explained that Thomas Fox, an official of the Defense Intelligence Agency, "advised that DIA was taking action to 'dry up' Fall's sources in the Defense Department and the military. All individuals who have been dealing with Fall are to be instructed that they are to have no further contact with him and he is not to be used for briefings or lectures before Defense groups or at Defense schools. The Bureau will not be mentioned by DIA in this matter and the individuals approached will be told that the Secretary of Defense considers it unwise for them to closely associate with a foreign national. No word will be given to Fall, he will just not be asked to participate in any Defense programs."

I spoke with two military men who were pressured to cut off relations with Bernard. Walter Kersey had met Bernard at SAIS during the summer of 1952. He later became an Army officer and in November 1963 was assigned to the psychological warfare school in Saigon. He thought the U.S. military personnel there would benefit from reading *Street Without Joy* and other books that dealt with counter insurgency. In 1964 he wrote to Bernard suggesting that if Bernard would send him five copies of each of his books, he would send Bernard copies of the *Saigon News*, a weekly newspaper. Bernard agreed and the exchange took place. Counter intelligence came to see Kersey and he showed them what he was sending. He was told that "Fall is not a reliable source. He is biased." Years later he told me, "If I did not want to lose my top secret clearance, I was to cease contact with him. It seemed to be something that carried over from the Nuremberg trials or the war. They felt that he represented the Communist point of view."

In another instance, on August 6, Maj. Gen. William P. Yarborough, the commanding general of the Special Forces School, home of the Green Berets, at Fort Bragg, North Carolina, wrote to FBI assistant director William Sullivan:

Dear Mr. Sullivan,

My G-2 informs me that your local FBI representative expressed interest in the recent visit of Dr. Bernard B. Fall to the USA John F. Kennedy Center for Special Warfare. . . . Official FBI interest in Dr. Fall is of concern to me, particularly because he has been an effective and interesting guest speaker and one who has contributed much to the edification of our students in our regular course as well as those high ranking officers attending the Senior Officers' course.

This is not the first time Dr. Fall has been here, and I hope not the last time that we would have had him here as a guest speaker. I am sure you know that Dr. Fall has spoken to other distinguished audiences at the Industrial College and similar gatherings.

If within bounds of your security you can release to me your specific interest in Dr. Fall, I would appreciate knowing the reasons behind . . . [your] queries. If this is not possible, do you have any official or unofficial advice from the FBI regarding the continued use of Dr. Fall here to augment our instruction with one of the best authorities and expertise available in the USA today on the North Vietnamese.

Sincerely,
General William P. Yarborough
Major General, USA
Commanding

J. Edgar Hoover himself responded, writing to General Yarborough that "I have taken the liberty of bringing your requests to the attention of the Assistant Chief of Staff for Intelligence Department of the Army and you should be hearing from that office concerning Mr. Fall in the immediate future."

In other words, since General Yarborough had questioned the FBI's objections to a man he considered an expert on military issues, Hoover—rather than answer his questions—attempted to intimidate the general by contacting his superiors at the Pentagon.

The Pentagon officials did write General Yarborough a letter that said in part:

Through established and reliable sources, we have learned he [Bernard] has been critical of U.S. military efforts in Vietnam and that he has supported the French Government's position in Vietnam of negotiation between the interested parties. He is in an excellent position to influence U.S. thinking on our efforts in Vietnam through his published writings and speaking appearances. The Defense Intelligence Agency, the Pentagon, Washington, D.C., advised the Bureau in April 1964 that it was issuing instructions to the U.S. Military services that Fall was not to be used for briefings or lectures before Defense groups or at Defense schools.

In spite of these pressures, General Yarborough continued to have Bernard speak at the Special Forces school at Fort Bragg. On July 29–30 of 1964 I accompanied him there. After his lecture, we watched a military exercise that included an airborne operation. It was an amazing experience for me, watching the soldiers preparing for action in Vietnam. It was Bernard's world, not mine.

In 1998 I visited with General Yarborough and his wife at their home in Southern Pines, North Carolina. He told me, "Bernard Fall was one of the acknowledged experts on Southeast Asia, Vietnam, Indochina. He was certainly one of those who had the necessary background, understanding, and expertise to help us and so, very early in the game, I contacted him along with other types that had been with the British in Malaya. Certainly, we wanted to know what had happened at Dien Bien Phu and places like that and Bernard Fall had a grasp of the whole, not only physical environment, but psychological and political environment. I had read *Street Without Joy* and I felt that the lessons for the U.S. Army in *Street Without Joy* were many." When his superiors in the Department of the Army said he should cut off relations with Bernard, the general said, "If you don't want him to come you'll have to put it in writing because we've learned more from him than from any half a dozen other guests that I can remember." They never did.

During my visit with General and Mrs. Yarborough, I learned that he too was an artist. He showed me paintings, colorful organic forms in acrylics. He kindly offered me my choice of two of his works, which I now have hanging in my home.

On October 10, 1964, the FBI discontinued its telephone surveillance. On February 25, 1965, they wrote, "Our investigation of subject has developed no evidence to indicate he [Bernard] is engaged in any intelligence activities against the U.S. government. Although in frequent contact with military personnel, members of Congress, and government officials, there has been no indication that he has solicited intelligence information.

> Since intensive investigation has failed to develop any admissible evidence which indicates subject has acted on behalf of the French, either for intelligence or propaganda purposes, it is felt the only logical investigation which could yet be conducted would be an interview of subject.
> In the event the bureau finds an interview of the subject could be a cause of embarrassment, noting his own occupation as author and lecturer as well as the current delicate situation in Vietnam, in which an interview with him at this time might be construed by subject or others as politically motivated, since he has criticized U.S. Government policy, WFO [Washington Field Office] will consider closing this investigation.

On April 22, 1965, two agents did come to our house to interview Bernard. I later read their summary of the discussion in his FBI file. It was a long and generally accurate account of his life and work, as he related it to the agents. It says in part: "[H]e considers his position as a permanent resident of the United States as such that he can criticize the United States from the viewpoint of a scholar, but that any attack political in nature would be morally indefensible since he is a guest of the United States." It was a distinction that was important to Bernard but that clearly did not impress the FBI or the Johnson administration.

As this ordeal had progressed, Bernard had expressed indignation at the false accusations and at the lack of respect for his efforts at informing the American public and the military. He rarely showed it, but I knew these pressures were agonizing to him. There was always the fear that the FBI could somehow force him to leave the country that had become his home. Even during the final interview, he was angry at being subjected to what he considered humiliating questioning. But the FBI investigation was over. There would still be an occasional item added to his file, when this or that person reported Bernard's criticisms of the war or the government, but the active snooping had stopped.

The years of surveillance had been heavy-handed at best and stupid at worst. If Bernard had been a spy or even a propagandist, he would surely have gone underground or at least changed his tune. It is likely that the FBI was less interested in proving espionage than in intimidating Bernard. Many people, without his courage and his connections, would have surrendered to the pressure. Certainly, as its own memo concedes, one reason the FBI finally backed off was its fear that because of Bernard's widespread contacts with radio, television, and newspaper personalities, he could make trouble.[1]

The FBI's powers to harass and intimidate are deadly serious, but in the execution they are sometimes comic. You get the impression that the agents, busily employed in digging through our trash and watching Bernard wash the car, didn't know South Vietnam from South Dakota. They were just bureaucrats doing what J. Edgar Hoover wanted them to do, seeing Communists behind every bush.

On January 31, 1965, Bernard was interviewed on *Meet the Press*. It was the biggest forum for his views since his *Saturday Evening Post* article more than two years earlier. The panelists were Robert Goralski of NBC News, Marguerite Higgins of *Newsday*, Peter Lisagor of the *Chicago Daily News*, and Lawrence E. Spivak, founder of the program and permanent panel member. The interview came in the aftermath of President Johnson's landslide election victory and at a time when he was starting a massive buildup in Vietnam. The panelists asked good questions and

Bernard responded with candid answers that went far beyond the official clichés about "saving Vietnam" and "stopping Communism."

Spivak asked the first question: What were the American "illusions" in Vietnam that Bernard had written about?

Bernard replied that the first illusion was thinking that an insurgency is mainly a military operation, rather than a political problem. He continued, "The second illusion has been that the defeats in Vietnam, as they have occurred over the past five years, can be ascribed to any particular group, whether it is the Buddhists or the students or let's say incapable Vietnamese military leaders. That too is an illusion. The faults, the mistakes, go far deeper than that."

Bernard added that one U.S. mistake was to put forth President Diem "as a man deeply interested in democracy. Diem was a dictator, and Diem failed to recognize precisely that one of his problems was lack of contact and progressive loss of contact with his own people."

Asked if the U.S. could win in Vietnam: "I would say the United States has the wherewithal to stay in Vietnam if she so desires. The whole point is, of course, what is the price tag?" Later, on the question of "winning," he added, "Neither side can win. This is going to be one of those guerrilla stand-offs, of which we have several on record."

Bernard dismissed the "domino theory," and said of American interests in Vietnam: "I would say American interests are involved. Whether vital or not, I don't think so."

He pointed out the French in Vietnam and Algeria, and the British in Cyprus, as examples of counterinsurgency efforts that failed either militarily or because they became too expensive or too unpopular. When Ms. Higgins pointed out that the United States was not a "colonial power" as the French had been, Bernard pointed out that this was true, but it was a distinction lost on the Vietcong fighter who had Americans shooting at him.

Bernard agreed that U.S. bombing could do great harm to

North Vietnam, but, "it is militarily meaningless. This is exactly it. All we would do is knock out factories which the Communists did not have in 1954 when they defeated the French, and all we would get in return is probably fourteen Communist divisions down our necks in South Vietnam."

Meet the Press enabled Bernard to reach concerned Americans across the country. The response was electric—requests for speaking engagements, calls from senators and congressmen, more interviews on television and in print. Bernard felt a new respect and a far greater audience. Perhaps this contributed to the FBI calling off its investigation.

After his appearance on *Meet the Press*, Bernard was increasingly called upon to write for national publications, but one major exception was the *Washington Post*. Bernard had previously written three articles on Vietnam, the last one on November 5, 1964. After that, managing editor Alfred Friendly, with whom Bernard dealt, rejected his articles. The *Post*, at that time, was supportive of the war. Bernard was angry and frustrated to be denied access to his prestigious hometown newspaper, with its influential readership among policymakers and journalists. We wondered if *Post* editors had been influenced by the hostile stories that the FBI and others in government were spreading about Bernard.

In the summer of 1980, I chanced to sit next to Alfred Friendly at lunch at a friend's house in the country. There was much discussion of politics. At one point, Friendly quietly turned to me and said, "I always regretted that I refused to publish your husband's articles."

I was too stunned to reply.

15

TO TEST ONESELF

Against his doctor's orders, and over my objections, Bernard insisted on returning to Vietnam during the summer of 1965. As he said once that year, "You cannot keep up your convictions if you don't base them on things that you have witnessed for yourself. Or, if you want to change your convictions, you had better do it on the basis of your own experience. So this is why I'm going back out there." He often spoke of his need to see things "first-hand" and obtain the "hard facts." The latter was a term he used relentlessly.

His health was a matter of grave concern. He still needed mandelamine pills to keep the infection in his remaining kidney under control, and cortisone to fight the inflammation. It caused his face to swell. I was fearful for his kidney as well as of the larger dangers of the war zone. I pleaded with him not to go into combat areas, not to exert himself or expose himself to disease. Yes, he vowed, he would be careful. Naively, I believed him. He was drawn not only by his need for research, but by the thrills, the danger, and the camaraderie of the war zone, the need to prove he could still be a soldier and could produce huge quantities of written material at the same time.

Bernard was able to enter Vietnam now, I think, both because Diem was dead and because of his increased celebrity. Bernard went armed with letters from the *New Republic*, the *New York Times Magazine*, and *Time*, all saying that he was on assignment for them. The *New York Times Magazine* was interested in a piece on the chances of ending the war in Vietnam as a result of the huge U.S. military buildup. *Time* had offered to pay his expenses should he succeed in again obtaining a visa to North Vietnam, in exchange for a first look at whatever he wrote about the trip. (He never got the visa.) And Gil Harrison of the *New Republic*, a fierce opponent of the war, would take all the pieces Bernard could send him.

Bernard put forth the usual bribe and took the girls and me to France before he set off. In Paris, he met with Mai Van Bo, the representative of the National Liberation Front of Vietnam, who expressed little or no interest in peace negotiations. Then he was off for Vietnam.

Upon my return to Washington, I had a letter from Dan Cordtz of the *Wall Street Journal*, who was writing at the request of Robert Kennedy, who had been elected U.S. senator from New York. He said Kennedy had just read *The Two Viet-Nams*, and felt it was the best thing written about the war. He said Kennedy had been quoting Bernard in his speeches and wanted to meet with him. I told him that was not possible, with Bernard on his way to Southeast Asia. I could only think that Kennedy's newfound enthusiasm for Bernard was a far cry from the time, not so far back, when he had approved the FBI wiretap on our telephone.[1]

Bernard wrote from Phnom Penh on August 10 that he was taking his medication and drinking a lot of liquids. He said the city was more beautiful than ever. It had changed, however, in that Prince Sihanouk had expelled the Americans three months earlier, in May, because of air space violations by U.S. aircraft and because of ground fighting between ARVN (South Vietnamese) and Vietcong troops along the Cambodian border. Bernard said the absence of the Americans was reflected in smaller cars and less traffic.

Attempting to reassure me, he wrote, "Dorothy, I feel so good here away from the damn rat race and in the midst of sane people." He declared himself in good shape and added that the next day he was driving down to the Vietnamese border to see what was happening. He did in fact drive to the Vietnamese border and walk across, and wrote to me about it. "I went to the market, bought a Vietnamese product as proof and walked right back into Cambodia." He said a Cambodian border commander told him, "Look at the VN army post there (a mile away)—they're so scared of the VCs they don't even come out and patrol the boundary. And look at the special housing for the 10 U.S. advisors. They get brought in and out by helicopter. Nobody patrols."

Bernard had often said that the South Vietnamese army did not fight well because the soldiers had no real motivation to fight. Here, at the border, he'd gotten one more piece of evidence to support his charge.

He went with a provincial governor to the border area where Cambodia had claimed the U.S. had violated its neutrality: "And as I stood there with the provincial governor, there was a mighty roar and *five* US F-105s came right over us! A charming shrug from the governor: 'You see, we arranged even a border violation for you.'"

Bernard had an audience with Prince Sihanouk during

which, among other things, he told the prince about U.S. Army Captain Humbert Rocque (Rocky) Versace, who was believed to be a prisoner of the Vietcong. Versace's mother, writer Tere Rios Versace of Baltimore, had asked Bernard to help. Her son was a Special Forces captain who spoke Vietnamese and French, an outstanding young man who had served in Vietnam for two years and had planned, when leaving the military, to become a priest, and return to Vietnam to work with children. But he had been taken prisoner and his mother had been told that he and other VC prisoners were dragged through the jungle by ropes around their necks.

Bernard had told Tere that he would discuss the matter with Prince Sihanouk, who had a relationship with the National Liberation Front. Bernard kept his promise and the prince said that as a personal favor to Bernard he would take the soldier's case up with the NLF. Bernard wrote me this and I relayed the message to Tere.

Bernard left Cambodia for Vietnam on August 15. I was to send him mail care of Charles Mohr, an outstanding reporter with the *New York Times*. Bernard said he had the full cooperation of reporters like Mohr and Neil Sheehan. Sheehan later wrote, "Bernie was using the *Times* office as a kind of Saigon headquarters. I took a call for him from one of the public affairs officers at General Westmoreland's command. Since Bernie had been in the country a couple of weeks, the officer said, General Westmoreland was wondering why he had not requested an interview. I relayed the message. 'Tell him I'm spending my time in the field trying to find out what's really going on,' Bernie replied. 'I'll call for an interview just before I leave if there's still time to spare.'"[2]

Bernard wrote to me that upon his arrival in Saigon François Sully found a room for him at an acceptable rate. "It *must* be a brothel. In any case it sure looks like it."

He took off with Sully on a night helicopter mission with the 197 Helicopter Company, an operation called Skunk Hunting. The idea was that one helicopter would draw fire and others would respond to VC firing from the ground:

> It's a newfangled thing: one helicopter with a set of projectors [searchlights] flies at low level along a road or river and tries to pick up sampans or carriers. Other choppers fly alongside, completely darkened, and open fire with machine guns and rockets on the target.
>
> We went with the choppers, Sully and I, northeast to Zone D. The eerie light of the projector meandered up the Donnai River as we flew above and alongside: in the rear of the thing and with the doors wide open. We wore nylon body armor and sat on steel armor plates. (I hugged my kidney.) No helmets, though. There weren't enough to go around, but the shots come from the bottom anyway. Saigon soon disappeared and all that was left was a pitch-black jungle and the deafening noise and the red instrument panel lights of the pilots. On both sides of us were the chopper gunners, looking like Martians with their huge goggles, round helmets, body armor, and intercom wires.
>
> And then the 'lightship' picked up an elongated shadow—a sampan. At that hour of the night it could only be VC. The engine noise deadened the roar of the rockets as they streaked down. And then the left gunner leaned over. 'They're firing at us,' he said. But the sampan disappeared. The mission later was termed unsuccessful by the pilots.

That letter was my first indication that Bernard had no intention of avoiding danger on this trip. I received many more like it. He wrote of the excitement, the thrill of the battles. He was the old Bernard, intoxicated with his experiences, reliving the death-defying moments of his youth. It was like an addiction I feared he would never overcome.

Next he spent two days in the Mekong Delta with John Paul Vann, the legendary soldier that Neil Sheehan, in his book *A*

Bright Shining Lie, later revealed to be not entirely the hero he was first thought to be. Bernard wrote that the Army had flown him out to Hau-Nghia via helicopter, then he and Vann had driven all over the province and to Saigon. He said they went to places that neither the Vietnamese army nor U.S. advisors had been to without heavy convoys or helicopters. "Between Vann and me we had a Colt .45, a carbine, and six grenades, and we just roared over the washboard unpaved roads at 120 KM/H hoping to be missed but probably (of course we did) enjoying the whole goddamned dare . . . and *he* has *five* kids. Darling, I haven't felt so good since 1962. I walk a lot, have my wind back, resist the heat extremely well, have a good tan, sleep a lot (alone, dammit)."

Is this crazy or what? He has to do this to feel great? What was I thinking? Was I joining him in saving the world? Was his mission to warn the country more important than his children and me? Was I so without backbone that he and I were ready to sacrifice ourselves for this insane war that he knew we would never win? Or was it his search for the camaraderie, for the last hurrah? He must be thinking that if he were to die soon anyway, why not in the thrill of battle.

On August 24 he flew northward on a military plane. He wrote to me about the coastline—magnificent beaches, totally deserted, and few fishing boats to be seen. He said that Nha Trang, once a sleepy harbor town, now had "100,000 people— 60 percent refugees from outlying areas. And its airfield looks like Idlewild. The U.S. buildup here is truly fantastic, beyond all proportions. One simply has no idea in the U.S. This *is* a war and, unless somebody does something about it, it's going to make Korea look like a Sunday outing."

The next morning he proceeded to Cam Ranh Bay, another huge new Army base. Again he wrote that it was incredibly large and expensive. Mountains were being leveled, he said, and a port as big as the one in Charleston, South Carolina, was being built.

He hitched another ride in a U.S. helicopter from which,

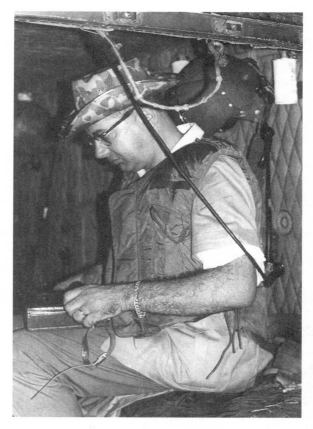

Bernard prepares to go up in a bomber, summer 1965.

only a few hundred feet up, he could see "his" Road 19, of "his" Mobile Group 100 that he had immortalized in *Street Without Joy*. Below, white and tiny, he could see the marker for the dead French soldiers who fought there. Now, he said, the area was mostly held by the Vietcong.

On August 26 he and Charlie Mohr joined a day-long reconnaissance patrol with "E" troop, Seventeenth Cavalry, 173 Airborne Brigade, in the north, near Konbrai. The force included 148 soldiers, thirteen jeeps armed with machine guns and 106mm recoilless guns, five armored personnel carriers, two 105mm howitzers, and two reconnaissance planes. "Look for Aug 27, 28, or 29. You'll find the stories under Charlie's byline." By the time

211

Bernard's letter arrived I had already seen the stories and was again furious. Mohr wrote:

> On February 9, 1954, during the French Indochina war, a French platoon was almost wiped out and a lieutenant named de Bellefont was killed about six miles northeast of Kontoum on Route 5.
>
> Today troops of the 17th cavalry, part of the independent 173d Airborne Brigade, moved with 106-mm. recoilless rifles cautiously into the same gorge where the French had been ambushed. Until this morning not one of the Americans in the detachment had known of the 1954 battle, but with them was Bernard Fall, a professor of political science at Howard University and student of the Indochina War.
>
> Mr. Fall, author of a book on the war titled *Street Without Joy*, had written of Lieutenant de Bellefont's fate and he told the respectfully attentive Americans of the story.[3]

The piece goes on to say that as the U.S. force advanced, they fired shells into the hills on each side of the road. Something looked suspicious and two men were sent ahead to investigate. The article rather frighteningly ended there.

Mohr later completed his story with a light-hearted description of how correspondents behaved during an ambush: "Near Kontoum author Bernard Fall and I found ourselves in a mild road ambush and raced each other to a ditch where I fell into a nice hole concealed by bushes while Fall had to flatten himself on the hard bare ground. This led Fall to comment on 'my natural talent for self preservation.'"[4]

In a letter, Bernard gave me a more detailed account of the ambush. They had started at six thirty in the morning. The plan was to push northward along Road 14 and to secure the road to Dak-To, an abandoned district seat. He boasted that he felt "fit as a fiddle" and "covered 5 km in high-stand jungle, crawling in part on all fours up steep hills and down." Then:

Combat reconnaissance toward Konbrai with Troop "E," 17th Cavalry.
Left to right: Lieutenant Sawczm, Lieutenant Minnefield, Private First Class
Morey, New York Times Correspondent Charlie Mohr, and Bernard Fall,
August 26, 1965.

The VC had blown all the bridges ahead of us and even blocked the possible bypasses with felled trees. That is where the fuckup began—incredibly it took the Fourth Battalion four hours to clear the road. By then about seventy trucks had built up at the last unpassable crossing near half-way to Dak-To and it was 1700. That washed up the mission and it was decided to turn back. The column was totally disorganized, armor mixed in with civilian trucks, troops mixed in with coolies—and so on. Then the news came that two VC companies were on our flank, and you could hear the rattle of small-arms fire. We put two of our mortars into position. That operation (normally a matter of seconds) took 45 minutes. Needless to say, the VC didn't wait. We now moved back helter-skelter, with the trucks bunching up at every detour as fat targets for any sniper.

And at the last detour it finally happened. Our little pickup truck had just reached a sort of small pass and the infantry fire had steadily increased when, all of a sudden, we heard the characteristic zing-zzzingg of very close incoming fire and decided that discretion was the better part of valor. [This must be when he and Mohr took cover.] . . . Pandemonium reigned for a few minutes, though there were maybe 30 shots, all from rifles and carbines. Finally we got organized and got through. But I shudder at the thought of what would have happened had the VC brought an automatic rifle or machine gun up there.

It was so incongruous—a man so brilliant, with so much to live for—who eagerly placed himself in such danger.

Near the end of his trip, on September 2, Bernard wrote from the Mekong Delta that he was about to leave on another military operation. He added that he had been almost in tears when he heard the news that Rocky Versace had been seen a short time earlier with other American prisoners and seemed in good shape. He felt this meant the chances were good that he would be freed. I phoned Tere to give her the news, but in fact her son was not freed. Sadly, Bernard learned that he was executed by the VC later that month.

More letters arrived from Bernard detailing his adventures and joking about defying his doctors. He wrote that he might come home early and added: "I might even settle down yet (haha!)."

By then I was livid and wrote him a furious letter:

You obviously don't care about those who love you—only about yourself. As for Vann, I'm not interested in the fact that he has five children. I know that you have to prove to yourself that you are still healthy, but you don't have to go to that extreme. I hate your wars and killing—the things you really do love. I don't know why you ever left the army. When and *if* you get home, you'll hear more about this. You made a promise which you broke. You can't tell me you couldn't get enough information without going *all over* Viet-Nam and into the jungle. I was up worrying about you most of the night and actively considered divorcing you—which you would love anyway—but no such luck for you.

He returned safely, of course, and I didn't divorce him, and soon he was hard at work writing about what he had seen and learned. One of his articles appeared in the *New Republic* of October 9, and another in *Ramparts* in December. Both articles focused on the unprecedented amount of military might the United States was deploying. The *New Republic* article, in particular, was one of the most brilliant pieces Bernard ever wrote. Called "Blitz in Vietnam," it was later reprinted in *Reporting Vietnam*, the Library of America's collection of outstanding pieces on the war, along with work by David Halberstam, Neil Sheehan, Charles Mohr, Ward Just, Peter Arnett, and other distinguished correspondents.

Bernard, having been a guerrilla fighter, was awed, even stunned, by the force the United States could apply against the Communist guerrillas in Vietnam. He said of the killing power of the bombs dropped by American B-52s:

> Against that kind of slaughter, the teachings of Mao Tse-tung, superior tactics, popular support for the VC, or, conversely, poor motivation among the Arvins [the South Vietnamese army] and patent ineptness among many of their officers, and even the 'mess in Saigon' are totally irrelevant. If tomorrow morning Mickey Mouse became prime minister of South Vietnam it would have precious little influence on the men of the U.S. Army.

He continued by saying that the B-52 raids

> do one thing regardless of whether they hit a VC installation or a totally innocent and even pro-government village—they keep the Viet Cong on the move, day and night, in constant fear of being hit. Gone are the days of large and even comfortable jungle hospitals above ground; of the VC rest

camp with warm food, clean clothes, and a good swimming hole; of the large ammunition depot and weapons repair plant. . . . The heavy bombers have changed all that. The VC is hunted down like an animal. His wounded die unattended. A VC combat unit returns from an operation only to find its camp area destroyed and its painfully amassed rice and ammunition reserve shattered.

Bernard was clearly troubled by the spectacle of the greatest nation on earth bringing such power to bear on soldiers who wore sandals, rode bicycles, and were only fighting to control their own country. He wrote about the moral questions in such a war: "To me, the real moral problem which arises in Vietnam is that of torture and needless brutality to combatants and civilians alike." He wrote that few U.S. officers had any understanding of the rules of war and some argued that the VC were "traitors" who deserved to be shot on sight. He described various U.S. and South Vietnamese atrocities and pointed out that these only justified North Vietnamese torture and killing of U.S. prisoners, including U.S. pilots who were shot down. He mentioned a French general, "a much-decorated combat veteran, who resigned from his command in Algeria because, in his words, he was a paratrooper and not a Gestapo torturer."[5]

Whatever his moral concerns, he recognized that American military power meant that it could not lose militarily. He wrote that "the immense influx of American manpower and firepower, and the ruthless use of the latter, have made the South Vietnam war, in the *short run, militarily* 'unlosable.'"

But eventually, he warned, the U.S. had to decide whether to show statesmanship in seeking a nonmilitary solution or "fall prey to the attractiveness of its own deployed firepower." In the latter case, he warned, South Vietnam, "still in the hands of a politically irrelevant regime, may become the victim of aroused social and political forces for which no aircraft carrier and eight-jet bomber can provide a ready answer in the long run." In short, as he had said many times, Vietnam was ultimately a political problem.

Bernard's *Ramparts* piece explored some of these same themes but also described some of his adventures out with the soldiers:

It is a brutal war. . . . The impact of the war right now is not literally the killing of individuals by individuals—you do not often see heaps of the dead lying around. But what you do see is the impact on the countryside. In Asia the countryside is always lush, but now when you fly over parts of Vietnam you can see the dead, brown surface of the areas which have been sprayed with seed killers. You see the areas that were sprayed on purpose, and the places defoliated by accident. This picture is of a Catholic refugee village, Honai, along Highway 1 in South Vietnam. It was sprayed by mis-

Bernard in a Vietnamese village, 1965.

take. All its fruit trees died. United States Air Force planes were defoliating the jungle along highway 1, but the wind shifted and blew the killer spray towards the villages instead. In a supreme irony, the jungle now stands in the background, lush and thick, while the villages are barren. . . . The Vietnam conflict has become an impersonal, an American war. I was with an American airborne unit operating strictly on its own. There was not one Vietnamese with that unit.

He went on to describe a bombing mission on Saturday, September 11, in an area near the Cambodian border controlled by the Vietcong:

Our "Skyraider" was loaded with 750-pound napalm bombs and 500-pound napalm bombs plus our four 20-millimeter cannon. Our wing plane carried 7,500 pounds of high explosive anti-personnel bombs plus our four cannon. We were the lead plane going in. . . .

We were airborne for one and one half hours before we reached our primary target. But as we came over the target the monsoon came down with incredible force and completely obscured the ground. Then a decision was made, in accordance with established procedures, to switch over to the alternative target which was described as a 'Communist rest center' in the Camau Peninsula. A rest center may of course be anything, any group of huts, or it may be just a normal village in which Viet Cong troops have put down stake for, perhaps, 48 hours.

As we flew over the target it looked to me very much as any normal village would look: on the edge of a river, sampans and fish nets in the water. It was a peaceful scene. Major Carson put our plane into a steep dive. I could see the napalm bombs dropping from the wings. The big bombs, first. As we peeled back from our dive I took the picture you see here—an incredibly bright flash of fire as napalm exploded at the tree level. The first pass had a one-two effect. The napalm was expected to force the people—fearing the heat and burning—out into the open. Then the second plane was to move in with heavy fragmentation bombs to hit whatever—or whomever—had rushed out into the open. So our wingman followed us in and dropped his heavy explosives. Mushroom-like clouds drifted into the air. We made a second pass and dropped our remaining 500-pound napalm bombs. Then we went in a third time and raked over the village with the cannon. We came down low, flying very fast, and I could see some of the villagers trying to head away from the burning shore in their sampans. The village was burning fiercely. I will never forget the sight of the fishing nets in flame, covered with burning, jellied gasoline. Behind me I could hear—even through my padded helmet—the roar of the plane's 20-millimeter cannon as we flew away. . . .

There were probably between 1,000 and 1,500 people living in the fishing village we attacked. It is difficult to estimate how many were killed. It is equally difficult to judge if there actually were any Viet Cong in the village, and if so, if any were killed.

Bernard ended the article with this:

The incredible thing about Vietnam is that the worst is yet to come. We have been bombing for a relatively short time and the results are devastating. The United States is probably only operating at one percent capacity in Vietnam. Everything could be escalated vastly—in the North, major industrial targets, major towns, and then the irrigation dams; in the South, more powerful bombs on more vulnerable targets. (It is strictly a one-way operation in the South. The Viet Cong do not have a single flying machine. We can literally go anywhere and bomb anything. The possibilities of devastation are open-ended.)

He spoke finally of means and ends:

Looking back at the Vietnam I left, I can see the means only
too clearly, and so can everyone else who is not altogether
blind. But I cannot say that I have found anyone who seems
to have a clear idea of the end—of the "war aims"—and if
the end is not clearly defined, are we justified to use any
means to attain it?[6]

Both articles contained beautiful writing and brilliant reporting. They have a timeless quality, like Ernest Hemingway's
best writing on World War I. But were they worth the risk of
Bernard's life? The readers of *Ramparts* and the *New Republic* were
already against the war. Many other fine reporters tried to tell
the truth about Vietnam but our government and many of our
people didn't want to hear it. More than 50,000 young Americans had to die before our political leaders decided they had
done enough harm.

Bernard on a bombing run, camera in hand, 1965.

16

OPPOSING THE WAR

THROUGHOUT 1965, as the U.S. war effort in South Vietnam intensified, so did opposition to it at home. Liberals who admired President Lyndon Johnson's achievements on civil rights and his Great Society programs were deeply disturbed by rising American casualties in a small, poor, distant nation where we seemed to have no vital interest. Many people felt instinctively that the war was wrong, even when they knew little about Vietnam's history, culture, or politics.

In time, many leaders of the anti-war movement would emerge. Senator William Fulbright held early hearings, in his Foreign Relations Committee, which accused the administration of "the arrogance of power." Senator George McGovern was an early critic and in 1972 would lead a brave, but ill-fated, anti-war presidential campaign against President Richard Nixon. Robert Kennedy, as a newly-elected senator from New York, began to question the war he had once supported. Establishment figures like the Rev. William Sloane Coffin and Dr. Benjamin Spock spoke out in opposition to the war, and young radicals like Tom Hayden rallied students against it.

In many ways, Bernard became the intellectual leader of the budding anti-war movement. More than anyone else in the public eye, he knew Vietnam's history, knew its leaders and its politics, and knew the realities on the ground. The proponents of the war did their best to ignore him, but millions of people were looking for answers, and many found guidance in Bernard's lectures, articles, and books. It was an electrifying time, as many nonpolitical Americans felt compelled to speak out against the violence that was being carried out in their name. Increasingly, politicians and journalists flocked to our home to get ideas, news stories, or inspiration from Bernard.

A whirlwind of visitors arrived. Senators Edward Kennedy, George McGovern, or Frank Church might come by, or Congressmen Don Edwards and Jonathan Bingham. Walter Cronkite came one day, to discuss Bernard's script for a CBS documentary on Ho Chi Minh; my daughters found him lovable and had no idea that millions of others did too. One evening our dinner guests included Senator McGovern, *New York Times* columnist Tom Wicker, and Robert Komer, who had just been named President Johnson's special assistant on Vietnam, although he knew little about the country. Bernard lectured him at length on the realities he would encounter there, but to no avail—the *Times* would later write of Komer's "deathless optimism that the war could be won" when he headed the "pacification program" there.[1]

Bernard had a bigger impact on another young policymaker he met that summer. Our friend Vince Davis, a professor of international relations at the University of Denver, was spending his annual two weeks of active duty as a Naval Reserve officer at the Pentagon. He was assigned to help a young analyst named Daniel Ellsberg prepare material on Vietnam for his boss, Assistant Secretary of Defense John McNaughton.

One morning, Ellsberg asked Vince who was the leading American scholar on Vietnam. Vince replied, "There's only one valid expert, Bernard Fall."

Ellsberg said he wanted to meet Bernard, so Davis picked up the phone. They arrived at our house at three that afternoon. Bernard escorted them down to his study, where an intense discussion went on for six hours, with no break for dinner, until the three men finally came upstairs at nine. Vince later told me he thought the afternoon had been an epiphany for Ellsberg:

Bernard discusses a documentary about Ho Chi Minh with Walter Cronkite, 1965.

"It was an intellectual awakening. He was too smart not to know that a lot of stuff he was hearing around the Pentagon was fallacious, deceptive, wrong. Yet he adored McNamara, who was his idol, an intellectual genius, but he [McNamara] was totally ignorant of the history of this culture, this society, the general circumstances of this part of the world, although he thought he was not. Dan said to me, 'You absolutely must get Bernard in to talk to McNamara.'"

Bernard never talked to McNamara, but Ellsberg became famous in 1971 when, risking serious legal consequences, he leaked the Pentagon Papers to several newspapers, including the *New York Times* and the *Washington Post*.

It was during this period that Bernard and Marc Raskin, the cofounder of the Institute for Policy Studies, compiled their *Viet-Nam Reader*. Their guiding principle was that if they could get enough information out to the American people those readers would see the folly of the war and demand a negotiated settlement. More than a dozen publishers rejected their book proposal, on the theory that the war was not important, not interesting, or not likely to last long. Finally, Marc called Jason Epstein, a highly regarded editor at Random House, and told him, "You have to publish this book!" He did.

The anthology covers a full spectrum of points of view about the war: Lyndon Johnson on American goals; Mao Tse-tung's comments in an interview with Edgar Snow; diaries of Vietcong soldiers; essays by Charles de Gaulle, McGeorge Bundy, Robert McNamara, J. W Fulbright, I. F. Stone, Chalmers Roberts, and North Vietnamese Premier Pham Van Dong. Marc and Bernard coauthored a final chapter on how to achieve a negotiated peace. That chapter was printed in the *New York Review of Books* of September 17, 1965. The *Viet-Nam Reader* became the bible of the teach-in movement.

Another friend in those days was Gilbert Harrison, the editor of the *New Republic*, who published at least eight of Bernard's articles between 1962 and 1967. Gil was obsessed by the war. Many years later, he told me: "I remember going to the White

House and begging McGeorge Bundy, *begging him*, to back off. 'This is a hopeless proposition,' [I said]. They smiled at you, a condescending smile as if to say, 'Well of course, we know things you don't know.' They weren't rude. They were just condescending. The atmosphere was poisonous. I remember [my wife] Nancy and I being invited to dinner at some journalist's house and I was seated across the table from Chal Roberts, who was chief diplomatic correspondent for the *Washington Post*. In the middle of the dinner he suddenly stood up, pointed his finger at me and said, 'You're a traitor!'"

Another good friend and ally in 1965 was Sanford (Sandy) Gottlieb, director of the National Committee for a Sane Nuclear Policy (SANE). Sandy and Bernard would talk and share information several times each week. He recalls, "Bernard was a fountain of knowledge and information and research on Vietnam. I depended on him a very great deal for background, for information, for counsel, for advice. He talked to hundreds of people. Most of them were starting from zero. None of them had the background to deal with the issues."

Sandy recalled one pivotal event in the escalation: "One early morning in February 1965, I was awakened by a phone call from Bernard. He said, 'They've done it. They've started bombing North Vietnam.'"

On February 7, Pleiku, in the Central Highlands of South Vietnam, had been attacked by Vietcong guerrillas. Eight Americans were killed and 126 were wounded. White House advisor McGeorge Bundy was in Vietnam at the time and he and his staff were shaken by the attack. Bundy immediately phoned President Johnson and recommended that the bombing begin. The bombing that followed against the North became an early catalyst for the anti-war movement.

The first teach-in was held on March 24 by faculty members at the University of Michigan who sought to inform students on the history, politics, and morality of the war. The first wave of teach-ins culminated on the weekend of May 15–16 when 122 college campuses were connected by radio hookup to hear debates on the war. Bernard was a participant in the afternoon's policy debate which included more than two dozen men and women from universities, government, and other institutions.

The bombing raids also spurred the growth of the student movement. Students for a Democratic Society (SDS) organized a march on Washington for April 17, and other protests were scheduled throughout the country. In November 1965 Sandy coordinated a Peace in Vietnam march on Washington, and year after year the marches became larger.

Many journalists came to talk with Bernard. Some knew him only through his writings and others had met him in Indochina. David Halberstam, tall and intense, visited several times. Stanley Karnow of the *Washington Post*, who had first met Bernard in Laos in 1959, came by. Our friend Richard Dudman, of the *St. Louis Post Dispatch*, went to Vietnam many times to report on the war. At one point, our forces in South Vietnam had begun the so-called Strategic Hamlet program. The idea was that good Vietnamese would be herded into fortified villages, and then we could shoot all the bad Vietnamese who were out running loose. Richard recalled that Bernard alerted him of what to watch out for. On his visit to one of these fortresses, Richard told me: "They had the moat and the barbed wire and the punji stick stockade all around it. They had a big gate to check people in and out and to register who was there and who wasn't. But along the back fence there was a little gap in the moat. There was a little building on the inside that came right up against the fence. It was a rice storage shed. They had it fixed so that the Viet Cong could come and get the stuff without wrecking the place. So, the whole thing was a fraud."

Among the journalists who contacted Bernard was Walter Lippmann, the most respected columnist of that era. Lippmann was a friend of Charles de Gaulle and accepted the general's argument that Vietnam and all of Southeast Asia be neutralized.[2] He invited Bernard to his home to discuss the Vietnam situation and he called subsequently to test ideas for his columns.

In mid-May, we gave a dinner party to which we invited French ambassador Charles Lucet, Walter Lippmann, I. F. Stone, and their wives. Izzy was just back from Saigon, where he had gone at Bernard's urging, and gave us his report. A few weeks later, when Bernard was out of town, we were invited to a cocktail party at the Lippmanns' home. The Stones took me and on the drive back Izzy was critical of Lippmann's circle of elite guests, all of them, except us, pillars of the establishment. It's true that Izzy was an unusual guest for Lippmann's party. But now that Lippman was opposing the war, he too was moving outside the mainstream, although he would never be as far outside it as Izzy Stone.

Don Oberdorfer, who later joined the *Washington Post*, went to work in 1965 for the Knight newspapers. He recalled,

That was the year of escalation. It became apparent to me that I would have to spend a great deal of my time on Vietnam, about which I knew nothing. One of the first things I did was to phone Bernard. I saw him a couple times, because he obviously was an authority on the subject and I was a neophyte. One day I went to a briefing with McNamara at the Pentagon. McNamara had a big blackboard and two big chalk lines plotted out. One of them was diagonally going up and the other was diagonally going down. The one that was going up, he explained to us, was tonnages of bombs dropped on North Vietnam by American planes. And the one coming down was tonnages of supplies going from north to south. How he thought he knew that number, I don't know. He said, 'Gentlemen, when these two lines meet, we will have started to win the war.' I remember that evening standing on the front steps of your house telling this to Bernie, what McNamara had said about these two lines meeting. 'That poor man,' he said, 'That might have something to do with operational research or maybe the Ford Motor Company, but it has absolutely nothing to do with the war in Vietnam. He's going to end up like Forrestal.'"

James Forrestal, Harry Truman's first secretary of defense, suffered a breakdown and killed himself. McNamara kept a portrait of him on his office wall.

Bernard continued to be denied access to top policymakers. Years later, I interviewed Jack Valenti, a White House aide close to Johnson. He told me that he had read that Bernard was the leading expert on Vietnam, so he thought it would be a good idea to bring him in to brief the president. "I mentioned this to President Johnson and he said, 'Well, talk to the National Security people about it.' So I discussed this with McGeorge Bundy and he did not eagerly jump on it. He said, 'Well, I'm not sure we need that. We've got people who understand that part of the world.' I said, 'Like a doctor, why don't we get a second opinion and bring this man in?' But it didn't happen."

Bernard did meet with Assistant Secretary of State Eugene

Bernard, in his study, gives information to I. F. Stone, 1965.

Rostow, brother of President Johnson's National Security advisor, a key advisor on Vietnam. Bernard's comment to me when he returned echoed what Gil Harrison had said about McGeorge Bundy: "Rostow listened, but he didn't *hear* me."

In his book, *In Retrospect*, Robert McNamara wrote, "When it came to Vietnam, we found ourselves setting policy for a region that was terra incognita. Worse, our government lacked experts for us to consult to compensate for our ignorance." In truth, there were plenty of experts, inside and outside of government. The problem was that Johnson, McNamara, and the others didn't want to listen to them.

Although McNamara never talked to Bernard, in his book he describes Bernard as someone who "initially supported U.S. policy in Vietnam, but grew increasingly skeptical and critical." This is not so. Bernard was critical of U.S. intervention from the beginning. What he did say in one of his 1965 articles, and McNamara quoted, was that U.S. power had made the war militarily "unlosable." But McNamara ignored the rest of what he said: that a war could be militarily unlosable and yet politically unwinnable.

It pained Bernard that he was denied access to the decision-makers. Not because of ego but because people were dying, the country was being torn apart, and he thought he could help. He would read McNamara's statements and in despair say to me, "They're lying to themselves."

After his death, I found a page in his files on which he wrote:

Statement to AP   21/2/66
I have at no time whatever been consulted by, or been in contact with, the White House in regard to any matter whatever concerning Vietnam. The White House has its own vast sources of information on Vietnam, which thus far have excluded me.

In retrospect, I wonder if any communication was possible. Bernard was entirely grounded in reality. The people who pursued the Vietnam policy, in three administrations, were obsessed with politics, with not "losing" Vietnam. They pursued their fantasies until the bitter end.

If we could put aside the war—and it was necessary, in those days, to put it from your mind sometimes, just to keep functioning—1966 was a splendid year for both Bernard and me. It was the peak of Bernard's career. He had won universal recognition as a scholar and journalist. In March he received a George Polk Journalism Award for Interpretive Reporting. For my part, my design work was recognized with gold medals from art directors' organizations, and I was preparing for a "Four Women" exhibit of my work for January 1967.

Viet-Nam Witness, a compilation of Bernard's articles since 1952, was published in the early spring. He said of it: "It tells how this avoidable war, the most avoidable conflict of the twentieth century, came into being through a series of misjudgments and misunderstandings."

Howard University President and Mrs. James Nabrit, Bernard's guests when receiving the Polk Award for Interpretive Reporting, 1966.

After three years of intensive research, he finished *Hell in a Very Small Place: The Siege of Dien Bien Phu*. Bernard dedicated the book, *To Dorothy, who lived with the ghosts of Dien Bien Phu for three long years.*

On our second spring trip to Treasure Cay in the Bahamas, we finally bought Bernard's dream plot of land on the island of Abaco. We promised ourselves that one day we would build a house there, facing the azure sea, surrounded by tropical pines and breezes.

In that spring of 1966 Bernard received another honor. He was awarded a Guggenheim fellowship for a study called "The Viet Cong: Rise and Development of a Peasant Guerrilla Movement." He said in his application:

As the situation stands in Viet-Nam in the fall of 1965, there exists, aside from the South and North Vietnamese regimes, a "Third Viet-Nam" which exercises effective control over perhaps 35,000 square miles of territory, 4 to 5 million people, and armed forces numbering close to 180,000. By present-day United Nations standards, those figures would rank what is commonly called the Viet-Cong at the top of the twenty-five smallest UN members. There exists a considerable body of honest disagreement as to whether such a movement can be anything else but an appendage or puppet of an outside power: and, if so, whether it can nevertheless have a life of its own. In the South Viet-Nam of today and of the next few years to come, the political outcome of the struggle may well depend upon one fact: whether the United States and South Viet-Nam can convince the population that the Viet-Cong, in spite of the fact that the great majority of its fighters are indigenous, is basically an 'alien' movement; and that the Saigon government, in spite of the presence of perhaps 200,000 white foreigners, nevertheless represents Vietnamese national objectives. . . . I hope to make a limited but significant contribution to the under-

standing of the phenomenon of peasant guerrilla movements. Their rise and evolution may well turn out to be one
of the most important socio-political events of the latter
part of this century.

Bernard always understood that this project would involve a
return to Vietnam. He wanted to interview Vietcong prisoners in
South Vietnamese custody; he sought documentation from Western sources in Vietnam and France, and interviews with American and South Vietnamese officials. And he still hoped to make
a second trip to North Vietnam.

After the Guggenheim fellowship was announced, Jim
Hoagland wrote an article in the *Washington Post* of April 10,
1966, "Professor to Study Vietcong in Action," in which Bernard said: "We don't know whom we're fighting. I want to find
out what makes the Vietcong fight and what makes them willing to suffer the tremendous pounding they take and keep
fighting. You've got to seek a more rational explanation than
just 'motivation.' What's important are the conditions that created this conflict, and whether these conditions can be created
or can arise elsewhere. Is this an isolated case or are there going
to be more peasant rebellions throughout the world? . . . The
United States has proven in Vietnam that she can make a war
militarily unlosable. What remains to be proven is that such a
war can be won."[3]

Bernard intended to carry out the project between June 1966
and September 1967, during the sabbatical he was due after ten
years at Howard. The fact that I became pregnant with our third
child, due in September 1966, complicated but did not halt our
planning. We agreed that Bernard would leave after the baby was
born and the children and I follow later. We would live in Hong
Kong while Bernard did his work in Vietnam. He would visit us
often. I looked forward to the adventure of living in Asia again. I
thought that exposure to British education in Hong Kong would
be beneficial for the girls.

Of course, I dreaded his going back to Vietnam. But I knew that I could not stop him. I had become his collaborator, his facilitator, his accomplice. Once again I accepted his assurances that he would avoid danger. This time he gave me a special reward: "When I come back I will become an American citizen."

That fall of 1966, as we awaited the baby's arrival and Bernard's departure, he lectured and wrote but was not teaching, so he had more time for me and the children. He would come up from his basement office to play with the girls after school. They raked leaves together and he worked on their math with them. As a father, he could be kind and loving, and he could also be impatient and even harsh. Nicole recalls his impatience in going over her homework with her. She wasn't getting it. He flicked her in the head with his fingers, saying "stupid," or gave her backhanded compliments like, "You're smart, you should be doing better than that." Both girls remember how he could tease them. Elisabeth recalls that when she was young he would threaten to take her to the doctor when she cried.

But he could be wonderful as well. Elisabeth also recalls the time a bird hit our window and Bernard brought it inside. He somehow fixed the bird's wing and she remembers it flying inside the house before he freed it. Another time, in our back yard, he found box turtles for her. Her greatest thrill came at the age of five. We had gone to a Chinese restaurant for dinner and her fortune cookie said, "You are going to have an exciting adventure." As we left the restaurant he made the fortune come true. Next door was a fire station. Bernard took her in, talked to the fireman there, and they sat her atop a fire engine, an experience she has never forgotten.

After Patricia Madeleine Marcelle, our third daughter, was born in September, Bernard brought the two girls to the hospital to see her. Of course, it was taboo, but Bernard slipped them in. Nine-year-old Nicole felt very grown up, because her father had told her to pretend she was twelve years old. I vividly recall the morning my labor pains started. Elisabeth had gone off to start first grade that day. Bernard and I looked at each other. For the first time in nine years we were responsibility-free during the day, basking in our newfound freedom. And now we were embarking on a new baby, a very sweet baby. Less preoccupied with my design career, I had evolved into a doting mother. The other two girls were old enough to be helpful, particularly Nicole, who reveled in having this little baby to hold and love. Elisabeth's place as the youngest had been usurped but she merrily tolerated her new sister. In our Christmas letter that year, Bernard admitted that he "could not tell his 'x' from his 'y' chromosomes to produce a boy. I'm busy inventing a chromosome sieve."

Hell in a Very Small Place was almost finished and would be out in January, soon after Bernard left for Vietnam. He was updating *Street Without Joy* for a second edition. Bernard edited, and wrote an introduction for, a collection of Ho Chi Minh's writings, called *Ho Chi Minh: On Revolution*. My design for the cover completed the work and it was sent to Praeger for publication.

Bernard was also rewriting the sections on Vietnam and Laos for the Encyclopedia Britannica. *Horizon*, a beautifully illustrated hardcover quarterly of the arts, had asked him to write its major article, "Two Thousand Years of War in Viet-Nam," for the Spring

A special farewell luncheon at the French Embassy, November 1966.
Left to right: Walter Lippmann, Bernard, French Ambassador
Charles Lucet, and Senator William Fulbright.

1967 issue. In it, Bernard wrote, "It is Viet-Nam as a cultural and historic entity which is threatened with extinction. While its lovely land has been battered into a moonscape by the massive engines of modern war, its cultural identity has been assaulted by a combination of Communism in the North and superficial Americanization in the South."

Bernard was writing "Seventeen Little Wars Nobody Talks About" for *Esquire* magazine, then at its peak of popularity, and was pleased to have his article "Vietnam in the Balance" leading the October issue of the prestigious *Foreign Affairs,* long a forum for establishment views.

The *Foreign Affairs* piece was long, grave, and scholarly. Bernard began by comparing the situation in Vietnam in late 1965 with the first battle of the Marne in September 1914. The point was that the 1914 battle prevented the collapse of the French, and the recent introduction of large numbers of American combat troops had similarly prevented the collapse of South Vietnam. Yet, even granting the power of the American military, Bernard painted a dark picture for the U.S: "Years—perhaps a decade—of hard fighting could still be ahead. And the political collapse of the government in Saigon is still a distinct possibility."[4]

In anticipation of his trip, Bernard had once more contacted Premier Pham Van Dong, seeking permission to come to North Vietnam. The return cable said:

DEAR FRIEND

I HAVE GIVEN MUCH THOUGHT TO YOUR LAST TELE-GRAM BUT UNTIL NOW WE HAVE STILL NOT ACCEPTED VISITS FOR THE SAME PURPOSE OF A NUMBER OF FOR-EIGN WELL KNOWN PERSONS BECAUSE OF THE US BAR-BAROUS AIR RAIDS IN THE FUTURE THERE WILL PROB-ABLY BE GOOD OPPORTUNITIES FOR TRUE FRIENDS OF VIETNAM TO VISIT

REGARDS

PHAM VAN DONG

The last family photo taken just before Bernard's departure for his final trip. Left to right: Elisabeth, Nicole, Dorothy holding Patricia, and Bernard, December 1966.

On November 19 we celebrated Bernard's fortieth birthday. Charlotte Sorkine Noshpitz, Bernard's friend from the Resistance, was living in Washington with her American husband, psychiatrist Joseph Noshpitz. Bernard and Joe loved to talk about philosophy and the role of psychology in each others' work; about children and adolescents, Joe's specialty; and about war and its consequences. Joe collected medals and brought one as a gift for Bernard's trip. It depicted Dagobert, the seventh-century Frankish king. His reign was prosperous and he was a patron of learning and the arts. "Take this with you," Joe said. "It will protect you."

17

RETURN TO THE STREET WITHOUT JOY

Shortly before he left, Bernard gave a long, informal, sometimes humorous interview to Dick Hubert on his *Celebrity's Choice* radio show. He spoke of his health and the dangers he faced with humor and candor. His kidney problem, he said, had a long Latin name, had cost him five operations and $18,500, and "I came out of the hospital and I felt pretty despondent about the whole thing. But I had a very good surgeon . . . and finally he said, 'Look, you idiot, so, all right, you've only got one kidney—if the kidney stops, obviously you're in trouble. So quit talking about it and start living.' And I did. It's never stopped me from anything. I'm just now going back to Viet-Nam for another year's stay, and [my] chances of dying in Viet-Nam are much better from any other cause but the trouble I have."[1]

On December 8, Bernard departed for Vietnam. He stopped first in Hong Kong to arrange housing for us and schools for the girls. He wrote to me daily as I spent the next two months preparing for my "Four Women" exhibit and giving Patricia a start in life before we took her halfway around the world. Soon Washington was blanketed by seven inches of snow, and while I sent out our Christmas letters Patricia brightened my lonely evenings with her smiles and coos.

Bernard wrote that I would find companionship in Hong Kong among the many journalists' wives there. He learned that most apartments required a year's lease, but then he found a couple that was going on home leave to Germany for six months. Their house sounded lovely, set on narrow Lugard road, which winds around the top of Victoria Peak, near the tram's last station. It offered both a magnificent view and a large garden. The owners, Richard Loeschel, an employee of a Dutch printing company, and his Chinese wife, Ling Ling, were leaving behind their Volkswagen Beetle and their chow chow, Whiskey. I thought a good watchdog would be comforting in the isolation of the peak.

Bernard found that the international school was fully booked, so he talked to British schools and sent me their brochures. Students wore a uniform, including a school blazer, tie, white socks, and black or brown shoes. "When you come, bring the kids' French blazers. N. and E. will love going to school by cable car."

Soon Bernard was in Vietnam, his natural element. He would be based in Saigon and travel with the military on operations. For the first month he bunked with François Sully, whose big, French-style apartment was in the Eden building, overlooking the big Le Loi traffic circle. According to Gerald Hickey, an expert on the small villages of Vietnam, François' apartment was often the scene of lively parties. Sully provided buffets with pastries from Givral, the coffee shop around the corner, where journalists gathered. Hickey saw Bernard at Sully's one evening and offered him a Coke. Bernard refused, saying that he had only one kidney and could not even drink a Coke. Without the kidney, he said, he would be dead.

Bernard's first stop was the huge airbase at Danang. He arrived in a steady downpour; the mud was at least calf-deep. Further northward lay the 17th parallel and the Demilitarized Zone that was no longer demilitarized. He wrote, "I'm spending X-mas with a Forward Marine Platoon on the 'rockpile' on the 17th parallel, but I'm thinking of you all."

He had met Jim Pringle, a correspondent with Reuters, on the C-130 flight north. Together they hitched rides on military vehicles from Dong Ha to Camp J. J. Carroll. Bernard explained to Pringle about the vulnerability, as he saw it, of the American bases, drawing examples from the French war. Bernard would be giving a talk at the camp, at the invitation of the U.S. commander, whom he had met when lecturing at a military college in the United States Pringle wrote to me that "Bernard's pessimism about U.S. prospects made the officers a little wary of him, though they respected his learning—if only they had listened to him."

In an article in the January 14 issue of the *New Republic*, Bernard described his adventures on the way to the Demilitarized Zone for Christmas:

Out on the road at the checkpoint, two soggy MPs stood near a flimsy shelter covered with graffiti, one of which masterfully expressed the whole situation: "I can't relate to this environment." As flies assembled around exposed food, a handful of Vietnamese children trooped around the checkpoint, begging. "Ho Chi Minh number 10," says a little boy in English, repeating an American-Vietnamese neologism according to which good things are number one and bad things scaled at 10. "Do you know where Ho Chi Minh is?" I say in Vietnamese. "No," says the child.

The mail truck. Red and yellow mail bags. Two GIs, young, one a Negro. As we leave the checkpoint, the driver

Bernard with journalist Jim Pringle of Reuters hitchhiking from Dong Ha to Camp Carroll for Christmas, December 1966. Photo courtesy of Jim Pringle.

passes his rifle and ammo clips back to me. "Sir, would you mind covering my side?" It's an M-14, looking very much like its older brother, the M-1. Familiar gesture of pulling back breech, inserting the first round, learned two decades ago; of locking safety, of looking warily at jungle closing in on the road. On the right side, the other GI cradles his submachinegun on his legs propped up high on the dashboard as we pick up speed, rocking crazily on the washboard road. The roar of the engine does not entirely drown out the sound of Christmas caroling up front in the truck's cab:

Jingle bells
Mortar shells
VC in the grass
You can take your Merry Christmas
And shove it up your ass.

In the mounting darkness, we began to climb out of the bushes and trees into a flat expanse of shrubless ground completely churned up by the tracks of tires and tank treads. The sharp outline of a tank hull mounting twin guns whizzes by.

"Home," says a voice in the truck cab. "We done made it again."

As I climb out of the truck with my pack and hand back the M-14, the voice in the truck says: "And you can tell 'em, buddy. War is shit."

This was Camp J. J. Carroll, also known as "Artillery Plateau," probably the most incredible single assemblage of groundborne firepower anywhere in the country. [2]

Bernard at Camp J. J. Carroll, in front of mountains in the demilitarized zone, Christmas Day, 1966.

Monday, the day after Christmas, Bernard left Camp Carroll at 4:00 a.m., just before the post was hit by 107 rounds of enemy mortar fire. He wrote, "They got badly zapped *one* hour after I left! The Dagobert Medal which I carried already has worked. It was just damn blind luck, like everything else in life, I guess."

On New Year's Eve he was back in Saigon where an old acquaintance, the chief of the French technical mission, invited Bernard for festivities. He was given champagne and told they were celebrating his promotion. "My promotion?" He learned that the French government had named him "Chevalier de l'Ordre National du Mérite" (Knight of the National Order of Merit) for scientific research abroad. He wrote to me, "Obviously, I'll hold off the Medal awarding ceremony until I return and we'll start off our return with a bang: the ceremony at the French Embassy and a dinner and reception at home. Right? Love, love, love, Bernard."

On December 28, Nicole and Elisabeth wrote to Bernard to thank him for their Christmas presents. They wrote that they missed him. On January 6, he sent them a reply from Saigon:

> Dear Girls,
> I was so happy to receive your two letters today. That is why I am writing you immediately. As you know, here we have no snow at all, but it is very warm, instead, because we are in the Tropics.
> I spent my Christmas with American soldiers. They had lots of very big guns (they're called ARTILLERY) and it rained constantly and it was very, very muddy, all the way up to your ankle. And instead of sleeping in a bed with sheets, I slept in a tent on a rubber mattress which I had bought in Washington.

Bernard described the soldier dressed up as "Père Noel" (Father Christmas) in his red suit, the soldiers singing Christmas carols, and the fact that because it was Christmas the soldiers decided not to shoot at each other that night. "But a lot of people, even children, get killed in this war." He said that both sides believe that they are right in fighting, "War is a very bad thing, and let us hope it is soon over." He went on about their coming trip, where they would live, asked them to keep a diary and a scrapbook, and to send letters to their school about the trip. "Lots of kisses to Nicole and Elisabeth and Patricia—Your Papa."

He wrote to me the next day about receiving the program for my exhibit: "I was so damn proud. . . . I went around with it throughout JUSPAO [Joint U.S. Public Affairs Office] like with the picture of a new baby!" Two weeks later the *Washington Post* published a one-and-a-half-page story of the exhibit. To my delight, a large color photo of me with my paintings opened the piece.

After staying with Sully for a month, Bernard found an apartment of his own at 211, Nguyen Van Sam. It contained plenty of bookshelves and a window overlooking the pagoda next door. He wrote to me of life in Saigon: "We may be winning the war, but for the last four days the artillery around Saigon hasn't let up. It got so that they finally flew an air strike (!) in Saigon's 8th district. It's like living where we are and somebody has himself an aerial bombardment at Howard University [four miles away]."

As my departure date neared, the British refused to grant me a visa for the six-month stay in Hong Kong. Moreover, I had found no tenant for our house. In desperation, I phoned Assistant Secretary of the Navy Robert Baldwin, who had just returned from Vietnam, where he had been with Bernard on a trip to Pleiku. Baldwin promised to contact the British Embassy. I held my breath and proceeded with preparations to leave. It took another week, and delayed my departure date, but Baldwin's intervention must have helped, because my visa came through. Also, at the last minute, Congressman Sidney Yates rented our house. He asked that I remove my work from the walls so that he could hang pictures from his own collection, some by Joan Mitchell, an artist of international stature. I was inconvenienced, but impressed that he was a patron of contemporary American artists.

In his next letter, Bernard told me to bring the short boots I recently bought, which I could wear there in lieu of heavier combat boots. He said he would stay with the children while I visited the war in Vietnam. What was he thinking? I would never compromise the future of my children by taking such a risk. Besides, I was nursing Patricia, a trick he couldn't manage. I ignored his advice about the boots.

On January 9, Bernard received his first copy of *Hell in a Very Small Place* from Lippincott and wrote to me: "I'll say that much for it: it's handsome as all hell. And the *Library Journal* reviewed it magnificently, saying that 'contrary to Roy's book [Jules Roy's book on Dien Bien Phu] with its obvious padding and editorializing (!!!), Fall's book has the facts and is much to be preferred for libraries.' That does it for libraries."

He continued: "This p.m. I'm going to Long Binh (the ammo dump the VCs blew up several times) to interrogate 3 U.S. civilians let go voluntarily by the VC. I've already interrogated a No VN Lt-Colonel who defected (hell, not for some ideology, but because he found a pretty girl he liked better than his wife . . . some victory). Fascinating stuff." After meeting the men freed by the Vietcong, he wrote: "Their story was extremely interesting and surely won't hit the U.S. press that way. In brief, they were treated exactly according to the Geneva Conventions, given the same rations as the rest of the Vietnamese." As Bernard had made clear in his articles, such civilized treatment of prisoners was increasingly rare on both sides.

His health was fine, he said. No pains, no aches. He had arranged for his tests with a French doctor. It was a busy time. He gave several interviews about his book, including one that led to a long piece by United Press International. He was trying to find U.S. officials who would give him data on the Vietcong, and he was juggling several magazine articles.

On January 17, he wrote to me: "You don't know how much I do wait for those letters of yours, and how terribly much I love you. It sort of grows (my love) that is, as I think of you. You're

Bernard interviews a Vietcong colonel who was taken prisoner, January 1967.

just wonderful, you know." He asked for news of my show and the reviews. I had sold a number of paintings at substantial prices. He joked that he had counted on me as a financial failure so that he could use my art as a tax write-off.

Jonathan Schell, who would later become famous for *The Fate of the Earth* and other books, arrived in Saigon about this time. He had completed his graduate studies in Japan and his plane ticket allowed him to stop anywhere in the world on the way home. He picked Vietnam, although he knew little about the war, and read *Street Without Joy* on the plane from Hong Kong to Saigon. He told me later:

> Bernard Fall was the acknowledged authority and writer on the subject. He was the man to read, who people turned to, if they wanted to find out about this country that we were tearing apart. I got to Saigon. I had no experience as a writer. But I had one contact. That was François Sully, whom I met at Harvard. [Sully had been a Neiman Fellow after being expelled from Vietnam by Diem in 1963.] I called the *Newsweek* office there. François answered and very kindly

invited me to come over, my one chance to get hooked up with anything whatsoever. I went into the office. It had two desks. François was at one desk and there was another gentleman at the other desk, who asked me what I was reading. I said, "I'm reading *Street Without Joy* by Bernard Fall." He said, "Let me see it." I handed it to him and he signed it for me. He was Bernard Fall! He and François, out of spontaneous friendliness, took me under their wing.

They took him along to press conferences and concocted a story that Schell was a correspondent for the *Harvard Crimson*. Later they came up with a press pass. "It was a ticket to the war in Vietnam. It was absolutely essential. Without it there would have been no writer named Jonathan Schell, certainly not about the Vietnam War."

One day they phoned Schell and said something newsworthy was happening and he should go to a certain place at 4:00 a.m. and board a military bus. He didn't know it, but Bernard and Sully were sending him to the biggest operation of the war, Operation Cedar Falls in the Iron Triangle. There was a briefing with a jaunty captain at a blackboard, outlining the different combat operations they could accompany. One of these involved forty-eight helicopters that were going to fly directly into the village of Ben Suc, which traditionally had been held by the NLF. "We were going to take it over, move the people out, and then destroy it," Jonathan recalled. His trip resulted in *The Village of Ben Suc*, first published as an article in the *New Yorker* and later as a celebrated and moving book.

The path of veteran correspondent Peter Arnett also crossed Bernard's from time to time:

I held Bernard in incredible respect. At the time, his books, particularly *Street Without Joy* and *The Two Viet-Nams*, were the only written works freely available. Bernard's works on the French Indochina war were the reference works. We read the books avidly, and looked for parallels in our early coverage because in those days we had no guidance on how we were going to cover the war. We were feeling our way. Therefore, the reference to the French experience was an important one to use to evaluate what was going on. So when Bernard started coming to town fairly regularly by '65, it was always an occasion to have him around. In the press corps he was an immensely popular man and always available to converse and to freely give of his opinions and to tell wonderful stories about his own experiences. We'd meet at Bodard's or Givral's. He'd be holding court there. Bernard gave us the moral support to look at the negative aspects of the war at a time when U.S. authorities were insisting we look only at the positive.

At the end of January, Bob Silvers of the *New York Review of Books* sent Bernard a telegram. Mary McCarthy would be arriving in Saigon on February 3 to report for that publication. He would be grateful if Bernard would reserve a room for her at the Caravelle or Continental and also for any help he could give her. Bernard did not mention McCarthy in his letters, but he must have introduced her to people and given her a tour of Saigon.

She proved to be more interested in the social side of the war than the military side. According to Carol Brightman's *Writing Dangerously: Mary McCarthy and Her World*, McCarthy was pressed by Bernard to go on a bombing mission. She refused. She had promised her husband that she would not go on combat missions. The biographer continued: "Fall had argued that she should train herself to go up and feel nothing, as he had; maintaining one's detachment made one strong and proud. She would rather 'be weak and humble. Or, rather, I *was* weak and humble', McCarthy decided. For a 'natural civilian' such as herself, 'insentience' would have been the last thing to seek, while for Bernard Fall, 'who loved war and its implements, it was the opposite; he responded to the thrill of danger, and it was this he had taught himself to curb.'"[3]

On February 5, after a delay of eleven days, the girls and I left Washington. We stopped in California, where I took them to Disneyland and visited my brother Morris, who came down from San Francisco with his eleven-year-old son Tony. After that, our trip was not smooth. Plane reservations were not honored. In Tokyo the worst snowstorm in ten years forced me to cancel a trip to Kyoto. Finally, in Hong Kong, a dockworkers' strike paralyzed transportation. Our landlords, the Loeschels, kindly came to fetch us at the airport in their tiny Volkswagen. With all our luggage and baby gear, we also needed a taxi. But the cab drivers, in sympathy with the dockworkers, were on strike too. And it was the Chinese New Year. I watched in disbelief as Richard Loeschel somehow loaded our two huge suitcases, a smaller one, the baby stroller, the girls, the baby, and me into the tiny VW Beetle along with himself and his wife. Upon arrival, a telegram was waiting for me:

WELCOME DARLING TET PARALYZES NORMAL MAIL TILL
NEXT WEEK LOVE BERNARD

Flares illuminated the sky as David Hackworth ("Hack") sat with Gen. S. L. A. "Slam" Marshall on the roof of the Rex Hotel. Hackworth was a living legend, the most decorated soldier in the Army's history. His illustrious career had begun in the Korean War. He had finished his own Vietnam tour and was stationed at the Pentagon when the well-known military historian Marshall requested that he accompany him to Vietnam. Among other works, Marshall had written *Pork Chop Hill*, about a famous battle of the Korean War. On this night in January, Bernard was brought to their table by the U.S. public affairs officer who was Marshall's Saigon contact. He wanted Marshall to meet the author of *Street Without Joy*. I'm sure Bernard relished the idea as well.[4]

"I will never forget the evening," Hackworth told me in 2001.

I met Bernard perhaps at ten o'clock at night. It was going to be a drink and a quick hello, and we ended up talking until three in the morning. He and I were in total synch regarding our conclusions on how the war was going. An animated conversation, the kind you find very rarely in your life, that just rocked on for five or six hours, nonstop. I had just returned from interviewing thousands of frontline soldiers about their experiences. They were telling me exactly what my experiences were the year before. Bernard well knew, from *his* experience, and his great intellect, the name of the game, and he was trying to tell everyone what the story was.

In the middle of this sat Slam Marshall, who was from a completely different school, believing that the firepower and this enormous, massive U.S. military would overpower the opponent much as they did the Germans, the Italians, and the Japanese. Bernard gave Marshall a quiet education on the Vietnamese—their culture, their history, their unflagging determination to rid their country of outside invaders.

Bernard told Marshall that bombing the Vietcong into oblivion was not the answer. Social reform was.

At some point, Marshall, a small man in his mid-sixties, called it a night and the two younger men talked for another two hours. Bernard did most of the talking. Hack recalled, "I was so mesmerized. As a kid, I had read what Bernard Fall had written. I was getting ready for the Indochina war when I left Korea. Even to a dumb kid it was obvious what was happening. In the fifties I got attuned to this guy and I read and reread what he wrote, like so many of us.

"The great irony was saying to Bernard, where are you going next? He said, 'I'm going with the Marines.' I said, 'Look, this is coming from an infantryman with eight Purple Hearts. You cannot just continue rolling the dice. You're going to crap out. You just can't go with the squad and with the platoon again and again and again, because you're going to get killed.' He just smiled that big cheery smile."

Hack eventually left the military to write and found himself a reporter covering Somalia and Operation Desert Storm, doing exactly what he told Bernard not to do. He told me that, finally, his wife put her foot down. "That's the end of that for you, Buster," she said.

I told him I couldn't have done that. Bernard had to always go to the source. He had a passion for Vietnam, an obsession. He was at the center of the biggest story in the world—how could he quit that and return to the classroom?

On February 18, 1967, Bernard wrote me a note to say he was well and in good shape. He was with the Third Marine Division near Hue. "Tomorrow morning I'm going into a heliborn assault with the First Battalion, Ninth Marines, and guess where: the Street Without Joy. The VC is still in it, still holding it."

Starting on February 19, the Marines were conducting Operation Chinook II. It was raining and overcast that morning and the helicopters could not take off. The men waited until the next day when they were trucked out at dusk from Phu Bai to Lai Ha, their jumping-off point. From there, Bernard trudged overland with the men on the Street Without Joy, the string of villages twelve miles northwest of the coastal city of Hue. During the French war it had been a haven for the Vietminh and now it was the home territory of the 802nd Vietcong battalion. Bernard must have felt young again, perhaps recalling the camaraderie of his days in the *maquis*. This is where he wanted to be: out with the grunts, exhilarated, feeling so alive while risking death.

In the morning of the second day the company came under fire and returned fire. They were walking along the sand dunes of the Street Without Joy, where the French fought in 1953.[5] On the morning of February 21, the path was reduced to a wide, rice-paddy dike.

Bernard was narrating into his tape recorder. The tape was still in the recorder when it was returned to me:

Well, we're moving out again on the Street Without Joy—it's the third day out now and what you've heard before were the noises of the crickets and the frogs next to us where we were sleeping out in the open. It started to drizzle afterward and now we've got thick-packed fog at nine o'clock in the morning. Supply chopper couldn't come in but we had enough food for this morning and on we go now.

Charlie Company picked up two Viet Cong suspects, which within a few seconds were confirmed to be Viet Cong supply carriers. Yesterday evening also we captured two of them: a little girl about twenty—strapping girl—and a boy about sixteen, in the village. By the time the Vietnamese had left us they were already beating them and, of course, it's no small wonder no civilians stay behind except a few old women.

We have been walking now for two and a half days in a virtual desert. Now we're with Able Company on the road and Able has found a mine. Charlie Company already exploded a mine with a trip wire and apparently one fellow is hurt.

He continued his taping:

Afternoon of the third day. Still on the street. Now bunker system out there they're going to blow up. The weather is finally cleared and we have an observation plane over our heads, turning around, shepherding us. But Charlie Company has fallen very badly behind; now there's a big hole in our left flank and there's some people running away from us. . . . Charlie Company is moving right through the area and by tonight we will know whether what we killed were genuine VC with weapons or simply people. . . . This is Bernard Fall on the Street Without Joy.

251

Bernard continued taping. He was number six in the line of soldiers as they moved along the Street Without Joy:

> First in the afternoon about four thirty—shadows are lengthening and we've reached one of our phase lines after the firefight and it smells bad—meaning it's a little bit suspicious. . . . Could be an amb. . .[6]
> [*End of tape*]

In Hong Kong, on February 19, I enrolled the girls in school. They were to start the following week at the British Royden House School, near the stop halfway down on the peak tram.

Bernard had told me to be sure and call Annette Karnow, Stan's wife, and I did. Annette invited me and the girls to lunch the next day, February 21. She was pregnant with her fourth child. She asked who I knew in Hong Kong. I told her I knew a photographer named Frank Wolfe and his wife, whom I'd met in Phnom Penh in 1962, and that my artist friend Kathleen Bruskin lived there with her husband, Bob, who worked for the Army.

The rest of the day was spent bathing and walking Whiskey, the dog we'd inherited. Nicole wrote a letter to her father:

> Dear Papa,
> The trip was very nice. In Disneyland I liked the Peter Pan ride because you really feel like your floating in the air.
> And in Hawaii I saw some Polynesian dancers.
> In Japan we saw an all girl dancing group.
> Now we are in Hong-Kong.
> We like Whiskey very much and we went on a picanic with the Loeschels.
> I hope to see you soon.
>
> Love,
> Nicole

We were finally settling in.

Stanley Karnow was then a Hong Kong-based correspondent for the *Washington Post*. Because of the twelve-hour difference between Hong Kong and Washington, Stanley worked late at night. He was in his office that night when the message came over the wire. He called Annette.

I was sound asleep when I heard a loud knocking. I opened the door and found Annette there with my friends Frank Wolfe and Kathleen Bruskin. I don't know how she located them.

They did not have to tell me why they were there.

Bernard had always been fatalistic. He had talked about the possibility that he might die, but in a joking way, making light of it. Maybe he thought his jokes would ward off the possibility.

Now it had happened. The fear I had lived with since 1953 had finally been realized.

One is never prepared. To ward off the tragedy, my mind traveled to other things. I said, "Poor Annette. In your condition, to have to come out in the middle of the night." I thought of my children—how to protect them, how to tell them, what to do. Kathleen stayed with me that night.

Maj. Gen. Wood B. Kyle, commander of the Third Marine Division, was in Hong Kong soon after. Bernard had given him my address and he came to see me and told me how Bernard had died. It had been a sunny afternoon. Bernard had decided to accompany the Marines on Operation Chinook up by the Street Without Joy. Following the group along a dike, he detonated what the Marines called a "Bouncing Betty" land mine and was killed instantly. Gunnery Sergeant Byron Highland, a Marine photographer and fourteen-year veteran from Detroit, died with him. He had volunteered to go with Bernard to take photos of the Marines in action.

The only thoughts I allowed myself were caring for my girls, the sadness that Patricia would not know her father, and that Nicole and Elisabeth would grow up with only childhood memories of him. I had to be strong to care for them and that necessity was a godsend. It helped postpone the agony. I decided to return home as soon as possible. U.S. Consul Allen Whiting helped arrange my trip. He asked me what I needed and I said milk for the two older girls.

The flight home was a nightmare. We arrived at Dulles airport at 6:00 a.m. My sister Mary was there with Jack Berteling, her sister-in-law Polly's husband, a Marine colonel who loved Bernard. So were the Leprettes (friends from the French Embassy), Pierre Feron, and another French veteran. We had no house—it was rented. Congressman Yates generously offered to find another place and asked for a month to do so. Our neighbor, Frances Zirkin, was going on a round-the-world trip and offered me her home for that month. That same morning, once we were installed in Frances's house, the girls ran off to school, to the same classes they had left only three weeks earlier. But their lives and mine were changed forever.

In a letter to me, Bernard's surgeon, Dr. Herbert Goldberg, wrote, "He died as he had lived—trying to do a job in the most complete and in the most honest and efficient way it could be done. Bernard's greatness was not apparent to me during his surgery. I have never known *anyone* to uphold a grave illness with such fortitude and, after the doctor had done all that could be done, refuse to accept the fact that his health was anything less than perfect. Feeling that way he could only live his life to the absolute fullest—and he did that."

In his tribute to Bernard in the March 13 issue of *I. F. Stone's Weekly,* Izzy wrote:

Like Mr. Justice Holmes, whose experience in the Civil War left a similar mark upon him, Fall understood the soldier's devotion. He could say with Holmes "in our youth our hearts were touched with fire." In Vietnam he avoided the high brass to be with the troops, and he would much have preferred to die as he did, with the Marines, on combat patrol along that road one of his earlier books made famous as

"The Street Without Joy." His was truly a meteoric career—short and dazzling—but he will long be read and remembered as a soldier-scholar, and I will miss him as a friend.

The Dagobert medal was with Bernard's personal effects when they were returned to me after his death. He had not taken it into the field. His typewriter and new Polaroid camera were not there and I assumed they were stolen. His Leica was returned to me. It had been torn apart by the explosion but the lens was intact. Separate, among his personal effects was a letter addressed to me:

X-mas eve, 1966
Darling,
You will see this only if anything has happened. I want you to know that I loved you and the children terribly much and was proud of you.

If I assumed the risks I did in this incredibly stupid and brutal war, I did so because somebody *had* to be a witness to what was happening. I hope that those poor blind men who direct America's policies will awaken to the real facts before it is too late. In that case, whatever happened to me will not have happened in vain. I know that you will be thinking of me as I will think of you—no matter where I will be.

Love,
Bernard

EPILOGUE

Eᴌɪsᴀʙᴇᴛʜ and I peered out the window, hoping to see the rice fields below. It was February 1997 and our plane was approaching Hanoi. I wanted a glimpse of the landscape Bernard had described as he arrived in North Vietnam in 1962. In his *Saturday Evening Post* article, he wrote about how the small, individual plots of land he had seen in 1953 had been replaced by large, communal farms. But this time there was cloud cover and we could see little as we approached Gialam airport.

I had been hesitant to return to the country where Bernard died thirty years earlier. But I wanted to write this book and Bernard always said that if you want to write about a place, you must go there. My daughters Elisabeth, a photographer, and Patricia, a writer, made the trip with me. Nicole, with two children at home, waited and accompanied me on another trip I made in 2000. Elisabeth, Patricia, and I were joined by my friend Harvey Resnik and his son Seth.

After we were settled in Hanoi, and had done some sightseeing, we were invited to meet with Ho Chi Minh's private secretary, Vu Ky, at Ho's house, which is maintained as a shrine. It was a modern-looking wooden house on stilts, with large windows and few rooms, sparsely furnished, well polished, and immaculate. Ho died there on September 2, 1969, a few days after suffering a heart attack. There, too, in his final days, with the war

*Patricia, Dorothy, and Elisabeth in Lai Ha, searching for
the Street Without Joy, March 1997.*

still raging, Ho had written his "testament," an inspirational
message to his people that promised, "We are bound to win total victory."

A spry, wizened man with a smiling face, Vu Ky took my arm
and escorted us through the door into the main room, which
was used for dining and meetings. On the large table in the center were a few books, and on top was Bernard's *Ho Chi Minh: On
Revolution*. Vu Ky also showed us a copy of *Le Viet Minh*. I knew
that Ho Chi Minh had read it because he and Pham Van Dong
discussed it with Bernard in 1962. Vu Ky insisted that we be photographed next to the bed where Ho died. A building next door
contained an underground bomb shelter. Vu Ky said that Ho
never stayed there during the American bombings, because he
rejected special privileges. He said that because of Ho's frugality,
any new construction on the house had been done when he was
away. After giving us branches of a fragrant bush, Vu Ky took us
to the pond where Ho often fed the fish. He said that even now,
when he goes and feeds the fish he thinks of his great friend and
leader. Vu Ky was using the house to work on his memoir. I gave
him a collection of Bernard's books for the house.

At the press center of the Foreign Ministry, we met with the director, Do Cong Minh, along with two other visitors. Minh, speaking in French, offered his help on our trip. He told me that he, too, had a loss in the war—his brother disappeared in battle in the South and his body was never found. He asked the girls about their professions. One of the men was impressed to learn that Patricia worked for Morgan Stanley, an institution known even in this Communist outpost.

I had not received a reply to my request for interviews with Gen. Vo Nguyen Giap and former Premier Pham Van Dong, so we continued our trip. From Hanoi we flew to Hue to visit the Street Without Joy. In the tape he made shortly before his death, Bernard said that he was in Lai Ha, the site of a battle described in his book. With a driver and a van, we headed north along Highway 1. The road was roughly paved, and there were many bicycles and motorbikes around us. We passed trees and palms, little shops, a gas station, a truck filled with soldiers. A train zoomed by. We saw workers in the rice paddies, women working alongside men to build a road. We saw boys and girls in blue pants, white shirts, and red string ties, outside their school on recess, and another school with children exercising. There were mountains in the distance.

We made a right turn toward Lai Ha. Suddenly the road was muddy, made soft and mushy by a recent rain. We waited for oncoming traffic at a one-lane bridge. A sign said we were entering Quang Tri province. There were many small shrines along the muddy river. We turned onto a narrow road that we shared with people walking and riding bicycles. Finally, Lai Ha was announced by an archway over the entrance to the village. Small children ran up to stare at us. Harvey amused them while the girls and I explored. An old woman carried a basket with tiny clams. A woman in a boat fished the river, using an American GI's helmet as a scoop. We walked to an isolated spot on the edge of the village that looked like the start of the Street Without Joy. For all its fame, it was only a path into swampland. We didn't follow it. We were close enough.

My daughters and I reflected on the destiny that had brought Bernard here to die on the "street" he had immortalized.

Bernard's entire life had been one of destiny. His destiny had enabled him to survive the Germans, to find his job at Nuremberg, to win the Fulbright grant to study in the United States, to take the summer course at SAIS that led to his focus on Vietnam, to make his six trips to Vietnam, to write brilliant books and articles about it, and to become, although French, one of the leaders in the American effort to stop the war. I believe, moreover, that in his final years, after he lost one kidney and suffered the impairment of the other, he thought that disability was going to kill him and he didn't intend to die in bed. He wanted to be out with the soldiers, doing his work and recapturing the glory of his youth. So he returned—as we did thirty years later—to the Street Without Joy, for his final rendezvous with destiny.

From Hue we went to Saigon, now Ho Chi Minh City, where I met with the academic dean of the university, Professor Lien, and a group of writers. I spoke with a seventy-year-old man who had been a war correspondent with Giap's army during the French war and had met Bernard in Hanoi in 1962. He cried as he told me about his sister, who had stayed in the South, then moved to the United States with her American husband. He had not seen her in forty-five years.

Patricia returned to New York and the four of us remaining went to Cambodia. By then I was glad I had come to Vietnam but I was still reluctant to return to Cambodia. I had such special memories of our time there in 1961–62, and I was horrified by what had happened in 1975–79, when Pol Pot's Khmer Rouge killed nearly one-fourth of the Cambodian population, some 1.7 million people. But the others wanted to see Angkor and I agreed. Indeed, I found the monuments of Angkor more spectacular than I remembered them. But Cambodia was heartbreaking, its people ravaged. Phnom Penh was a more modern city now but with too many ghosts. Elisabeth said that she felt death close at hand, that the dust had not settled. We were happy to leave.

The others returned to the United States and I flew back to Hanoi alone, still hoping to see Pham Van Dong and General Giap. The press center had not obtained the interviews. Both men were well up in years, and I was told that Pham Van Dong had returned to his native village. I ran into *Time* correspondent Tim Larimer, who said that he knew someone who wrote for General Giap, Huu Mai, one of the best-known writers in Vietnam. Tim spoke to Huu Mai, who then called me. He told me that he had read all of Bernard's books. He said that General Giap, his friend for forty years, had visited his home the previous weekend. He would call him. Soon Huu Mai phoned and said the general would see me the next afternoon at his home.

The general's secretary met me at the gate. He apologized for not having arranged an appointment earlier and asked about my daughters. I entered a comfortable-looking room with a low table ready for tea with small cakes and huge grapes. Madame Dang Bich Ha, the general's wife, came in. Youthful-looking, warm, extremely intelligent, she, too, asked about my daughters in her beautiful French. We sat down to tea, joined by her youngest son, who was tall and handsome and resembled his father. Soon the parlor doors opened and Gen. Vo Nguyen Giap entered in dress uniform, his shoulders marked with red epaulettes. He was eighty-five, a proud old man who was one of the greatest generals of the twentieth century.

Bernard never met General Giap, but in one of his lectures he said of him:

"On December 22, 1944, a young doctor of history by the name of Vo Nguyen Giap took a first platoon of thirty-four guerrillas into North Viet-Nam's Dinh Ca valley. Here again, a photograph has been preserved: it shows us a short, pudgy man, wearing a rather formal Borsalino hat, knickerbocker trousers but no shoes, and a U.S. Army .45-caliber pistol. Ten years later, a commander of the Viet-Nam People's Army, he was to defeat the French at Dien Bien Phu and ten years later again, as vice premier and minister of defense of North Viet-Nam, he was to face the United States in South Viet-Nam."[1]

The general and I had a friendly chat. He said he had read extracts of Bernard's books and that Bernard had made a great contribution to the understanding of his people's struggle for liberation. "Your husband was the first person to foresee the defeat of the Americans. Even during the war, after Dien Bien Phu, the Americans thought that with their power—so much greater than the French—that they could defeat us. I was very moved when your husband wrote that we fought the war for peace. He studied our people."

He said an American visitor had asked him, "What is your strategy?" "My strategy is the strategy of peace," he answered.

Giap said he knew there were those in America who were against the war; he mentioned Senator Fulbright and George Ball, under secretary of state in the Johnson administration. He added, "After the war, many American veterans came to see me—*très amis* [very friendly]. The Vietnamese people are people who appreciate friendship." He said former American soldiers sometimes asked him, "Why did we come here?"

He said that they were always appreciative of those writers who wrote objectively, like Bernard Fall and Philippe Devillers, our friend in Paris who had written *Histoire du Vietnam de 1940–52*.

At the end of the visit, I told General Giap how glad I was to meet him (*je suis ravie*). He said he was "not glad, very moved (*ému*)." He had a profound recognition of Bernard's sacrifice, as another casualty of the war. "I hope you will remember your visit," he said. "Please give my best to your daughters."

The general and his wife explained that it was very rare for them to receive foreign visitors in their home. We embraced with kisses on both cheeks.

Huu Mai and I have maintained a correspondence via the Internet, recently in English, which he has learned. His son Viet, a poet and journalist, visited me in Washington when he was in the United States to study at the University of Iowa Writing Center.

I returned to Vietnam twice in 2000. I went to Ho Chi Minh City on April 30. It was the twenty-fifth anniversary of the fall of Saigon. A group of American journalists was holding a reunion, organized by photographer Horst Faas, and invited me to join them. Among them was Tim Page, who with Horst edited the book and exhibit *Requiem*, a tribute to photographers who had died in the war. Richard Pyle and Edie Lederer of the Associated Press showed me François Sully's former apartment. They all remember Bernard fondly and I was honored to be with other men and women who had risked their lives to bring Americans the truth about the war. One of the highlights of the celebration was an all-but-endless parade of Vietnamese of all descriptions— soldiers, farmers, workers, young people, government officials. As I photographed each passing group, I was impressed by the women veterans, so proud and strong, many of them dressed in long trousers and colorful tunics. A tall woman walked past and we smiled at each other. We clasped hands, bonding for a brief moment. It was a moment I will always remember, along with the kindness of the Vietnamese, who showed no animosity toward those of us from the country that had done their country such harm in a long and costly war.

Nicole joined me on my return in December. We brought an exhibit of works on paper by fourteen American artists, to be shown with the art of fourteen Vietnamese professors at the Hanoi Fine Arts College. U.S. Ambassador Douglas "Pete" Peterson made opening remarks at the exhibit. He was an Air Force pilot who was shot down in 1966 and endured six years as a prisoner of war in Hanoi. Back in the United States, he was elected to Congress, and then appointed by President Clinton to be our first ambassador to the People's Republic of Vietnam. He spoke to me of the importance of Bernard's writings and said he had always been right in his appraisal of the war. I was deeply moved to hear that from this good and brave man.

Dorothy meets Gen. Vo Nguyen Giap, March 1997.

I once asked my three daughters for their thoughts about their father.

"I felt that Papa was mindful of teaching me to really think about things," said Nicole, the oldest. "To enjoy life, have humor about it, and above all persevere in what you do, be liberal-minded and tolerant. I think I was lucky to be his oldest child. I simply had more years with Papa than the others."

Nicole added, "I didn't realize how Vietnam weighed on me until 1975 when the U.S. pulled out of Vietnam and we stopped seeing the war on the news. I felt that I had been holding my breath for years and could finally let go." She was eighteen when the war ended.

Patricia said, "Though I was only five months old when Papa died, I don't think I truly understood his death's impact on our family until I had children of my own. When [my two-year-old son] Drew cries for his daddy when he's been away for a few days, I can't even imagine how devastating Papa's death must have been on a six- and nine-year old child. I always felt that I had suffered the least since I had never had the opportunity to truly know him. There had been no precious moments together to recall, no reminders of our life together before he was gone, simply photographs of someone who represented my father."

Elisabeth said, "He had idealism. He wasn't out of touch with people, although he dealt with facts. He embraced a part of America. He was open to people, engaged people of all walks of life." She quoted Colette, "It is the image and the mind that binds us to our lost treasure. But it is the loss that shapes the image."

During my third and final visit to Hanoi, General Giap and his wife again invited us to their home. It was another warm visit, and as it ended the general gave me a statement that he said I could use for my book. It said in part:

> I had read a number of Bernard Fall's researched works on the Vietnam War. At first, he was only looking for the truth. But day by day he became more deeply moved by the victims of the war. . . . He was a great friend of the Vietnamese people, a fighter who sacrificed himself in the struggle for truth, freedom, and peace on our Earth, which so often is not peaceful.

Bernard's books are still read today, and the lessons and warnings he gave us on Vietnam can still serve us well. The United States is now engaged in a horrifying war in Iraq, which it entered, again, with total lack of knowledge of the country's history, culture, or politics, with no foresight, and from which it cannot extricate itself. Bernard's words become even more relevant in today's world as we see the United States repeating the tragic mistakes of Vietnam.

NOTES

T HIS book contains statements from individuals who, for the most part, are cited in the text. With very few exceptions, interviews were taped, so that I have used the exact quote from the person I cite. These go back to 1971 and were converted from reel to cassette tapes at the Kennedy Library where the originals reside. In the few cases where I was not able to record a conversation, I made careful notes at the time of the interview.

Notes to Preface
1 Robert S. McNamara, *In Retrospect* (New York: Times Books, 1995), 32.

Notes to Chapter 2
1 Bernard Fall, *Last Reflections On a War* (New York: Doubleday, 1967), 16.
2 An autobiographical unpublished piece by Bernard.
3 Fall, *Last Reflections*, 18–20.
4 Bernard B. Fall, "Liberation vs. Pacification," (lecture, Yale University, March 3, 1966).
5 Susan Zuccotti, *The Holocaust, the French, and the Jews* (New York: Basic Books, 1993), 216–217, and Lucien Lazarre, *Rescue As Resistance* (New York: Columbia University Press, 1996), 193.

6 This was a communal burial for the the poor with no money. After the war, Leo was reburied in a cemetery in Cimiez.

7 Fall, *Last Reflections*, 20.

8 Michel Aguettaz *Francs-Tireurs et Partisans dans la Résistance Savoyarde*, (Grenoble: Presses Univesitaires de Grenoble, 1995), 217–221.

9 Fall, *Last Reflections*, 21.

10 La Foux, in the Ubbaye above Barcelonnette, is near the mountain pass Col d'Allos, from which there is a beautiful panorama of the region below. The two probably skied there.

Notes to Chapter 3

1 Bernard B. Fall, "The Case of Alfred Krupp," *Prevent World War III*, Summer 1951, 39.

Notes to Chapter 5

1 Fall, *Last Reflections*, 23.

2 Bernard B. Fall, *Street Without Joy* (Harrisburg, PA: Stackpole Company, 1961), 19.

3 Bernard Fall, "Insurgency and Counterinsurgency in Vietnam," (lecture, U.S. Naval War College, Newport, Rhode Island, April 21, 1966); also "Counterinsurgency: The French Experience" (lectures, National War College, Washington, D.C., June 27, 1966, and the Industrial College of the Armed Forces, Washington D.C., January 18, 1963).

Notes to Chapter 6

1 Bernard B. Fall, "Solution in Indochina: Ceasefire Negotiate," *The Nation* (March 6, 1954): 193.

2 Letter from Donald G. Bishop, Syracuse University, April 6, 1954.

Notes to Chapter 8

1 François Sully "To Each His Turn: Today Yours, Tomorrow Mine," obituary, *Newsweek* (March 8, 1971): 75.

2 While the date of the first document in Bernard's FBI file number 97–3489 is not visible, the second document is dated January 15, 1958. It begins: "A confidential informant, who has furnished reliable information in the past, advised that—." The rest is blacked out. There are many 1958 investigating documents noting "Registration Act investigation re Fall," trying to prove that Bernard was a foreign agent for France.

3 Fall, *Last Reflections*, 198–99.

Notes to Chapter 9

1 Bernard B. Fall, "Will South Vietnam be Next?" *The Nation* (May 31, 1958): 489.

2 FBI Headquarters File 97–3489, July 9, 1958.

Notes to Chapter 10

1 Stokely Carmichael with Ekueme Michael Thelwell, *Ready For the Revolution: The Life and Struggles of Stokely Carmichael (Kwame Ture)* (New York: Scribner, 2003), 131, 596–97.

Notes to Chapter 11

1 Fall, *Street Without Joy*, 12, 13.

2 Fall, *Street Without Joy*, 243.

3 Tillman Durdin, "Enemies Everywhere," *New York Times Book Review*, June 4, 1961, 3.

4 Philip Foisie, "Our Street of Sorrow," *Washington Post*, 1961.

5 Colin Powell, *My American Journey* (New York: Random House, 1995), 147–48.

6 FBI Headquarters File 97–3489, June 2, 1964, regarding "Bernard Fall being retained as a consultant at Cadillac Gage during November and December 1961."

Notes to Chapter 12

1 David Chandler, interview with the author, taped September 15, 1997.

2 Claudia Gertie Hall, interview with the author, taped August 20, 2001.

3 Z [Bernard Fall], "The War in Vietnam: We Have Not Been Told the Whole Truth," *New Republic* (March 12, 1962): 21.

4 Bernard B. Fall, "Master of the Red Jab," *Saturday Evening Post*, November 24, 1962: 18.

Notes to Chapter 13

1 Chalmers B. Wood to Ambassador Fritz Nolting, *State Department History* (Washington, D.C.: December 7, 1962): 757.

2 Bernard B. Fall, *Two Viet-Nams* (New York: Frederick A. Praeger, 1963), vii.

3 Bob Woodward and Carl Bernstein, *The Final Days* (New York: Simon and Schuster, 1979), 39–40.

4 Stanley Karnow, *Vietnam: A History* (New York: Viking, 1983), 279, 281.

5 Madame Ngo Dinh Nhu, interview for the television documentary *Vietnam: The Deadly Decision*, April 1, 1964 (John F. Kennedy Library, Boston).

Notes to Chapter 14

1 FBI Headquarters file 97–3489, February 16, 1965.

Notes to Chapter 15

1 Woodward and Bernstein, *The Final Days*, 39–40.

2 Quoted in Horst Faas and Tim Page, eds., *Requiem: By the Photographers Who Died in Vietnam and Indochina* (New York: Random House, 1997), 158.

3 Charles Mohr, "Saigon Offers Troops in Outpost Promotions If They Can Hold It," *New York Times*, August 26, 1965, 51.

4 Charles Mohr, "Times Talk," *New York Times* (February 1966).

5 Bernard B. Fall, "Vietnam Blitz," *New Republic* (October 9, 1965): 17.

6 Bernard B. Fall, "This Isn't Munich, It's Spain," *Ramparts* (December 1965): 23–29.

Notes to Chapter 16

1 Tim Weiner, obituary for Robert Komer, *New York Times*, April 12, 2000.

2 Ronald Steel, *Walter Lippmann and the American Century* (Boston: Little, Brown and Co., 1980), 549.

3 Quoted in William Hoagland, "Professor to Study Vietcong in Action," *Washington Post*, April 10, 1966, A16.

4 Bernard B. Fall, "Vietnam in the Balance," *Foreign Affairs* (October 1966): 1.

Notes to Chapter 17

1 Fall, *Last Reflections*, 25.

2 Bernard B. Fall, "You Can Tell 'Em Buddy," *New Republic* (January 14, 1967): 17.

3 Carol Brightman, *Writing Dangerously: Mary McCarthy and Her World* (New York: Harcourt Brace, 1992), 536–37.

4 David Hackworth, *About Face* (New York: Simon and Schuster, 1989), 579–580.

5 Report from Commanding Officer, Headquarters, First Battalion, Ninth Marines, March 8, 1967, and Tom Evans, "Death on the Street Without Joy," *Leatherneck* (July 1996): 22–25.

6 Fall, *Last Reflections*, 268–271.

Notes to Epilogue

1 Fall, *Last Reflections*, 112.

BIBLIOGRAPHY

Aguettaz, Michel. *Francs-Tireurs et Partisans dans la Résistance Savoyarde.* Grenoble: Presses Universitaires de Grenoble, 1995.

Anderson, David, ed. *The Human Tradition in the Vietnam Era.* Wilmington, Delaware: SR Books, 2000.

Appy, Christian G. *Patriots: The Vietnam War Remembered From All Sides.* New York: Viking, 2003.

Arendt, Hannah. *Eichmann in Jerusalem: A Report on the Banality of Evil.* New York: Viking Press, 1963.

Arnett, Peter. *Live From the Battlefield.* New York: Simon and Schuster, 1994.

Becker, Elizabeth. *When the War Was Over.* New York: Simon and Schuster, 1986.

Borton, Lady. *After Sorrow.* New York: Kodansha International, 1995.

Brightman, Carol. *Writing Dangerously: Mary McCarthy and Her World.* New York: Harcourt Brace and Company, 1992.

Carmichael, Stokely. *Ready For the Revolution: The Life and Struggles of Stokely Carmichael (Kwame Ture).* New York: Scribner, 2003.

Dougan, Clark, Samuel Lipsman, et al. *A Nation Divided (The Vietnam Experience Series).* Boston: Boston Publishing Company, 1984.

Ehrlich, Blake. *Resistance France, 1940–1945*. Boston: Little, Brown and Company, 1965.

Emerson, Gloria, et al. *War Torn*. New York: Random House, 2002.

Faas, Horst, and Tim Page, eds. *Requiem: By the Photographers Who Died in Vietnam and Indochina*. New York: Random House, 1997.

Fall, Bernard B. *Hell in a Very Small Place: The Siege of Dien Bien Phu*. Philadelphia: Lippincott, 1966.

———. *Ho Chi Minh: On Revolution*. New York: Praeger, 1967.

———. *Last Reflections On a War*. New York: Doubleday, 1967.

———. *Le Viet-Minh*. Paris: Armand Colin, 1960.

———. *Street Without Joy*. Harrisburg, PA: Stackpole, 1961.

———. *The Two Viet-Nams*. New York: Praeger, 1963.

———. *The Viet-Minh Regime*. New York: Institute of Pacific Relations and Cornell University, 1954.

———. *Viet-Nam Witness*. New York: Praeger, 1966.

Field, Michael. *Witness in Indo-China*. London: Methuen, 1965.

Giap, General Vo Nguyen. *People's War, People's Army*. New York: Praeger, 1962.

Graham, Lawrence Otis. *Our Kind of People: Inside America's Black Upper Class*. New York: HarperCollins, 1999.

Hackworth, David. *About Face: The Odyssey of an American Warrior*. New York: Simon and Schuster, 1989.

Halberstam, David. *The Best and the Brightest*. New York: Random House, 1969.

———. *The Making of a Quagmire*. New York: Alfred A. Knopf, 1964.

Karnow, Stanley. *Vietnam: A History*. New York: Viking Press, 1983.

Latour, Anny. *La Résistance Juive en France, 1940–1944*. Paris: Stock, 1970.

Lazarre, Lucien. *Rescue As Resistance*. New York: Columbia University Press, 1996.

Library of America. *Reporting Vietnam*. New York Literary Classics of the United States, 1998.

Mabbett, Ian, and David Chandler. *The Khmers*. Oxford: Blackwell, 1995.

MacPherson, Myra. *Long Time Passing: Vietnam and the Haunted Generation*. New York: Doubleday, 1984.

McNamara, Robert S. *In Retrospect: The Tragedy and Lessons of Vietnam*. New York: Times Books, 1995.

Mecklin, John. *Mission in Torment*. New York: Doubleday, 1965.

Meyer, Charles. *Derrière le Sourire Khmer*. Paris: Plon, 1971.

Mollard, André. *Les Mouvements Unis de Résistance: La Résistance en Savoie, 1940–1944*.

Moore, Lt. Gen. Harold G., and Joseph L. Galloway. *We Were Soldiers Once . . . and Young*. New York: Random House, 1992.

Powell, Colin. *My American Journey*. New York: Random House, 1995.

Prochnau, William. *Once Upon a Distant War*. New York: Times Books, 1995.

Sheehan, Neil. *A Bright Shining Lie: John Paul Vann and America in Vietnam*. New York: Random House, 1988.

Shirer, William L. *The Rise and Fall of the Third Reich: A History of Nazi Germany*. New York: Simon and Schuster, 1960.

Stafford, David. *Secret Agent: The True Story of the Covert War Against Hitler*. London: Overlook Press, 2001.

Steel, Ronald. *Walter Lippmann and the American Century*. Boston: Little, Brown and Company, 1980.

Taylor, Telford. *Nuremberg and Vietnam: An American Tragedy*. New York: Bantam Books, 1970.

Woodward, Bob, and Carl Bernstein. *The Final Days*. New York: Simon and Schuster, 1976.

Zaroulis, Nancy, and Gerald Sullivan. *Who Spoke Up?: American Protest Against the War in Vietnam, 1963–1975*. New York: Holt, Rinehart, and Winston, 1985.

Zuccotti, Susan. *The Holocaust, the French, and the Jews*. New York: Basic Books, 1993.

INDEX

Bold font indicates Photograph

A

Abadi, Moussa, 23
Algiers, arriving in, 182
Alsop, Joseph, 193
American Witness, 153
Amerika Illustrated, 105–106, 113, 125
Anciens Combattants Français, 107
Anderson, Will, 105
Andreani, Jacques and Huguette, 106–107
Andrews, Marshall, 151, **152**
Angkor
    temple city of, 162
    wonders of, 79
Anschluss of March 1938, 12–13
anti-war movement
    basic text of, 224
    leaders of, 222
Appenzeller, Oury (Ernest), 25
Armée Juive, 21
Army Intelligence, G-2, 195
Arnett, Peter, 215, 246
Artillery Plateau. *See* Camp Carroll
Australian army's survival school, speaking at, 179
Automobiles. *See* Citroën Deux Chevaux; Fiat; Jeepster, the infamous

B

B-52 raids, 215
Baldwin, Hanson, 182
Baldwin, Robert, 243

Bamboo, The Yellow, 74, 83
Ben Suc, village of, 246
Bernard's death, 253
Bernard's personal effects, 255
Berteling, Jack, 254
Berthold, changing of Bernard's name to, 22–23
Bingham, Jonathan, 222
Biret, Auguste, 10, 42, 83
Bishop, Donald, 85
Black Bourgeoisie, 140
Blackstock, Paul, 102
blitzkrieg, early days of 1940, 14
Bourdet, Claude, 96
Brandes, Jean (friend of Aunt Lotti), 37–38
Bright Shining Lie, 209–210
Brightman, Carol, 247
British Royden House school, 252
Brooke, Senator Edward, 140
Brown, Sterling, 140
Browne, Malcolm, 173, 183
Bruskin, Kathleen, 252–253
Buddhism, 162
Bunche, Ralph, 140–141
Bundy, McGeorge, 224–225, 228–229
Burlingham, Lloyd, 160

C

Cadillac Gage Company, design of "Commando" warfare vehicle, 159
Cambodia
    Dorothy's reflections upon returning to, 263

living in, 160–178
post-Cambodian readjustment, 180
Camp Carroll, **240**, **241**, 242
Cam Ranh Bay, 210
Cans, Michel, 62–63
Cao Dai, 77–78
Cap St. Jacques (SEATO Base), 114
Carmichael, Stokely, 144–145
Celebrity's Choice (radio show)
humorous interview with, 237–240
summary of Bernard's Resistance work, 28–29
Chevalier de l'Ordre National du Mérite, 244
Christmas eve letter, Bernard's, 255
Church, Senator Frank, 222
Cistaro, Jean, 6
Cistaro, Tony, in Chau Doc, 6–7
Citroën Deux Chevaux, 165
Clément, Monseigneur, as a key ally, 22
Coffin, Rev. William Sloan, 22
Compagnons de France
activities under cover of, 26–27
Bernard's membership in, **11**, 18–21, **20**
Cordtz, Dan, 206
Cronkite, Walter, 222, **223**
Culas, Madame, 13
Culas, Monsieur
as resistance leader, 28–29
stories of Cambodia, 56
Culas, Monsieur and Madame, school run by, 13

D

Davis, Vince, 225
Dê, Nguyen, 96
de Gaulle, Charles, 130, 224
Demilitarized Zone, Christmas in the, 239–240, **241**
Der Weltkrieg in Bildern, 10–11
destiny
Bernard's life as one of, 260
on what rests our, 9, 35
Deuve, Col. Jean, 121–122, 141
Devillers, Philippe, 96, 262
Diem, President Ngo Dinh, 115–122, **116**
Diem Regime, 117–118

American Friends of Vietnam, 171
correspondents' visits with Bernard, 173
economic aid to, 126–128
Dien Bien Phu
book on the battle of, 7
death marches after, 118
French defeat at, 88–89, 127, 154
researching at French Army files, 187
researching at Service Historique de l'Armée, 182
writing book on the battle of, 182, 231
Disaster Through Air Power, 151
domino theory, 203
Dong Ha, 239, **240**
Dorsey, Emmet (Sam), 141
Dudman, Richard, 226
Durdin, Tillman, 151–152

E

Eclaireurs Israélites de France (EIF), 25
Edwards, Don, 222
Ellsberg, Daniel, 223
Emmanuelle, Sœur 24, 26, 41–42, 131
Epstein, Jason, 224
Europe, Dorothy's first trip to, 96

F

Faas, Horst, 263
Fall, Bernard
birth of, 10
bombing run, on a, **220**
Christmas eve letter from, 255
death of, 253
FBI surveillance of, 189–202
interviewing a Vietcong Colonel, **245**
marriage to Dorothy, 86–88
personal effects of, 255
Vietnam, 2, 55–81, 111–124, 138, 205–220, 240, 244–245
Fall, Dorothy
Civil Service investigation of, 191
designing campaign posters for Prince Sihanouk, 166
first pregnancy, 111, **113**
"Four Women" exhibit, 230, 238
furious letter to Bernard, 214–215
Grange League Federation (GLF), 89

Kal Ehrlich and Merrick, 105
living with the ghosts of Dien Bien
  Phu, 231
marriage to Bernard, 86–88
in Nice, **131**
with Nicole and Elisabeth (1960),
  150
Night Patrol, 150
return to Vietnam in 2000, 263
searching for the Street Without
  Joy, **258**
Fall, Elisabeth Anne (second
daughter)
  approaching Hanoi in 1997, 257
  birth of, 150
  with Dorothy and Nicole (1960),
    150
  memories of Bernard, 233, 265
  in Paris 1961, 158
  searching for the Street Without
    Joy, **258**
  sixth trip to Vietnam, 3
Fall, Leo
  birth of Bernard and Lissette, 10
  capture and death of, 24
  in hiding, 19
  marriage of, 9
  as teenager, 10
Fall, Lisette, 24
  Free Zone of France, 13
  Paris visit with, 83
Fall, Nicole (first daughter)
  with Dorothy and Elisabeth
    (1960), 150
  letter to Bernard, 252
  memories of Bernard, 233, 265
  in Nice, **131**
  in Paris (1961), 158
  sixth trip to Vietnam, 3
  visit to Vietnam in 2000, 263
Fall, Patricia Madeleine Marcelle
(third daughter)
  birth of, 2–3, 236
  memories of Bernard, 265
  searching for the Street Without
    Joy, **258**
  working for Morgan Stanley, 259
Fall family photograph, **11, 236**
Far Eastern Survey, 88
fascism, Bernard's opposition to, 143
Fate of the Earth, The, 245
Federal Bureau of Investigation (FBI)

1965 interview by, 201
Bernard's file with, 190
copy of documents from Bernard's
  file, **196–197**
early 1963 memo, 190
scrutiny of Bernard, 129
surveillance by, 189–202
Feron, Pierre, **108**, 254
Fête de Genie (festival), 172–173
FFI, 2e Bureau, Bernard assigned to,
  28
Fiat, Paris 1961, 158–159
fisurs, spot (physical surveillance),
  190–191
Foisie, Philip, 152–153
Forces Françaises de l'Intérieur, **19**
Foreign Affairs, October issue, 235
"Four Women" exhibit, 238
Fox, Thomas, 197
France, 1964, Bernard, Lisette, Uncle
  Auguste, Aunt Marcelle, **186**
Frankiel, Henry, protecting of Bernard
  from raids, 16
Frazier, Franklin E., 140
Free Zone of France
  German invasion of, 24–25
  Vichy government and, 15
Freistedter, Franz (Uncle), 84
Freistedter, Hilde (Aunt), 84, 97
French Intelligence Service, suspicion
  of intelligence activities for, 190
French regular army, Bernard linking
  up with, 33, **34**
Friendly, Alfred, 204
Fulbright, Senator William, 5, 137,
  222, 224, **234**
Fulbright Fellowship, 43–44, 137

G
George Polk Journalism Award for
  Interpretive Reporting, 230
Gertie, Lt.Col. Ray, 168
Gialam Airport, 257
Giap, General Vo Nguyen, 264–265,
  264, 267–268
Gillespie, George Ann, 172
Glenn Miller, music of, 33, 177
Goldberg, Dr. Herbert, 254
Goralski, Robert, 202
Gottlieb, Sanford (Sandy), 225
Great Battles Series, 182
Greenhouse, Ralph, 101

Gregory, Ann and Gene, 91–92, 117, 173
Guggenheim grants
    application for, 233–234
    sixth trip to Vietnam, 3
Guidon, Father, **133**

H
Hackworth, David, 248–250
Halberstam, David, xi–xiv, 215, 226
Hansberry, Leo, 140
Hanoi
    Bernard's arrival in, 60–61
    Dorothy's third and final visit to, 265
    Fine Arts College, exhibit at, 263
    interview of Ho Chi Minh, 175–176
    landscape after Bernard's death, 260
    University, research at, 67
Harrison, Gilbert, 206, 224–225, 229
Hayden, Tom, 222
Heilprin, Marilyn, landscape painting with, 113
Hell In A Very Small Place
    completion of, 231, 234
    Dorothy's artwork for, 95
    Kulski's praise for, 94
    packing galleys for his new book, 7
    receiving first copy of, 244
Hickey, Gerald, 238
Higgins, Marguerite, 202
Highland, Gunnery Sergeant Byron, 253
Highway 1, 259
Hirschfeld, Tom and Hana, 167, 173
Histoire du Vietnam de 1949-52, 262
Ho Chi Minh
    CBS documentary about, 222
    Dorothy's drawing of, 150, 178
    interview of, 171, 174–176
    introduction by Bernard to writings, 234
    leading war of liberation, 61
Ho Chi Minh City, 263
Ho Chi Minh: On Revolution, 234, 258
Hoach, Dr. Le Van, 77
Hoagland, Jim, 232
Holland, William, 107
Holmes, Eugene C., 140

Honey, P. J., 154, 157
Hong Kong, 232
Hoover, J. Edgar, 190, 192, 199
Horizon, spring 1967 issue, 234–235
Howard University
    1966 sabbatical, 2
    Bernard lecturing at, 139–147
    FBI surveillance of, 194
    Madame Ngo Dinh Nhu's visit to, **183**
    spring garden party, **146**
Hubert, Dick, Celebrity's Choice radio show interview, 28, 33, 237
Human Relations Area Files (Washington Branch), 97–106
Hutchinson, Colonel, 103
Huu Mai, 261–262

I
"Impressions du Cambodge", (Dorothy's exhibition), 174
In Retrospect, 229
Indochina
    Bernard's 1953 trip to, 58–80
    Bernard's second (1957) trip to, 111–124
    job offer in, 74–75
    spending 1961–1962 academic year in, 157–158
    third trip to, 130
International Control Commission, using data from, 123
International Position of South Viet-Nam, 1954-58, The
    Institute of Pacific Relations report, 125–126
Iraq, similarities to Vietnam, 265
Iron Triangle, 246

J
Jeanne d'Arc monument, **108**
Jeepster, the infamous, **104**, 105
Johnson, Lyndon, 221, 224
jungle rot, 75
Just, Ward, 215

K
Karnow, Annette, 252
Karnow, Stanley, 226, 253
Kennedy, Senator Robert, 222
kidney problems, 184–185
Komer, Robert, 222

Konbrai, 211, **213**
Kramer, Lucy, landscape painting with, 113
Krupp, Alfred (Alfried), trial of, 38–41, **39, 42**
Kulski, Dr. Wladyslaw
  Bernard's doctoral dissertation, 86–94
  reconciliation with Bernard, 94
Kyle, Maj. Gen. Wood B., 253

L

la Médaille de la France Libérée, 36
la Rue Sans Joie (Street Without Joy), 130
Lafont, Pierre-Bernard, 134
Lai Chau, French outpost at, 72–73
Lai Ha, 260–262
Lancaster, Donald, **166**
Lanselle, Pierre, 21
Laos
  1959 trip to, 133–137
  corruption and incompetance in, 115
  flight to Ban-Ban, 64, **65**
  supply drop mission, **66**
Laotian Rebellion of 1959, 134–135
Larimer, Tim, 261
Le Viet Minh, 258
Lederer, Edie, 263
Leffler, Harry, 86–87
Lévy, Roger, 96
Lewis, Harold, 140
Librairie Biret
  Aunt Marcelle and, 42
  Marcelle and Auguste operating, 83
Library Journal, review of *Hell In a Very Small Place*, 244
Lippmann, Walter, 5, 226–227, **234**
Lisagor, Peter, 202
Loeschel, Richard, 238, 248
Long Binh, 244
Lucet, Charles (Ambassador)
  farewell luncheon, 5
  at farewell luncheon, **234**
  at Jeanne d'Arc monument, **108**
Lynch, Acklyn, 141–142

M

"machine", Bernard's, 187
Maison de France, Dorothy's exhibit-
ion at, 173–174
Malot, Rémy, **31**
  with Bernard at Bastion IX, 31–36
  as Bernard's friend, 35
  serving in Vietnam, 56
  visiting at Fontainebleau, 96
Mao Tse-tung, 215, 224
Marshall, Gen. S.L.A. (Slam), 248–249
Marshall, Thurgood (Supreme Court Justice), 140
Mathews, Claude, 145
McCarthy, Mary, 247
McCarthyism, 155
McGovern, Senator George, 192, 222
McNamara, Robert (Secretary of Defense)
  Bernard's criticisms of, 193–194
  briefing with, 227
  essay by, 224
  similarity to James Forrestal, 228
McNaughton, John, 223
medical afflictions, 75–76, 184–187, 206, 254
Meet the Press (television), 202–204
Mekong Delta, 209, 214
Mendenhall, Joseph, 181
Mestrovic, Maté, 52
Meyer, Charles, 165, 173
Meyer, Sika, **166**
Military Review, "Indochina: The Seven Year Dilemma", 69–70
misur (microphone), 190–191
Mitchell, Joan, 243
Mohr, Charles, 208, 211, 215
Morrison, Toni, 140
Murray, Marie, 145
Mus, Paul, 96
Mutual Security Program, 115

N

Nabrit, James, **230**
New Republic
  "Blitz in Vietnam" article, 215
  first article for, 170
Newton, Henry G., 158
Nha Trang, trip to, 118–119
Nhu, Madame Ngo Dinh, 108, **183**
Nhu, Ngo Dinh, 115
Nice, France, Bernard with Dorothy and Nicole, **131**
Normandy, Allied invasion of, 27

Noshpitz, Charlotte Sorkine, 236
Nuremberg Wars Crimes Tribunal
  Bernard in uniform, **38**
  U.S. Chief of Counsel's office, 38–
  42

O
Oberdorfer, Don, 227
Operation Cedar Falls, 246
Operation Chinook II, tape recorded
  notes of, 251–252
Orchid, The Purple, **111**, 112

P
Pacific Affairs, 88
Page, Tim, 263
Pathet, Lao, psychological warfare of,
  136–137
Pentagon Papers, 224
People's War, People's Army, 170
Peterson, Ambassador Douglas (Pete),
  263
Phnom Penh
  arrival in, 161
  boulevards of, 162
  city of intrigue, 167
  returning from, 179
  royal treatment in, 79–80
  teaching position in, 121
  writing from, 207
Pich Nil, Dorothy and Bernard at, **166**
Pierson, Betty, 52
Pleiku, attack by Vietcong guerrillas,
  225
"Ploughing of the Sacred Furrow"
  (festival), 172
Pohoryles, Henri, 25, 96
Pol Pot regime, mass slaughter in
  1970s, 174
Pork Chop Hill, 248
Powell, Gen. Colin, 153
Praeger, Frederick, 170
Price, Darrell, 173
Pringle, Jim, 239, **240**
Prune Tree, The, 74, 83
Pyle, Richard, 263

Q
Quang Tri province, entering, 259
Quang-Yen, inspecting training camp
  at, 64

R
Ralph Bunche Chair in International
  Relations, 141–143
Ramparts, 215–220
Raskin, Barbara, 5
Raskin, Marcus, 5, 141, 224
Ratanakiri province, day trip to, 169–
  170
Ready for Revolution, 144–145
Red River Delta
  armored task force, **71**
  Bernard's description of, 176
  military situation in, 67–68
  viewed from the air, 61
Reporting Vietnam (collection of
  outstanding pieces on the war), 215
Requiem, 263
resistance movements
  Bernard's records during, 30–31
  following Normandy invasion, 27
  while a teenager, 3
  Zionist and anti-Nazi, 18
Resnik, Harvey and Seth, 260
retroperitoneal fibrosis, 185
Ridenhour, Ron, 153
Rios, Tere, 208, 214
Roberts, Chalmers, 224–225
Rockefeller Foundation, 157, 161, 168
Rostow, Eugene, 228–229
Roth, Iris, 52
Roy, Jules, 244
Royal Lao Army, studying insurgency
  of, 136
Royal School of Administration,
  teaching at, 164, 170

S
Sacks, I. Milton, 157
Saigon
  Bernard's 1957 arrival in, 114
  Bernard's arrival in, 76–77
  Rotary Club speech, 119–120
Samneua, experiencing combat in,
  135
San Francisco
  Dorothy in, 68–85
  settling down in, 85
Savage, Frank, 143–144
Schell, Jonathan, 245–246
Seligmann, Anna, marriage to Leo
  Fall, 9–10
Sheehan, Neil, 208–209, 215

Sihanouk, Prince Norodom
    audience with, 207–208
    dinner invitations from, 168
    former king of Cambodia, 162–163
Silvers, Bob, 247
Snowden, Frank, 140
Sœur Emmanuelle, 22–24, 42, 130
Soukhavong, Gen. Amkha, **135**
Spivak, Lawrence E., 202
Spock, Dr. Benjamin, 222
State of Vietnam, 95
Steinberg, David, 101, 104–105
Stein Schneider, Herbert, 186
Stibravy, Roma, recollections of Bernard, 51
Stone, Esther, 155
Stone, I. F. (Izzy)
    in Bernard's study, **228**
    essay by, 224
    lunch meeting with, 154–155
    research techniques of, 123
    tribute to Bernard, 254–255
Strategic Hamlet program, 226
Street Without Joy
    flight to Hue to visit, 259
    Operation Chinook II, 250–252
    return to the, 237–255
Street Without Joy (book)
    banned in South Vietnam, 173
    beginning work on, 149–159
    Bernard's diary as basis for, 59
    French edition of, 157
    publication in 1961, 151
    speaking engagements resulting from, 154
    Stackpole Company contract for, 129–130
    updating of, 234
    work begun on, 149
    Yarborough assessment of, 200
Sullivan, William, 198–199
Sully, François, 116, 173, 208–209, 238, 263
Summerford, Joe, 105
surveillance, by FBI, 189–204
Sweet, Brig. Gen. J. B., 129
Syracuse University
    Alumni News eulogy, 94
    Bernard and Dorothy at, **49**
    Bernard's graduate work at, 44
    Bernard's PHD at, 58

dissertation deadline, 89–90, **90**
Dorothy's studies at, 47–52
Military Ball at the, **53**
ROTC classes at, **51**

T
Taborstrasse, special toast to, 170
Tahiti, visit to, 179–180
teach-in, at University of Michigan, 225–226
Terres Rouges, 120
tesur (phone tap)
    beginning of, 190–191
    discontinuance of, 201
Thailand, research in, 132
The Nation, 88
Thi Hai, 164
Times of Vietnam, 92, 117
Today Show (television), interview on, 181
Treasure Cay (Bahamas), 231
Troop "E," **213**
Two Viet-Nams, The
    1963 publication of, 181
    finishing of, 170
    research for, 157
    Robert Kennedy's interest in, 206
    second revised edition of, 157
    updating of, 4
    Vietnam handbook and, 104

U
USIS library, exhibition at, 173

V
Valenti, Jack, 228
Valeur, Robert, 112
Vandenbosch, Amry, 56–57
Vann, John Paul, 209–210
Versace, Rocky, 214
Vichy regime, running of Free Zone, 15–16
Vietcong, book about, 3
Vietmimh rebels, 56
Viet-Minh Regime, The, 94–95, 156
Vietnam
    American illusions in, 203
    B-52 raids, 215
    Bernard visiting a village in 1965, **217**
    Bernard's lessons and warnings on, 265

as Bernard's mistress, 2
Catholic Diem and Buddhist Repression, 182
Christmas in, 242–243
corruption and incompetance in, 115
departure for final trip, 238
Dorothy's return in 2000, 263
expanding U.S. involvement in, 180
first trip to, 55–81
flawed theories about, 138
lure for Bernard, 57
as political problem, 217
returning from, 80
summer of 1965, 205–220
tragic mistakes of, 265
visiting in 1957, 111–124
Viet-Nam, Bernard's preferred hyphenated spelling of, 101
Vietnam, North
    Bernard's storehouse of documents about, 156
    bombing of, 225
    industrialization of, 177
Vietnam, South
    antagonizing the dictator in, 170
    Communist plot to undermine, 137–138
    persona non grata in, 173
    situation in 1962, 171
    U.S. military intervention in, 137
    U.S. war effort in, 221
Vietnam: International Aspects, 95
Viet-Nam Reader, The
    anti-war movement basic text, 5
    compilation of, 224
Viet-Nam Witness, 230
Villa Beauregard

betraying of refugee families at, 21
Fall Family at, 13–15
victim of turnover edict, 15–17
Village of Ben Suc, The, 246
Vu Ky, Meeting with in Ho Chi Minh's house, 257–258

W
WAHRAF
    Bernard working with, 97–105
    Bernard's resignation from, 103
Walton, Hanes, 145, 194
wars of liberation, Bernard's feelings toward, 141–142
Washington, move to house in, 185–186
wedding scheme, 87–88
Whiskey (the dog), 238, 252
White House, The, disavowing contact with, 229
Whiting, Allen, 254
Wicker, Tom, 222
"Will South Vietnam Be Next?", article in The Nation, 126–127
Winer, Isadore and Esther (Dorothy's parents), 45–47
Wolfe Frank, 252–253
Wood, Chalmers, 181
Writing Dangerously, 247

Y
Yarborough, Maj. Gen. William P., 198–200
Yates, Congressman Sidney, 243

Z
"Z", Bernard's nom de plume, 170
Zielony, Colonel Alex, 131
Zirkin, Frances, 254

ABOUT THE AUTHOR

DOROTHY FALL is an artist, a former award-winning art director, and graphic designer. Her work has been exhibited interna-
tionally and is in collections throughout the world.

Shortly after her husband's death in 1967, she selected works
for the volume *Last Reflections On A War*, for which she wrote the
preface. Her December 13, 1970, article, "An Epitaph for Phnom
Penh," appeared in the "Outlook" section of the *Washington Post*.

Dorothy Fall lives in the house she shared with Bernard Fall
in Washington, D.C. Their three daughters are Nicole, a sculptor, Elisabeth, a photographer, and Patricia, a writer.